# Introducing Marketing

Martin Christopher, BA, MSc, PhD, is Professor of Marketing and Logistics Systems at Cranfield School of Management. The author of numerous books and research papers on marketing topics, he has held a variety of academic posts, including a period as co-director of the European Logistics Management Programme in Holland and later as Visiting Research Professor at the University of British Columbia, Canada.

Malcolm McDonald, MA, MSc, pursued a successful career as Marketing Director of Canada Dry and as a senior management consultant before taking up a Senior Teaching Fellowship at Cranfield, a post he now combines with varied consultancy work and a company directorship.

Gordon Wills, BA, DMS, FInsM, MBIM, is Professor of Customer Policy at Cranfield where he has been since 1972 and is currently also Director of the Cranfield Management Resource. He has held professorial posts at Bradford, Alberta, Prince Edward Island and Tulsa Universities, and has also lectured throughout Europe, Australasia and Central America. The author of over a score of books and editor or co-editor of several scholarly journals, he is a director of two companies and one of Europe's leading authorities on marketing.

Martin Christopher,
Malcolm McDonald and
Gordon Wills

# Introducing Marketing

Pan Books London and Sydney

First published 1975 by MCB Publications Ltd, Bradford
This revised and expanded edition published 1980 by
Pan Books Ltd, Cavaye Place, London SW10 9PG
4th printing 1983
© Martin Christopher, Malcolm McDonald and
Gordon Wills 1980
ISBN 0 330 26086 3
Set, printed and bound in Great Britain by
Cox & Wyman Ltd, Reading

# Contents

# Foreword

*Introducing Marketing* has been specially updated, amended and edited for this edition. The original title on which it is based, *Introduction to Marketing*, was prepared for practising managers whose business life thus far has been concerned either with partial activities within or totally outside the marketing department. Typically aged 30–45, such folk are to be found across Europe in their millions. A few are able to follow either Master of Business Administration (MBA) courses, or middle/senior management development programmes taken in-company, or at a business school. Most undertake no formal study of marketing at all however.

This audience is one which Cranfield School of Management, at which the authors work, has sought to address on the subject of marketing on an introductory level since the 1950s. It is a difficult audience. It knows a thing or two about business in general, but little about marketing, and what little it does know tends to be somewhat jaundiced. Somehow, marketing is seen as a less worthy social activity than the act of producing goods or services for society. Marketing's more strident activities like television advertising or personal selling are often not seen in their total perspective, and rare excesses therein by atypical companies are taken as typical of all such activity.

This response does not alarm us. It is perfectly natural and healthy because, in an affluent society, materialism – egged on by persuasive marketing – can pose very real social problems. Whilst not seeking to overlook the problems, *Introducing Marketing* seeks to place them in their proper perspective and, in this edition, to do so with a far wider audience than has hitherto been reached. As well as appealing to the primary readership described above, the book will serve as a stimulating 'refresher' for the experienced marketing practitioner, and as an easy-to-read introduction for marketing novices. In the language of our reply to Question 22, we are now seeking to penetrate a market we have hitherto only skimmed.

Our intention in *Introducing Marketing* is to demonstrate why, how, and with what effect marketing colleagues in business perform their role. It is not an overly complex role but its importance for society and any business is seldom overlooked without disastrous consequences.

Our method is to offer succinct answers to more than a score of the most commonly encountered queries about marketing. In each case we report real-life examples, recommend how to go into topics in depth with a short further reading list, and provide a few self-audit questions the reader should be able to answer effectively.

We recommend the use of this book either on a self-tutored basis or as a background text for training programmes. We have used it ourselves in both such ways and the Pan edition incorporates many of the comments received by way of reaction to the three previous editions that have appeared since 1975.

Those three earlier editions were jointly authored by Martin Christopher and Gordon Wills, with David Walters (now at the Oxford Management Centre) rather than Malcolm McDonald – who appears as a co-author for this edition. Malcolm McDonald has provided considerable additional materials in the planning, sales management and international marketing areas.

October 1979
Cranfield School of Management
Bedfordshire, England

# Question 1
## What is marketing?

*Marketing is concerned to match an organization's capabilities with the wants of its customers. It must do this against a background of the dynamic characteristics of the environment in which the matching takes place. This includes direct and indirect competition, economic uncertainties, legal and political constraints and institutional patterns.*

*The matching is typically undertaken for an organization by a formalized department headed by a senior executive at board level. He plans, coordinates and controls the product or service offered, the price that is charged, the style of promotion and the place where it is to be made available. In doing so he is concerned to master not only the separable effects of these four 'P's, but also their interactive effects. This management activity is the marketing function.*

Marketing is the way in which any organization or individual *matches* its own capabilities to the wants of its customers. Since most organizations continue in business over relatively long periods of time, it is necessary for them to plan both the particular capabilities they offer and the particular customer wants they wish to serve. It is this need to look ahead to develop products or services and/or groups of customers which normally requires all medium or large organizations to formalize marketing as a specific activity or function if the matching process is to be successfully accomplished.

Whether or not a formalized activity is present, the matching inevitably proceeds. Any mis-match leads to failure unless its causes are speedily detected since customers will simply refrain from acquiring the product or service offered. The customer is also undertaking a continuous process of matching between his or her wants and the capabilities offered by the organization.

In the simplest market place the customer and the marketer meet, personally. The customer can respond directly to the product or service offered and if any mis-match is present, inform the marketer in order that the offering can be adjusted to conform truly to customer wants. Regrettably, few organizations work today in such a simple situation. A successful German manufacturer of industrial pumps had some 6,000 customers throughout Europe and a further 4,000 in North America and Australasia. He offered a full range of products together with installation and maintenance servicing, as well as financial support for the purchase of specific items. He deployed technical sales representatives travelling to meet his major customers once or twice a year, but in many countries he dealt through agents rather than directly. His marketing activity was complex but its success was just as dependent on matching his organization's capabilities to the wants of its customers. And he will continue to succeed only if he gleans regular information about what customers want in the future as well as how they are reacting to his present range of products or services.

Lest any pump manufacturer should be daunted in his task, however, let him count his blessings whilst he compares his marketing challenge with that faced by a food manufacturer who sells his produce throughout the EEC. Whilst the preferences for pump technology the world over have some striking similarities, the diets of fellow Europeans in Denmark, Holland and the UK, to cite but three, differ distinctly. Just observe the Dutch preference for cheese at breakfast time in contrast to ours, or the Danish propensity to eat biscuits for breakfast with our observable preference for toast. Then recall that there are just short of 300 million customers in the EEC for breakfast most days and some 85 million housewives doing their shopping from something in excess of one million retail stores.

As one can well imagine, it takes a great deal of planning to meet the varied needs of so many folk successfully. Yet in the pan-European food manufacturing companies like Unilever, that's exactly the measure of the marketing task they face.

Fortunately, the task is not so daunting as it can sound. Organizations seldom grow so large that they either have the capability or the wish to serve such vast markets in a short period of time. They add to their capabilities and knowledge of customer wants as they go. The organization itself and its employees become a bank of information and knowledge about what customers want, although all too frequently much of that information is lost either by inadequate analysis or codification, and lessons have to be relearnt again at the expense both of customers and organizations.

This bank of information means that most established organizations know in rough and ready terms what customers will want in the immediate future. Excepting major upheavals, statisticians can also indicate the overall outlook somewhat further ahead.

## The marketing environment

Few organizations are left alone in our world to match their capabilities with their customers' wants. The process goes on in an open environment with varying degrees of competition either from similar or identical products or from quite different opportunities for expenditure by customers of their limited financial resources. A unit trust seeking to market its services to individual customers could be in competition both with building societies and with alternative uses of the available funds, such as a long holiday, redecoration of the outside of the home, or a pony tethered in a paddock for the children. The unit trust will also be in direct competition with other unit trusts. Such direct competition for customers is readily apparent to most organizations; the other forms of less obvious competition can also be extremely telling. In times of economic uncertainty, folk may reduce many expenditures on products or services which can be delayed without any undue difficulties occurring whilst holding or increasing expenditure for others. With the rapid rise in oil prices in recent years, for example, the demand for motor cars fell along with the level of economic activity, but the demand for holidays held up.

Equally, economic uncertainty reduced capital investment in new equipment and plant during the very rapid European inflation throughout the seventies, although the cost of labour was increasing relatively much more rapidly and substitution of capital goods for labour should logically have occurred. The movement towards more capital-intensive activities occasioned by such a change in the respective productivities of labour and capital did occur, but with a lagged time effect.

The environment in which the organization's marketer operates includes legal and political facets as well. Within the EEC there are community laws and regulations made as a consequence of the terms of the Treaty of Rome, which govern numerous aspects of trade, from transport and distribution to the description and packaging of products. Each nation within the EEC has its own laws in addition, such as the UK's *Fair Trading Act* or laws governing hire purchase or unsolicited goods and services. Outside the EEC, each and every country will have further laws and regulations governing export/import activities and trading terms. Many countries, for instance, require that products sold within their borders must be partly or wholly manufactured or assembled there, regardless of whether this is in the best economic interests of either an organization or its specific customers for any particular transaction.

Such legal issues merge into political issues very easily. Sanctions against Rhodesia for more than a decade, the long-term boycott of South African or Israeli goods by individuals or countries, oil sanctions against Holland and the USA by the OPEC countries – all are outstanding instances of international political environmental factors. Less apparent but nonetheless as effective in distorting a simple organization/customer matching process are quota schemes between countries, or barter deals such as have been widely concluded between Comecon countries and Western nations for the past two decades.

Within countries the extent of political pressures and influence will vary according to the tenor of national politics. Such influences in some EEC countries are far more potent than in others.

One final aspect of the marketing environment to which reference should be made is the institutions which previous years of trading activity bequeath to contemporary marketers. This point can perhaps be well illustrated by several examples. The Giro method of banking, invented in Austria and widely practised throughout Europe for half a century, only reached the UK in the 1960s and is only now beginning to make any real impact on the pattern of banking behaviour amongst the two-thirds of the population who made no use at all of the joint stock banks at the time of its introduction, and to whom the convenience of banking services had hitherto not been effectively available.

Until the late 1960s, the major pattern of food distribution throughout Europe was relatively small grocers or multiple chain stores operating through highly local retail outlets. The advent of mass car ownership has transformed this pattern in two decades to one of large-scale hyper/supermarkets in almost every EEC country. In doing so, several other traditional retail institutions have been undermined – the pharmacist, the butcher, the green-grocer, the fishmonger, the dairy, even the baker and the paint and wallpaper decorator.

These two recent instances of change focus the need for the marketer to identify the pace at which customers are willing and able to respond to new institutional forms in their market place. Should his capabilities be thrown behind the declining or the growing institutional forms and at what moment if at all should his allegiance be switched? Such a dilemma is more sharply focus-ed perhaps within the EEC as a whole as hitherto mainly national organizations develop their activities throughout many or all of the other member states. At what moment should they begin to sell directly, or establish local marketing capability rather than operate through licensees, agents or other styles of distributor-ship?

Save for the largest organizations of all (and only they in cer-tain circumstances which will normally be carefully circumscribed in law) the marketing environment must normally be accepted as it happens in the short and medium term. It is a dynamic back-cloth against which, and the milieu within which, the matching of organizational capability and customer wants must take place.

## The marketing activity

Formalized marketing activity in an organization is concerned with analysis, planning and control of the process of matching capabilities with customer wants. It has already been demonstrat-ed how vitally significant it is to have a flow of evaluative and behavioural information back from the customer in the market place. This, plus accumulated learning about the markets served, provides the effective basis on which marketing plans can be pre-pared, put into effect and performance thereon audited and controlled.

Successful matching depends on customers being aware of the products or services on offer, finding them conveniently available and most acceptable in the manner presented both in terms of price and formulation. This satisfactory state of affairs is best accomplished by attention to what are often termed the four 'P's – product, price, promotion and place. As will be demonstrated in some detail in answer to later questions in this book, each 'P' is a continuing problem to the marketer. It must be both attended to separately and as it interacts with the other elements in what is termed the *marketing mix*. Any sufficient answer for this year may well expect to be challenged in the next. Products or services will be installed, improved upon or made obsolete. Prices may be undercut or margins undermined. Promotion can be upstaged or drowned out. The place of effective sale at any time can become less satisfactory as alternative opportunities emerge or business develops.

And these comments all assume a sufficiently agreeable answer has been identified *ab initio*, which will take account not only of the separable importance of each of the four 'P's to the customer, but of their interactive impact as well. For example, to what extent can a higher price with more effective promotion improve the overall marketing effect judged in terms of profit contribution, rather than some other blend? To what extent can more rapid place availability of components or machine tools, involving as it often must a more expensive total distribution system, more than recoup those new costs in terms of extra sales and go on to add even more profit contribution? These are marketing mix problems.

To wrestle with such mixing problems and to plan for and to implement solutions most medium and large organizations establish a marketing department and charge one of their senior executives to coordinate all such activities at director or boardroom level. This is the marketing function.

*Further reading*
Levitt, T., 'Marketing Myopia', *Harvard Business Review*,
   July–August 1960, pp 45–56
Wills, G. S. C., 'Implementing the Marketing Concept' in
   *Exploration in Marketing Thought* (ed G. S. C. Wills), Crosby

Lockwood for Bradford University Press, 1971, ch 1, pp. 1–30
Rodger, L., *Marketing in a Competitive Economy*, Associated
   Business Programmes, 2nd edition, 1968

**Self-audit questions**

1.1  *How does your company continuously seek to match its
     offerings with market demand?*
1.2  *What elements of your marketing environment currently
     have the most impact on your marketing success?*
1.3  *How is the concept of the four 'P's applicable and
     managed in your organization on an integrated basis?*

# Question 2
# What is the difference between marketing and selling?

*Selling is simply that part of marketing concerned with
persuading customers to acquire the product or service which best
matches an organization's capabilities with its customer's wants.
If the marketing job has been well done, such selling may still
be tough, but it will be effective. If not, salesmen all too often
find themselves trying to sell what the producing organization
wants the customer to want.*

*Selling typically takes place through intermediate organizations,
either in terms of those undertaking manufacture or assisting
distribution. Equally, it can be undertaken at a personal level
with face-to-face contact, or impersonally as via mail order.*

Marketing has been described in reply to Question 1 as the matching of an organization's own capabilities to the wants of its
customers. It has also been indicated that the matching is achieved
by an organization's careful attention to the four 'P's – product,
price, promotion and place. Selling is one aspect of promo-

15

tion. It is quite specifically intended to clinch a transaction, to persuade a customer to agree to acquire the product or service offered at the prevailing price. As such, it should represent the consummation of marketing's efforts to match what the organization is offering with what the customer wants. If the marketing process has been well done then selling may be tough going, but it will not be impossible. If little or no marketing planning of the offering has been undertaken, all but the lucky must expect to fail. Only luck and good marketing can sell a product or service twice to a customer.

Selling any product or service to a customer the first time round is a somewhat different matter. Half truths or over-claims for efficacy can often convince folk to acquire a product or make use of a service once that is subsequently found wanting. No further sales follow and few organizations are in business where they can profit adequately from single purchases from subsequently dissatisfied customers alone. Naturally, in any circumstances some who acquire once will fall by the wayside later, but the selling effort of the well-organized marketing function gives rise to only a small proportion of dissatisfied customers. Furthermore, its information feedback from the market place alerts it to the main reasons why customers fail to acquire again. If necessary, this then becomes the basis for improving or modifying the product or service offered.

Selling is not about half truths or exaggerated claims for what is on offer – they are excesses and they are folly since they are counter-productive. Their frequency is overstated because when they do occur they make good copy for the news media.

Well-planned sales effort as part of a carefully thought-out marketing activity is about persuasion. The sales representatives or the direct mail leaflet or the industrial/technical advisory service, depending on the organization's chosen mode of selling, seeks to persuade the customer to take the leap from wanting to acquiring the product or service. The more care that the organization has devoted to knowing a customer's wants before his salesmen make the effort to persuade, the greater the probability of success. Conversely, if the marketing thinking has not pervaded the organization's build up to the sales effort, the probability of success is inevitably that much lower. What the salesman finds he has is a product or service in search of a customer. This cannot happen in a marketing orientated organization. Where it does occur, the phenomenon is normally described as *production orientation*. In other words, the organization's capabilities have led it to develop a product or service that it, the organization, wants the customer to want, and has the avowed intention of relying on its salesmen to persuade customers to acquire come hell or high water. If they fail, they tend to get the blame, rather than the organization's overall stance towards its customers.

Fifteen years ago a modest-sized European engineering firm developed a splendid idea into a viable technology. It harnessed the heat from factory chimneys, diesel exhausts and other industrial processes thereby recycling energy. The inventors believed in their process, but their potential customers even when assailed by salesmen did not want it and they did not acquire it. Only today with the massive escalation in world energy costs, has a viable market emerged for the long-viable technology. Its savings are now sufficiently attractive to command attention and custom, particularly in the hyper-conscious North American market. They have been one of the few organizations lucky enough to benefit from the OPEC cartel's activities. Their production orientation, no matter how clever, could have been their downfall and all too often it is.

In contrast is the marketing orientation of a large French printing engineering company which was established by an electronic engineer and a salesman from one of the more traditional industries. The salesman's frequent visits to printers had given him a clear understanding of the bottlenecks in production, especially the problem of maintaining a correct 'register' for long print runs. An automatic electronic process was perfected, specifically for printing which, although primitive in the sophisticated world of space electronics, exactly met a readily perceived need with printers across the world. Furthermore, it was engineered to give value in the context in which it was expected to operate. Its price was seen as realistic in terms of the savings it afforded on the more traditional processes of human adjustment. Technical selling of the electronic registration device was still needed, but it was undertaken on fertile, marketing prepared soil in some eighty-four countries throughout the world by the mid-seventies.

## Different levels of selling

Sales activities will seldom all be undertaken on a personal, face-to-face basis. In many markets, such as those where customers are purchasing low value items on a frequent basis like consumable household items, or where customers for industrial items are geographically widely spread, agents or intermediaries will be used. In such situations the organization initiating the product or service needs to sell first to the intermediary and then usually to assist the intermediary to sell to the eventual customer on his behalf. This is the way most retailing has worked since the start of the twentieth century, although the growth throughout Europe in recent years of 'own label products' has somewhat reduced its effect in groceries. It is also the way in which Svenska Cellulosa sell their pulp, paper and newsprint to European industry and that Courtaulds sell their synthetic fibres to cloth manufacturers or carpet producers throughout Comecon or EEC countries, and the rest of the world. In circumstances such as these, both the original producer and the intermediary must of necessity sell to their eventual newspaper readers or to the consumers of clothing, furnishing fabrics, carpets and the like; and their sales activities must be based on a careful analysis and understanding of the importance which the newsprint or the fibre used plays in the satisfaction of customer wants.

Such illustrations can also be drawn from service industries, such as tv rental companies or insurance brokers. The insurance broker, for instance, will devote the most careful attention to the individual needs of each customer in the same way as a traditional butcher can. In comparison the international insurance companies or the architects of the Common Agricultural Policy in Brussels concentrate on the overall relevance for the markets to be served.

Whilst the use of intermediaries to sell an organization's product or service extends its reach into the market place and can reduce the capital it needs to deploy throughout the market since intermediaries will often hold stocks and/or promote sales at their own expense, it also has disadvantages. The customer now stands at one or even more stages removed from the originator of the product or service. Agents or intermediaries will not necessarily either gain the same level of insight from their contact with end-users, or communicate what they do learn back to the originating organization. Further, their objective may be shorter term or different in other respects from the originating organization's marketing and sales objectives. Misguided selling can damage the originating organization's market standing. Accordingly, a policy of advice and normally gentle control of such activities by intermediaries is required.

In the paragraphs above, two types of selling through intermediaries have been identified. One is to intermediate manufacturers who use materials or semi-finished components in producing end products or services, the stimulation of end-user demand for which is indispensable to the originating organization. The second type is where the agent or broker offers stocks or service availability on a localized, more convenient basis for the customer. Any particular organization can have either, both, or neither types. It depends on the capabilities of the organization and the wants of customers, and how the organization chooses to match them.

## Different forms of selling

Any organization's sales activity can be accomplished in a variety of ways, but they can all be characterized as either personal or impersonal selling. Two of the most distinctly different are personal representatives calling at a customer's premises, or the use of advertising designed to elicit a direct response.

The personal approach can be well illustrated by the call of a representative at a customer's premises. Knowing whether this is the most fruitful form of selling, and if so how frequently to visit and how long to spend on each visit, are problems in themselves which call for careful analysis. Quite obviously the nature of the product or service will influence the requirements. Selling a complex technical product or service may well only be achievable after the most complex series of discussions and negotiations between teams of individuals. In industrial, particularly capital goods, markets a myriad of individuals may well be influencing the sales outcome within a customer organization, and some will play a more significant role at certain junctures in the process.

However, once a customer has become familiar with an organization's offering, a representative's call can often become a matter almost of courtesy or public relations – provided always that such a pattern is not indicative of complacency in an ever-changing marketing environment. It will be supplemented on occasions by telephone selling/follow-up calls – indeed this pattern is common amongst routine frequently ordered industrial components.

An interesting variant of direct calling by a representative on a customer is the use of exhibitions to which customers come to meet salesmen and technical advisers. In certain industries and especially in Eastern Europe, the use of exhibitions is a widespread technique of selling. The method is most widespread at introductory stages of new products where sufficient curiosity exists to persuade potential customers to travel at their own expense. The data processing industries have, for instance, used this method constantly, as do camping and caravan manufacturers.

It has the disadvantage to any sales organization that many of the competitors' products are normally arranged alongside one's own, but this can rebound to one's advantage when there is a clear product or service superiority.

Impersonal selling has grown massively in popularity throughout Europe in the past half century. Most typically it takes the form of orders placed as a direct result of promotion either in the main media or on the telephone. By offering a 'no questions asked' refund service, organizations have been able to persuade customers to acquire products or services simply on the basis of descriptions and/or pictures. In European retailing alone mail order is estimated at somewhere in the region of six to ten per cent of all activity today, although there are distinct differences of levels between EEC member states.

*Further reading*
Lonsdale, J. E., *Selling to Industry*, Business Publications, 1966
Bickers, R. L. T., *Marketing in Europe*, Gower Press, 1971
Morse, S., *The Practical Approach to Marketing Management*, McGraw-Hill, 1967

2.1 *How do you distinguish between marketing and selling in your organization? Who does what?*

2.2 *At what levels of selling does your organization operate?*

2.3 *What forms of selling does your organization utilize?*

2.4 *Are your activities at 2.2 and 2.3 similar to your major competitors? Why?*

## Question 3
# Are industrial marketing and consumer marketing different?

*On the face of it there are many differences between marketing to industrial customers and to so-called consumer markets. However upon closer examination many of these differences are more apparent than real.*

*An analysis of all marketing situations will reveal that the principles are constant but that it is in the application and the emphasis of these principles that the true differences between industrial and consumer marketing emerge. In practice the observable distinction lies in the particular blend given to the marketing mix, in other words consumer marketing may produce a certain mix with a certain emphasis, say on media promotion, whilst the industrial mix may place more effort behind direct selling.*

Any company wishing to achieve a profitable and durable penetration of a market must base its marketing strategy upon a thorough understanding of customer needs and wants and be totally familiar with the buying process utilized by that customer and the factors that influence that customer in his or her choice. This requirement holds for all companies, no matter what their products or the market to which they direct them.

Thus the immediate answer to our question might well be 'no'. However, this is too simplistic a conclusion and it is necessary to take a broader view of the question.

There are some obvious reasons for considering industrial and consumer marketing to be different. For example, it is possible to state that the demand for industrial products is ultimately derived from that for consumer products. Thus when a product is in derived demand, say a silicon chip, then the marketer is of necessity vitally concerned about changes in ultimate demand patterns. In some cases there are several intermediate levels between the sale of the product by one company and its consumption in the end market embodied in a consumer product. Thus the silicon chip might be sold as a chip to a company specializing in the use of microprocessors for use in control instrumentation. The producers of control instrumentation may be many and various, all of them manufacturing products – some for end markets and some for still other manufacturers! It can be seen therefore that the nature of the demand for that basic silicon chip can indeed be derived from the demand for several or many other products.

It might be useful to define industrial products as those products that are sold to industrial businesses, institutional or government buyers to be incorporated into their own products, resold or used by them within their own businesses.

But does this really make such products distinctive? Clearly it does not because in many instances the same physical product can be classified as either an industrial or a consumer good. An example of this is the electronic calculator. If it were sold to a business firm it would be classified as an industrial good; if it were sold to a student it would be considered to be a consumer good. There are many other examples. The same model of motor car is sold both as a representative's car to a business firm and as a family saloon.

If the product type cannot be used to differentiate marketing types, can the method of production be used? A power station, aircraft or ocean liner is usually custom built, on a one-off basis. The marketer is involved in developing the product with his customer for a period which could extend over a few months or for a number of years. But much the same could be said for a bespoke tailored suit. Again we find no clear-cut differences.

Perhaps the institution or outlets used to sell products could give a lead. Here, again, we find problems. The calculator and the car are sold by the same dealer. Builders' suppliers sell to do-it-yourself consumers as well as to professionals who use the goods in their own businesses.

Thus, developing a clear dichotomy between industrial and consumer goods is not easy. What can be shown is that while we can identify some principal types of industrial goods the approach to their marketing follows common basic principles. The principal types of industrial goods are basic raw materials, components, capital goods/equipment, and maintenance, repair and operating equipment.

Basic/raw materials are usually sold on a contractual basis. Often a tight specification is determined. Sales are usually determined by competitive pricing, credit terms and delivery reliability. For semi-manufactured items, e.g. steel, a standard industry specification can be set although some highly individual technical requirements are made and usually in these circumstances an associated technical service is vitally important.

Component markets differ from basic materials because of their wider variation. Product quality and reliability become extremely important. In these markets, e.g. plastic mouldings, a supplier can capitalize on a reputation for reliability. Capital goods markets are usually dominated by high technical ability on both sides. Because a total package is sold the marketer's sales team must be able to discuss all of the aspects of the equipment from installation through to maintenance scheduling. Maintenance, repair and operating goods are consumable items, usually of low unit value and often sold through distributors rather than directly.

It is sometimes suggested that a major difference between industrial and consumer marketing lies in the behaviour of buyers. Industrial buyers it is presumed tend to be 'rational' in their decision making whilst consumer buyers are open to influence from a whole range of sources such as media, merchandising, packaging, word-of-mouth and even impulse. Yet if we look more carefully at industrial buyers we also find that they are influenced by much the same factors. Many studies have been conducted of the industrial buyer and they all suggest that the buying process is highly complex, but no more complex than the consumer decision process, and that non-price factors tend to predominate in the purchase decision. Thus the marketer of industrial goods needs to pay careful attention to the nature of the buying process and to adapt the marketing mix accordingly.

## The industrial marketing mix

The concept of the *marketing mix* has already been introduced in the context of the four 'P's. We have found that it is difficult to make clear-cut distinctions between industrial and consumer marketing, indeed we might conclude that the principles for both are the same and that the significant differences lie in emphasis in the use of marketing mix elements.

Selling industrial goods usually requires a quite different emphasis from the salesman when compared with that required to sell consumer goods. The salesman makes far fewer calls than for consumer goods, say two or three per day as opposed to ten or more. His sales call is predominantly one of liaison and problem solving. He spends a lot of time with each customer.

Advertising in industrial marketing also works with a different emphasis. Because of the need to build a reputation it often takes some time before advertising can be seen to make an impact on sales. Apart from the need to build a reputation there is always the problem that unlike consumer goods, where many sales are made on a daily or weekly basis, the sales of many capital goods can occur but once in the life of a firm. This suggests that for many industrial goods advertising is often viewed as a source of information for industrial buyers, information on which they may not act for some considerable time. Clearly, the majority of consumer advertising is aimed at generating more immediate sales.

While some areas of marketing research may not be particularly appropriate to the industrial field generally all the research disciplines are relevant. Again it is a question of emphasis. For example, product testing is often a problem of developing a product in association with a customer to meet his specific needs and to solve his particular problems. A consumer product may be tested on a very much broader scale with far different parameters determining its success or failure. Industrial attitude surveys can

24

also be extremely useful when used to probe customer reaction to such things as technical service which is often a particularly important aspect of industrial goods marketing.

A number of differences of emphasis also exist in promotional media selection. For example the industrial advertising campaign is often aimed at reaching a comparatively small number of people across Europe whose reactions are vitally important rather than at ten million housewives in France or Italy. The technical press alternatives are many and varied making the task of media selection a difficult one.

Sales literature is a distinctly important feature of industrial marketing. The technical data and product specifications contained in leaflets are in many instances kept on file for reference purposes as well as being used for initial appraisal of competitive products. Certainly this is not usually the case for consumer goods, although for consumer durables such as cars, hifi equipment and other technically orientated purchases such comparisons are made.

Because industrial markets are usually well defined the industrial goods manufacturer can make very good use of direct mail advertising, personal postal advertising comprising a letter and often sales literature directly aimed at specific prospective purchasers. Accurate and current mailing lists are vital to the uccess of a direct mail campaign.

Although the sophistication of the computer enables direct mail techniques to be applied to consumer markets, success rates are generally lower and the cost continues to escalate making it non-viable for low value items.

Exhibitions are far more important to industrial marketing. They provide an excellent opportunity for both meeting prospective customers and demonstrating products. Similarly, public relations also forms a significant part of industrial marketing. Many prospective customers can be convinced of a product's performance and value to their business by reading about successful applications in other competitor organizations. Public relations in this case is defined as the management function which evaluates public attitudes, identifies the policies and objectives of an organization and plans and initiates a programme aimed at earning public understanding and acceptance.

In all our discussion so far we have been at pains to emphasize that there is no change in *principle* when marketing industrial products compared with consumer products. The major differences are in the *emphasis* that is placed upon each element of the mix. This emphasis is determined as a result of a careful examination and analysis of the industrial buyer's decision process just as the consumer goods marketer would attempt to build a strategy based upon an understanding of the consumer's buyer behaviour.

## Successful industrial marketing

A German manufacturer of commercial motor vehicle seating was faced with increasing competition by low-cost firms. For some time it met the competition's low prices but eventually reached a point where further price reductions were impossible. The company had mistakenly hoped that its reputation for quality and service would be sufficient to fight off the competition's low price levels. In addition to its commercial motor vehicle seating it made and sold a range of institutional furniture such as stacking chairs for churches and tubular steel canteen furniture. When it became clear that this strategy was not the right one it chose to develop a new product range. The new product range, office chairs, only had its steel tube construction in common with existing products. In almost all other respects there was no comparability.

Marketing seemed a problem. The new general sales and marketing manager had recently joined from a consumer goods company. After an initial appraisal of the situation he made plans to make the new range known both to end users and to office equipment dealers in what was at the time a very conservative market throughout the EEC. In addition, the trade structure differed in each member country.

To deal with the problem of the dealers, in-store displays were designed, stocking incentives were offered in the form of a bakers' dozen, i.e. for each order of twelve typist chairs an extra chair was delivered free. A dealer lottery was run in each country for a period of two months in which a minimum value of order entitled the dealer to enter his name into a lottery, with 'weekends in Paris for two' as the prizes (for the French traders it was Rome).

The approach to users was also unusual. Large companies were selected and offered substantial introductory discounts. Competitions were also used. The promotion featured the fact that the new range was ergonomically designed, but rather than stress the technical aspects of the design it majored on the benefits. The creative approach taken featured an attractive secretary enjoying after-work activities as well as working efficiently on her new typist chair.

This new approach took the trade by surprise. The results of this untypical industrial but thoroughly professional marketing approach were outstanding. Today the company has a profitable and established range of office furniture.

*Further reading*

Webster, F. E., Jr and Wind, Y., *Organizational Buying Behaviour*, Prentice-Hall, 1972

Robinson, P. J., and Faris, C. W., *Industrial Buying and Creative Marketing*, Allan & Bacon, 1967

**Self-audit questions**

3.1  *What are the key marketing features in your business that would make it appropriate to classify it as 'industrial' or 'consumer' ? Is the distinction fundamentally valid?*

3.2  *If the demand for your products could be termed 'derived' do you really understand the nature of demand in those end market(s)?*

3.3  *Are you truly sure that you cannot use the different emphases of consumer/industrial marketing in your industrial/ consumer business?*

## Question 4

# Does the marketing of services differ from the marketing of products?

*The principles of marketing apply in the marketing of services although differences of emphasis are present.*

*We can differentiate two basic types of service. The 'service product' offers the customer an intangible series of benefits which in most instances cannot be stored for future use; the 'product service' is vital to the functioning of the product and therefore an intrinsic part of it.*

*Service products can be usefully classified as either commercial or non-profit-making but in each case the marketing approach and the management of the marketing mix elements can be seen as appropriate. Product services are an inextricable necessity for the marketing of many products and interact with each of the four 'P's.*

Marketing seeks to establish what customers want, both explicitly and implicitly, and to provide for their needs. This sequence of matching wants with organizational capability is applicable to service products in the same way as it is to consumer and industrial products even though on occasion the criterion for success is less obvious. Take for example the range of government services. How can efficiency criteria be developed?

Because of the misconceptions in many minds concerning 'service products' and 'service offered with industrial or consumer goods' we should examine the difference between the two. Whereas the 'service product' is marketed purely as a service, e.g. banking, insurance, hotels, 'product services' are often an inseparable part of a package, e.g. computer installation and maintenance.

## Service products

Service products are those which produce a series of benefits which cannot be stored. They must be consumed at the moment of manufacture. If we consider this aspect for a moment we can see that a railway seat or a hotel room cannot be stored for later use. If it is not available when it is required, or not used when it is available, the opportunity for raising revenue is lost. The same seat or room may be required on an alternative day but it cannot be put into store on one day and sold on another.

This fundamental difference does not mean that marketing service products presents insurmountable differences. Rather it means that the marketing mix elements must be combined in a more suitable manner.

Consider for instance the problems of SNCF or British Rail. Many of the services to and from Paris or London are stretched to their limits for but a few hours each day while commuters are travelling to and from work. For the remainder of the day their trains travel far from full. To utilize this wasted capacity and to obtain a contribution towards profits SNCF and British Rail both offer lower-priced off-peak facilities.

It is not only the consumer or industrial goods manufacturer who attempts to establish his customers' needs and then tries to meet them profitably. British Airways developed the 'shuttle' service between London and Glasgow subsequent to extensive research into customers' requirements. It was found that for short journeys customers were much more interested in availability of service, punctuality, rapid embarkation and disembarkation than they were in in-flight meals or drinks. In response to this set of perceived needs they developed shuttle, a service that guarantees a seat provided that the passenger appears at an appointed time. In-flight ticketing dispenses with both pre-booking and lengthy check-in procedures.

In all these examples, and indeed for many other product services, their commercial success can be measured conventionally in terms of profitability. Clearly the lack of profit from a service product raises the same questions as does the lack of profits from either consumer or industrial goods. Is the service right? Am I promoting it in the appropriate way? Is the price too high or low? Is it being sold in the right places?

For some service sectors these questions are easily posed but difficulty exists in arriving at answers and solutions. Professional services in medicine, dentistry, accountancy, architecture, management consultancy are of this type. For such service products constraints are imposed in terms of promotion and pricing. Advertising a particular expertise is often forbidden, nor may prices be freely set. Nevertheless they can and do compete with each other by innovating within the marketing mix structure, for example their place of business or the mix of services that they provide.

There are other forms of service products for which the benefits accruing to the purchaser are not direct. For example, building societies offer the benefits of being able to determine where you live, in what type of house, and often afford an additional bonus in a capital gain through price inflation of property. Together with banks they also offer the facility, through numerous plans, to save for any one of a number of eventualities. Their marketing to potential users will emphasize derived benefits rather than the product itself.

Let us consider those service products for which profitability cannot be used as an efficiency measure. Primarily these are service products in the social or welfare field. The motor car has brought untold benefits to society. It has also provided many serious problems. For example, drinking and driving are unacceptable bedmates; poor driving standards exacerbate accident injuries, using seat belts can reduce injuries. Can marketing help to reduce drunken driving, discourage accidents or encourage the wearing of seat belts? How can the principles of marketing be applied here? Who are the customers? What are their needs?

Commercial organizations attempt to make a profit and satisfy customer needs by means of a profit objective. Reaching this objective or failing to do so is in fact the measure of their efficiency. Relating this to the social/welfare context, we can use as a measure of efficiency the success or failure in reducing social problems. Thus fewer road deaths at hours notorious for drinking and driving can be used as a measure of success. It is by no means perfect. There can be many extraneous influences at work as well but despite this it is better than no measure at all.

We have explored both commercial and social/welfare service products. We might finally add the dimension of service within a service product.

Many companies engaged in the marketing of physical products have found that they can develop profitable diversification spin-offs by marketing their 'know-how'. Thus, a Dutch company engaged in the production of dyestuffs found that there was a small but highly profitable market for the production knowledge and application techniques that they had acquired over the years. A separate company was set up to exploit these skills – a service product spun-off from an industrial product. Similarly British Rail have established a successful consultancy company which advises other countries on how to develop rail services.

## Product services

We must also consider our second major aspect of service. Many consumer and industrial goods are sold on the basis of service either before the sale is made, or after the sale, or indeed both. A British minicomputer manufacturer's sales staff spent considerable time with prospective customers determining their specific needs before attempting to sell them any particular computer. Highly trained systems analysts studied the prospective company in terms of the tasks done by company employees. In this way they traced the flow of information, decisions, organization inputs and outputs. Based upon these studies they made recommendations not only for the applications of their products, but also for improvements in the client company's operations. Following the sale and depending upon the size of the computer and its type of application, the company provided maintenance engineers to service the equipment. This detailed attention to product services built them a most successful business in a highly competitive market.

Very similar supplier/customer relationships exist for most capital goods products to a greater or lesser degree. In shipbuilding the before-sales service often extends into a complete bespoke service with extensive after-sales activity to maintain and service the product, although batch production can reduce some of these expenses.

Consumer goods can also be subject to both before and after-sales service facilities. Indeed for Germany's VW/Audi the reduced after-sales service requirement has been made a major sales feature. VW promote computerized servicing diagnosis, and

Audi prolonged servicing intervals. Washing machine manufacturers offer service insurance packages to consumers across Europe, whereby for an annual payment, the appliance will be serviced regularly and replacement parts supplied without charge.

A major Norwegian house builder has been developing a before-sales service which extends well beyond a choice of sanitary ware and paint colour finishes. Within the constraints of local authority planning permission, and of course customers' budgets, a complete design service is offered to purchasers once a building site has been purchased. The customer can specify number and size of rooms and to a degree their location. Sales have boomed.

Service is not confined to products. Many suppliers have found that the way they pack, deliver and process customers' orders has an impressive impact on the customer which usually results in increased sales. A study of actual customer uses of a product, its relative importance to his business and the effects on his business of failure to supply can only result in a better supplier/customer relationship.

However, service costs money and somehow this must be recovered either in higher product costs, a service charge, or through greater contribution from increased sales. Either way, such service must be seen as an element in the marketing mix. A few moments' thought will show product service to be a substitute for or a complement to other elements in the marketing mix. It can either extend the price element or again through convenience aspects be applied to availability. A leading Italian manufacturer charges a higher price for his machine tools because of a technical differentiation which reduces the servicing frequency and therefore the servicing bill. Mass distribution of newspapers, bread and milk on a door to door basis undoubtedly increases the price of the product. It also makes life a lot more convenient.

## The marketing of services

The implication of these various examples of service products and product services is that exactly the same principles of marketing apply as in the marketing of physical products.

It is always important in any company not to think in terms of products or services *per se*. Rather it is more helpful to inquire what *benefits* do our products or services provide? Customers do not buy products or services – rather they buy the benefits that those products or services provide. This is not just a semantic point; it is an important distinction which can be vital to the long-term survival of the firm. There are many examples of companies who have taken a narrow view of their business and defined it purely in terms of the products or services that they produce and as a result they were forced out of business when competitive products or services were introduced providing the same benefits but in a more cost-effective way.

When it comes to devising a marketing strategy for a company in the service business the same factors should be considered as with any other firm – who are the customers? What are their needs? What benefits do they seek? How sensitive are they to the various elements of the marketing mix?

There are clear signs that the marketing concept is being increasingly accepted by companies in many service industries where previously it was thought inappropriate or not applicable. This is true of banks, building societies, design consultancies, even professions where their regulations permit. Indeed with the growing recognition that all companies are in service marketing to one degree or another it may be that the distinction between different types of marketing will soon no longer be made.

*Further reading*

Wilson, A., *The Marketing of Professional Services*, McGraw-Hill, 1972

Kotler, P., *Marketing for Non-Profit Organizations*, Holt, Rinehart & Winston, 1975

**Self-audit questions**

4.1  *What are the service dimensions to your product?*

4.2  *What importance is attached by customers to these elements?*

4.3  *Can your company's product offering be enhanced by developing its service dimension?*

# Question 5
## Who are our customers?

*To define in precise and actionable terms just who an
organization's customers are or could be is the first stage in
planning and implementing an effective marketing strategy.
Knowing where our sales are coming from, and also the source
of our profits, is the key to understanding current market
positions and for assessing the potential for the future. A number
of definitional issues are raised, for example, are the customer
and the consumer the same? Who are the potential customers for
our products as distinct from the actual users? What are the
appropriate measures to define a market? The answers to these
questions are vital to a fuller understanding of the company's
markets.*

We have seen how marketing can be defined as the matching of
the firm's resources to the needs of the customer. This presupposes
both the identification of those needs, a subject to be dealt with
in later questions, and also the identification of the customers. The
nature and identity of the company's customers is not always
given the attention that it deserves. Some indication of the importance of this knowledge can be gained from the following data,
taken from a Dutch company's experience in the pipe tobacco
market:

- 18% of the customers of its best selling product accounted
for over 80% of its sales
- 61% of the sales of the product were to people aged 35 and
under
- the sales of the company's product accounted for 8% of the
total industry sales.

This data was gained from surveys and industry sources and it
was felt by company management that it could provide some useful cues for marketing action. The question asked though was:
what was the message that this information embodied? The
answer to the question is contained in understanding *why* those
people who bought the product in such quantity did so and con-

versely in understanding why a large number of potential purchasers did not.

## Customers and consumers

Firstly we should distinguish between customers and consumers. In many cases the customer is acting as an intermediary or an agent for the final user of the product. This difference is more than semantic. Consider the case of the industrial purchasing officer buying raw materials such as wool tops, for conversion into semi-finished cloth which is then sold to other companies for incorporation into the final product, say a suit or dress, for sale in consumer markets. Here we can see that the requirements of those various intermediaries and the end-user himself are eventually translated into the specifications of the purchasing officer to the raw materials manufacturer. Consequently, the market needs that this manufacturing company is attempting to satisfy must in the last analysis be defined in terms of the requirements of the ultimate user, the consumer – even though our direct customer is quite clearly the purchasing officer.

A further distinction can be made in that the purchasing officer is himself only an agent for the user; he attempts to represent the requirements of his firm through a purchasing specification, and to meet those requirements within a budget constraint. An analogous situation exists with the housewife who in her weekly shopping trip is acting as an agent on behalf of her household. She is the customer, her family are the consumers. Her motivations and her actions, like the purchasing officer's, can be explained, partly at least, by her perceptions of the needs of the consumers on whose behalf she is acting.

Given that we can distinguish between customers and consumers the next question to be faced is who are our potential customers – as distinct from our actual customers – and who are our 'lost' customers? The answers to such questions can often provide us with more valuable insights for marketing strategy than a simple analysis only of our existing customers. Being able to identify our potential customers is the first stage in converting them to actual customers. A definition of the potential market for any product or service must be grounded upon a clear view of what basic customer needs our product meets or is intended to meet. Do these people use alternative products or do their needs go unsatisfied?

It is common practice in marketing to refer to the *market share* that a product or brand currently holds. This is essentially a measure of the proportion of the total sales of similar types of products that our product accounts for. Thus Gerber baby foods could be described as having a percentage share of the Belgian or British market. This share could be expressed either in terms of the value of the market, often called the 'sterling' share, or it could be expressed in terms of units sold. Either way it is a measure of actual sales as a proportion of an actual market rather than a measure of actual sales as a measure of the potential market. The difference between these two measures gives some indication of the scope for extending the market penetration of our product.

Past or lost customers are equally difficult to identify but like our potential customers a knowledge of who they are could be invaluable in increasing our marketing effectiveness. When in answer to a later question we discuss the methods of market research we will see that there are ways in which both potential and past customers can be identified thereby enabling some explanation of their behaviour to be attempted.

## Describing the customer

Knowing who our customers are implies an ability to describe them in terms appropriate for marketing action. Depending upon the nature of our business we might usefully describe industrial customers in terms of their level of purchases from us, the size of their total turnover, or the sort of business that they are in. For consumer markets their geographical location, their age structure, their frequency of purchase of the product, their income or other such measures might be more appropriate. These typical measures of markets are termed *demographic character-istics*. One of the benefits of these measures is that they are commonly used bases for the majority of data collection exercises such as censuses and they have the additional advantage of being relatively straightforward features to measure. However, convenience should not be allowed to obscure the possible irrelevance of such measures to specific market circumstances and this is a point to which we will return in the next question. It is essential to be able to describe the company's markets in terms which will act as guides to marketing strategy – knowing the precise age structure of our market, for example, is of no use to us if we are unable to capitalize upon this fact in terms of advertising or distribution policies. Nevertheless, even basic demographic data can provide a valuable source of initial market information, even though we may then wish to look beyond that data. The tabulation below, for instance, demonstrates national differences in consumption of various foods:

% of households with:

| | instant coffee % | tea % | canned soup % | instant potatoes % | frozen vegetables % | corn/ olive oil % | crisp- bread % |
|---|---|---|---|---|---|---|---|
| Austria | 31 | 61 | 1 | 5 | 11 | 28 | 11 |
| Belgium | 38 | 48 | 25 | 9 | 12 | 83 | 5 |
| Denmark | 17 | 92 | 17 | 11 | 42 | 30 | 34 |
| Finland | 12 | 84 | 10 | 8 | 12 | 17 | 64 |
| France | 42 | 63 | 11 | 23 | 5 | 36 | 3 |
| West Germany | 49 | 88 | 19 | 21 | 21 | 74 | 26 |
| Great Britain | 86 | 99 | 76 | 17 | 24 | 57 | 28 |
| Italy | 10 | 60 | 3 | 2 | 2 | 94 | 18 |
| Netherlands | 62 | 98 | 43 | 7 | 14 | 13 | 15 |
| Norway | 17 | 83 | 4 | 17 | 15 | 28 | 62 |
| Spain | 40 | 40 | 2 | 14 | 7 | 91 | 13 |
| Sweden | 13 | 93 | 43 | 39 | 45 | 48 | 93 |
| Switzerland | 72 | 85 | 10 | 17 | 15 | 61 | 30 |

It will be apparent that the problem of defining who our customers are will be complicated by the scale of the markets in which we operate. Philips of Eindhoven have a pretty clear idea of who their customers for heavy electrical equipment stations are, for example. On the other hand the same company does face greater problems in defining their market for domestic electric light bulbs. A market which can be measured in terms of tens of customers is generally easier to define than one measured in terms of tens of millions of customers.

## The 80/20 rule

With the greater size of a market in terms of purchasing units there is almost always encountered a phenomenon known as the '80/20' rule or the *Pareto effect*. This simply means that it is usual for a small proportion of customers to account for the largest part of the business. It may not be 80/20, it could be 90/20, but there is rarely a proportional balance between our customers and the purchases they make from us. In many manufacturing companies this relationship can provide a viable means of describing a large market in terms of the importance to the business of individual customers. Let us say that we graph the proportion of customers that account for a certain proportion of sales then we might expect to find a relationship somewhat similar to that shown in FIGURE 1.

FIGURE 1

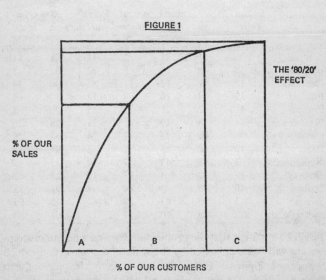

THE '80/20' EFFECT

% OF OUR SALES

A    B    C

% OF OUR CUSTOMERS

Here our customers have been categorized simply as 'A', 'B' or 'C' customers according to the proportion of our total sales that they account for. The 'A' customers, perhaps 25% of the total, account for 70% of the sales; the 'B' customers, say 55% of the total – account for 20% of total sales and 'C' customers – 20% of the total – account for the remaining 10% of sales. This type of classification can be extremely useful when it comes to developing a strategy for taking particular products to particular markets especially when it is realized that exactly the same phenomenon can be found if we plot the proportion of our products that provide a given proportion of profits.

The Pareto effect is found in almost all markets from industrial compressors to banking, postal services or dog food. The marketing man in consumer markets will frequently concentrate his efforts on the 'heavy half' as it is called in those circumstances where he believes that it is easier to sell more of something to people who are already committed users of the product. In the direct mail business, for example, it is an accepted principle that customers who have bought a product, any product, through direct mail in the past are the prime market for selling additional, even different, products to in the future.

Knowing the customer sounds easy enough. Detailed analysis of exactly who he or she might be is, however, vitally necessary if effective matching of capabilities with wants is to be accomplished.

*Further reading*

Boyd, H. W., and Levy, S. J., 'New Dimension in Consumer Analysis', *Harvard Business Review*, Nov/Dec 1963

For a fascinating study of consumers the following book is recommended for perusal:

Allen, D. Elliston, *British Tastes*, Hutchinson, 1968, and Panther, 1969

**Self-audit questions**

5.1 *What is the distinction in your organization between customers and consumers? Do you positively market and/or sell to both?*

5.2 *Does the Pareto effect apply in your business? What do you do about it?*

5.3 *What do you learn from your lost customers and consumers?*

# Question 6
# Are all customers the same?

*Recognizing that customers differ from each other in terms of their needs and wants provides opportunities for market segmentation. Segmentation, it is suggested, can provide the key to profitable marketing in competitive markets. The means whereby groups of customers are distinguished from each other is clearly important and attention has to be paid to the choice of criteria for segmentation. Customers can be categorized on many dimensions but only those criteria which relate in some way to purchasing behaviour and which are themselves actionable are of any use to the marketing strategist.*

Once an organization's customers, actual and potential, have been identified, the question becomes can it satisfy their wants? The problem would be more easily solved if all our customers exhibited the same requirements or, put another way, if their wants could be satisfied by the same product sold in the same way. However, as we saw in answer to the previous question there are differences in demographic characteristics between customers and closer examination reveals that other differences exist as well. An undifferentiated marketing campaign to a mass European market will seldom have a uniform impact across Europe because of these differences amongst customers.

On the other hand catering to what may be highly specific individual requirements within the market place is not a viable strategy for many products. Fortunately we often find that when a market is subjected to scrutiny the members of that market fall into natural groups or segments within which customers exhibit the same broad characteristics. These segments form separate markets in themselves and can often be of a considerable size. Looking at markets in this way is termed *market segmentation*.

By taking a segmented view, marketing can bring many advantages to an organization. In the first place many companies have found that if they can identify a viable sub-market they can cater exclusively for the needs of that segment and gain a degree of dominance that would probably not be possible within the total market. One German firm in the specialist instrument field took this view and discovered that it was more profitable to have a 50% share of a DMk 50 million market than to have a 5% share of a DMk 250 million market. They realized, as many other organizations in all fields of enterprise have recognized, that market segmentation strategies can be the key to profitability in competitive markets.

Recognizing that customers are different can enable the marketer to achieve a closer matching of customer needs to the firm's product or service offering. Thus the matching process that has been referred to since the outset is in fact facilitated by adopting a segmentation approach. Segmentation strategies have an additional value in that they allow the company to relate its strengths and weaknesses to its marketing approach by ensuring a concentration of resources in those areas where the company has the greatest advantage.

If segmentation of our markets has these positive advantages how may we actually identify such groupings of customers?

## Identifying customer groupings

Two approaches to segmentation suggest themselves:
- market segmentation through an analysis of the characteristics or attributes of the customer
- market segmentation through an analysis of the responses or behaviour of the customer.

Let us take a more detailed look at these approaches, which do not necessarily need to be mutually exclusive by the way. First of all segmentation by customer characteristics poses the question 'what sort of characteristics?' We saw in the previous answer that demographic features can be a useful way of looking at customer differences and they could indeed be used as the basis for a segmentation strategy. For example, a French commercial bank might decide to develop particular services that are angled at the young and newly married in the joint annual income bracket of Fr80,000–Fr90,000. Or a Danish manufacturer of marine engines might set up a division concerned with the sale of marine systems to the supertanker market. But such demographic characteristics are not the sole criteria whereby we can characterize markets. In consumer markets for example it might be appropriate to use personality factors or 'life style' types as the basis for segmentation. The pan-European marketing campaign for Martini, for example, has been aimed at penetrating a particular segment of the market that portrays, or aspires to, a particular life style and Israel's pan-European campaign to develop sales of avocado pears built on a similar dimension.

Segmentation on the basis of behavioural responses can either be in terms of an examination of usage characteristics such as how often the segment members purchase the product or how sensitive they are to price changes. On the other hand we can take an approach which is becoming increasingly popular which is to examine the benefits that the customer is seeking from a product or service and to use these as the basis for segmentation. This is called *benefit segmentation*.

The Italian toilet soap market can be looked at in a number of ways. It can be analysed in terms of the age and income of users for example or again it can be differentiated in terms of price sensitivity. These criteria in themselves may form useful bases for segmentation but the benefit-orientated approach described here confronts the problem rather differently. It is based upon the notion that the reason a customer purchases a specific product is to acquire the 'bundle of benefits' that he or she perceives it to contain. Because individuals will have different priorities when it comes to required benefits we can see that the rationale for segmentation under this scheme is the grouping of customers on the basis of the similarity of their perception of the benefits that a particular product contains. So in the case of toilet soap, market research might reveal that there is a segment that seeks mainly hygiene-related benefits such as cleanliness, deodorant properties, freshness. Another segment might be largely concerned with the cosmetic properties of the soap, e.g. skin care and perfume. Still another segment might be seeking 'value for money' as the main benefit and therefore is guided more by the unit price of the soap. These benefit segments could then provide the basis for the design of marketing strategies aimed specifically at them.

Similar examples could be taken from industrial and service markets as the principles are universal.

# Criteria for segmentation

Whatever the means whereby we distinguish between our customers the criteria that we use for categorization must be appropriate to the specific product/market situation. In other words why segment a market on the basis of age of customer in the case of consumer and service markets or on the basis of plant throughput in the case of an industrial market, if those attributes have no relationship to potential purchasing behaviour? This is the advantage of seeking to identify the benefits that the customer is seeking to acquire from a product purchase – once we know the nature of these benefits and the particular combinations that the market seeks then we are better poised to position our product offering to those customers who are most likely to be attracted to it.

Clearly, for a strategy of market segmentation to be successful there are a number of requirements that must be met:

– firstly, as we have noted, the criteria used to differentiate between customer groups – market segments – must be relevant to the purchase situation

– secondly, the segment should be of a sufficient potential size to ensure that an adequate return can be made on any marketing investment made within it

– thirdly, an identified market segment can only be exploited if it can be reached. It must be reachable both through the media (where media promotion forms a part of the proposed marketing mix) and through the appropriate channels of distribution

– fourth, for a segment to be viable in its own right it is necessary that it can be distinguished from other segments but at the same time its members must have a high degree of similarity on the criteria adopted for segmentation.

The realization that customers are different has led to many successful marketing innovations by a wide variety of companies. Banks and insurance companies have identified markets for specialist services, producers of industrial power plants have introduced new products on the basis of identified customer benefits, cigarette manufacturers have introduced cigarettes which

have been aimed at small – but profitable – segments of a very
large total market. These and other examples provide a testimony
to the value of market segmentation.

## Segmentation in action

A Danish brewer of lager developed a new approach to its product strategy based upon a fresh look at its markets as a result of
a segmentation analysis. The company knew that national differences existed in terms of preferences for beer and lager and it had
some idea of what the criteria for preference were. Scandinavians
preferred a lighter, drier drink than did the Germans and Dutch
who went more for a fuller, sweeter beer. Such knowledge was
useful but it did not provide great insight into why some beers
did better than others in some markets. Again the company knew
that the majority of beer was consumed by a minority of drinkers.

Evaluating their existing knowledge the company believed that
there could well be 'gaps' in the European market where minority
needs, which were not being currently met, could be filled by a
product aimed just at them. The question was: who were these
people and what attributes should the product possess to ensure
an appeal amongst these potential consumers?

It was decided that a multi-country study should be conducted
in Denmark, Sweden, Holland and Germany to ascertain the
nature of current preferences and to relate them to identifiable
market segments.

The means whereby this was done was through an attitude survey which questioned existing drinkers on their preferences for
beer and lager along a number of dimensions such as strength,
brightness, dryness and so on at the same time as deriving data
relating to demographic characteristics such as age, income, oc-
cupation. Information was also collected which was designed to
give an indication of the life styles that these drinkers associated
with the consumers of various existing brands of beer and lager.

The research established that people have 'images' of the type
of person who drinks particular drinks. Thus one drink might
be seen as being 'masculine' another as 'friendly' another as
'sophisticated' and so on. The segmentation study revealed that
amongst occasional drinkers there was a need, particularly dis-

played by younger respondents, for a 'potent but convivial' drink at a price that was not excessive but that was high enough to give a connotation of quality.

The outcome of this research was the successful development and launch of a 'German'-type beer with special packaging in the form of a foil top and a label that was closer in its format to a bottle of Château wine! The promotional appeal was very much oriented towards the status aspirations of the younger, sophisticated end of the market and the price was about twenty-five per cent higher than the regular beers in the market. This is just one example of the profitable exploitation of a market segment, based upon a careful analysis of market characteristics and the opportunities within that market.

*Further reading*

Frank, R. E., Massey, W. F., and Wind, Y., *Market Segmentation*, Prentice Hall, 1972

Wind, Y., and Cardoza, X., 'Industrial Marketing Segmentation', *Industrial Marketing Management*, vol 3, no 3, March 1974

**Self-audit questions**

6.1  *Are all your customers the same? If not, how do you classify them?*

6.2  *How does benefit segmentation apply to your customers and consumers?*

6.3  *Are there any market segments in which you are not present which meet the basic criteria outlined?*

# Question 7
# Why do customers behave the way they do?

*An understanding of the way in which customers behave in terms of product purchase decisions and the ability to explain that behaviour is an essential pre-requisite for marketing success. If we can better understand how and why our customers buy we are better positioned to sell to them. There is now a considerable body of knowledge available covering the mechanisms of customer choice – in consumer, service and industrial markets. This knowledge can be summarized and distilled in the form of a number of 'models' which themselves can afford an effective basis for marketing action.*

In a recent product test two well-established brands of margarine were tested against each other in 400 French households. One was the brand leader and the other was a much smaller brand in terms of market share. Half the sample were given the two brands in plain foil wrappers simply marked 'X' and 'Y'. The other half received the two brands in their usual, familiar wrappers. All 400 housewives were asked to state which brand they preferred overall. In those households where the brands were given in the anonymous wrappers there was approximately a 50/50 split in choice – neither brand emerging with a significant difference. However amongst those households where the brands' true identity was revealed the preference was 65/35 in favour of the brand leader.

Why?

Similarly a manufacturer of British defence equipment selling to the Middle East has found that price is of minor importance, that quality is taken for granted, that performance is assumed to be as specified but that the critical determinant of the purchase order is the ability to establish a personal rapport with the buyer. On occasions orders have gone to the most expensive tenderer where the performance levels have been lower rather than to the cheaper, competitor's bid.

Why?

These examples are not quoted because they necessarily demonstrate anything odd or out-of-the-ordinary on the part of the particular customers cited. Rather, they demonstrate the complexity of the mechanics of customer behaviour.

## How do people choose?

The study of customer behaviour in marketing is essentially the study of how people choose. What are the influences that affect these choices and how do they differ from person to person or from product to product? These are the questions that the marketer must answer if he is to build an effective marketing strategy for it is indisputably true that if we know more about how a customer chooses then we are in a much better position to present products or services that will lead to his or her choice being our offering.

This contrasts with the point of view, adopted by some, whereby the consumer is viewed simply as a 'black box'. This view holds that as long as one knows that for a given stimulus there is the likelihood of a certain response then what goes on in between does not matter. Such a view is too crude and limited for the development of creative marketing strategies. It postulates the customer reacting rather like one of Pavlov's dogs. If we expose him or her to a sales visit, for example, an order does or does not result. Now in reality we know that sales visits by themselves rarely generate orders because there are so many other elements at work as well. If there is a connection between sales visits and orders placed it will probably not be a direct one. It is more likely that a visit might influence the customer's attitude towards the product or service, and that influence along with many other factors might then influence choice behaviour in the direction we wish.

Accordingly it is more often the case that today's marketing practitioner is looking for *models* of customer behaviour which attempt to describe and explain the influences of several and hopefully all marketing actions upon choice. These models need not necessarily be over-elaborate or complex but they do need to be grounded upon a secure theoretical proposition. This need for theory should not dismay the practical marketer, indeed it has often been remarked that there is nothing so practical as good theory.

This requirement for a deeper understanding of choice mechanisms applies equally to industrial and service markets as it does to consumer markets. There is often a feeling that industrial buyer behaviour is somehow more rational or straightforward than consumer goods buying. This has repeatedly been demonstrated not to be the case. The marketer encounters the same patterns of interplay of behavioural factors in the marketing of machine tools or printing inks as he does in marketing toothpaste, canal barge holidays or education.

## Some models of buyer behaviour

Over the years a considerable body of theory and knowledge has developed about customer behaviour. Whilst there are almost as many theories and models as there have been major writers on the subject it is possible to categorize these developments under a limited number of headings.

*The rational customer* – the idea of the rational customer is based largely upon the writings of theorists in economics. In their attempt to understand how a customer allocates his resources of disposable income they suggested a model whereby the customer seeks to maximize his satisfaction or 'utility' in terms of what he or she gets for what he or she pays.

A whole corpus of micro-economic theory has grown up largely based upon the work of Alfred Marshall which attempts to demonstrate the basis for customer choice in terms of rational, economic criteria. Essentially this theory suggests that choice behaviour is determined by the utility derived from a purchase at the margin compared with the financial outlay necessary to acquire the item. As such it ignores all the many non-price factors that marketing practitioners know to exist in given situations. It also tends to suggest that there are laws of customer behaviour to which all will adhere. One obvious instance of this is the economists' concept of the *demand curve*, which postulates that in all but a number of situations (which are termed paradoxical by economists), as the price of a product goes up demand for it will fall. This does indeed happen in many cases but yet there are too many exceptions. A British company launched a new health-type apple drink on the market and because of new manufacturing technology was able to price it as low as ordinary lemonade. The launch was accompanied by extensive advertising describing the product benefits and stressing its quality. Demand was extremely disappointing and subsequent research revealed that potential customers felt that at the low price the benefit and quality claims being made for the product were just not believable. The price was therefore increased by twenty per cent and sure enough demand rose! In fact over the next two years the price was increased in stages until the price was double the original launch price and with every price rise sales rose also.

The implication of this example is that whilst economic factors are undoubtedly important in many situations they by no means explain the totality of customer behaviour. Price carries quality connotations for the customer which must be taken carefully into account once they have been understood.

*The psycho-social customer* – later developments in the theory of customer behaviour centred around the relationship of the customer to his environment, and to the impact of this relationship and his inner motivations and perceptions, upon purchasing decisions made. Thus contributions to this field of theory have come from sociology, anthropology and psychology. The general thrust of this school of thought is that customers' attitudes and behaviour are affected by such things as family or work organization, prevailing cultural patterns, customer reference groups and the like.

In consumer markets we are all familiar enough with the idea of 'keeping up with the Joneses' as a frequently encountered form of behaviour. This is one form of social influence upon choice behaviour, i.e. the customer takes into account the reactions of others. However such behaviour is by no means limited to consumer markets. A leading Italian manufacturer of word-processing equipment for office use has found that there is a quite definite imitation effect in that these fairly expensive units are frequently being purchased primarily because the customer feels that a company such as theirs should have one.

Often it is found that customers are influenced in their choices by so-called *reference groups.* These are groups to which an individual might aspire to belong and will thus try to emulate the behaviour of that group. Alternatively they might be groups or associations by whom they wish to be judged. Thus the teenager might seek to follow the dress and manner of a favourite pop star; a junior brand manager might emulate the style of his marketing director; the business school student of a professor of business policy; or an industrial purchasing officer might be influenced in his purchases by the behaviour of his opposite numbers in more successful firms.

One of the important issues arising from a study of the customer from this psycho-social point of view is the question of the link between attitudes and behaviour. Most marketing theorists accept that attitudes play a central role in choice behaviour – indeed attitudes towards a service or product will often ultimately determine whether it is purchased or not. Nevertheless the concept of an 'attitude' is fairly difficult to define of itself although it is generally agreed to comprise three components:

(i) a *cognitive* element, i.e. the beliefs and perceptions held by the individual about the benefits of and/or the product or service under study

(ii) an *affective* element, i.e. the feelings and emotions aroused by the benefits of and/or the product or service

(iii) a *conative* element, i.e. a tendency to take action in relation to the benefits of and/or the product or service.

Given positive readings for each of these three components then the customer will be as favourably disposed to buy the product or service as is possible. Clearly there will be many influences upon attitudes including word of mouth experience of a product or experience of competitive offerings. Nevertheless, inadequate resources can still prevent purchase taking place as can poor distribution.

It must also be recognized that it is possible for behaviour to influence attitudes as well as vice versa. This involves a concept of customer learning whereby experience of a product helps shape one's attitude towards it. It is often suggested, for example, that we change our attitudes to fit our behaviour. Whatever the complexities of the attitude/behaviour relationship it is quite clearly an aspect of customer behaviour which is of vital importance to the marketer.

*The problem-solving customer* – in contrast to any of the established theories of customer behaviour, particularly those based largely on economic or psycho-social precepts, is the concept of the problem-solving customer.

This view of the customer is based upon the notion that all behaviour can be seen as directed towards solving buying problems. A main theme in the problem-solving model is that customer behaviour, in seeking to satisfy buying goals, is essentially 'rational'. Customers will act to solve problems as they themselves perceive them within the constraints of their learning capacities and the available information. In other words the customer buys goods to solve problems as best he knows how. The choice of product will depend upon how well he perceives the product as solving that problem. Knowledge of the product, the information that can be gathered about it and all possible experience of it will act to influence choice.

Problem-solving activity is largely an information gathering and processing task. The sources of such information will not be solely confined to advertising or salesmen but may be acquired through every source of contact between the customer and the product. Thus we see the problem-solving customer as attempting to evaluate a whole array of pieces of information in its broadest meaning whether through word-of-mouth, own past experience, price, product design and quality, packaging or whatever.

The implication for the marketer, whether selling advanced technology to industrial markets or biscuits to housewives, is that the successful product must in some preferably unique way be capable of solving real customer problems. The marketing and communications mix must clearly be designed to aid the customer both in the initial identification of the problem and in pointing towards a solution.

## Customer behaviour in action

Every day millions of European customers make billions of buying decisions. Almost every single one involves choice – even when the choice is *not* to buy. Every one of those decisions can be looked at and analysed under the following headings, and effective marketing requires that they are:

- Problem identification
- Information seeking
- Recognition of alternatives
- Evaluation of solution
- Selection of strategy
- Decision
- Active implementation

A recent case study of a Dutch firm involved in road haulage looked at how that company made the decision to acquire replacement vehicles for its fleet. Examining the decision under each of the above headings it became obvious that the level of information seeking was high and a number of alternative vehicles were considered. The business eventually went to a supplier who as part of his marketing approach had put together a detailed cost-benefit analysis of how the vehicles would affect running costs and also improve performance. In addition a leasing package was prepared, again with a full analysis of the impact on the purchasing firm's cash flow. The successful supplier had recognized that the best way to market his product was on the basis of helping solve the customer's problem in its wider context.

*Further reading*
Lunn, J. A., 'Consumer Decision-Process Models' in Sheth,
   J. N. (ed), *Models of Buyer Behaviour*, Harper & Row, 1974
Tuck, M., *How do we Choose?* Methuen, 1976
Howard, J. and Sheth, J., *The Theory of Buyer Behaviour*,
   Wiley, 1971

**Self-audit questions**
7.1   *How and why do your customers and consumers choose to buy from you rather than your competitors?*
7.2   *How does your marketing effort match with your customers' and consumers' problem-solving activities?*
7.3   *How do attitudes affect behaviour in your market?*

# Question 8
# How do products make profits?

*Products make profits for the company by effectively providing customers with the benefits they seek within carefully controlled cost and revenue parameters. In this question we shall be concerned to discuss the ways in which the organization can develop a policy towards the products that it markets and how it might identify profitable opportunities for further development.*

'Customers don't buy products; they seek to acquire benefits.' This is the guiding principle of the marketing director of one of Britain's more innovative companies in the hair care business.

Behind that statement lies a basic principle of successful marketing. When people purchase products they are not motivated in the first instance by the physical or basic attributes of the product but by the benefits that those attributes bring with them. Let us take some simple examples. You, the reader, bought this book not because it was a book but rather because it gave the promise, one would hope substantiated, of bestowing certain insights about marketing. Even those who buy books to impress others still seek specific benefits, perhaps personal prestige. A purchaser of industrial cutting oil is not buying the particular blend of chemicals sold by Britain's leading manufacturer of industrial lubricants, rather he is buying a bundle of benefits which will solve a specific lubrication problem.

Indeed, this last example provides another guide to identifying what it is that people buy. People buy one product rather than another because they see in it the best way of solving a particular 'problem'. Here we are using the word 'problem' in the sense of a consumer need requiring satisfaction.

This is not just a question of semantics. It is crucial that a company wishing to develop its business profitably defines its scope of activity, present and future, not in terms of the products or services that it produces but rather in terms of the benefits that it provides or the problems that it solves. If the company takes too narrow a view of its business by defining its business as the manufacture of, say, fountain pens then it may run the risk of concentrating upon becoming better and better at producing fountain pens whilst gradually the market is turning to other forms of writing implement. The alternative approach would be for such a company to recognize that the benefits it provides are in the field of written communication and that if better or more cost-effective means of providing that benefit come along then people will naturally move towards the new product.

One famous marketing author called this narrow product-based view of the business 'marketing myopia' and that particular ailment has been the cause of the decline of many previously successful companies. To overcome this myopia the organization must continually review its product range by confronting the question: does each product provide relevant and desired benefits for today's needs? Answering this question objectively requires a knowledge of the market which goes beyond simple head-counting and demographics. To answer that question the organization must regularly conduct benefit-needs research. It is easier than one might think to ask customers to describe the benefits that they derive from existing products, it is rather more difficult to elicit information on benefits that ideally the customer would like but which currently are not provided. However, it can be done as one French manufacturer of floor polish has found. Based upon group discussions with housewives it was found that there were something like twenty benefits which to a greater or lesser degree were sought by users of these types of products. Such benefits as, for example, 'stands up to damp mopping', 'provides a lasting shine', 'no streaks', 'non-slip'. Using these features a further sample of housewives were questioned on what combinations of benefits they most preferred and also to rate existing products in terms of how well they provided these benefits. What emerged from this study was a detailed basis for the development of a new product and the design of a whole new approach to marketing that product.

## The product as a vehicle

Previously we have defined marketing as the process of matching customer needs to corporate capabilities at a profit to the firm.

We can now develop this concept further by recognizing that the vehicle whereby this matching is achieved is the product. Thus the product is central to the fortunes of the company and the need for a defined policy towards products is paramount. Put at its simplest the product will only continue to provide the means whereby *corporate* objectives might be met if it concurrently provides the means whereby *consumer* needs are met. FIGURE 2 illustrates this idea.

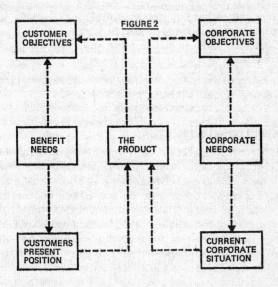

FIGURE 2

The art of successful product management therefore must be based upon a clear view of just *how* the present and future product range will continue to meet these twin goals of customer and corporate objectives.

As a first stage in successful product management it is essential to think of the 'product' as a variable in the marketing mix in the same way that we might consider price or promotion. The extent of freedom to manoeuvre on the product variable will be largely based upon the internal resources of the firm and where its strengths are in relation to the competition. We shall explore the technique of *strengths and weaknesses analysis* in more detail in answer to Question 10 in this book and at this stage it is sufficient to suggest a number of pertinent questions to aid in establishing the appropriateness of the current product strategy:

- What benefits do customers seek from this type of product? Does our product provide these benefits in greater proportion than competitors' products?
- What competitive product advantages are causing us to lose market share?
- Does our product range still provide 'value-in-use' to the customers in relation to its cost to them?
- Does each product in our range still meet the corporate objectives set for it?

The answers to these and other questions will then provide a firm basis for developing a product/market strategy.

## Product market strategy

What is product/market strategy? Very simply it is the totality of the decisions taken within the organization concerning its target markets and the products that it offers to those markets. Strategy implies a chosen route to a defined goal and an element of long-term planning. Thus the product/market strategy of the firm represents a commitment of the future direction of the firm.

The effective company is one which plans for growth, and in terms of its product/market strategy seeks to plan its product portfolio well in advance, in terms required or determined by product policy. The company must plan for growth and both product policy and product/market strategy must be growth oriented but clearly the growth must have purposeful direction if future profits and cash flows are to be maximized. The direction is provided through appropriate growth policies indicating the vectors along which the firm is intended to move. The two main vectors of commercial growth are product development and market development. The very simple matrix shown in FIGURE 3 depicts the concepts employed.

It is apparent that some product/market strategy alternatives are less costly to pursue than others and the marketing director must develop his strategy at all times with the cash flow and profitability

| MARKET | PRESENT | PRODUCT MODIFICATION −QUALITY −STYLE −PERFORMANCE | PRODUCT RANGE −EXTENSION −SIZE VARIATION −VARIETY −VARIATION | NEW PRODUCTS IN RELATED TECHNOLOGY | NEW PRODUCTS IN UNRELATED TECHNOLOGIES |
|---|---|---|---|---|---|
| PRESENT | MARKET− PENETRATION STRATEGIES | PRODUCT− REFORMULATION STRATEGIES | PRODUCT RANGE− EXTENSION STRATEGIES | PRODUCT− DEVELOPMENT STRATEGIES | LATERAL− DIVERSIFICATION STRATEGIES |
| NEW | MARKET− DEVELOPMENT STRATEGIES | MARKET− EXTENSION STRATEGIES | MARKET− SEGMENTATION −PRODUCT DIFFERENTIATION STRATEGIES | PRODUCT− DIVERSIFICATION STRATEGIES | LONGITUDINAL− DIVERSIFICATION STRATEGIES |
| RESOURCE AND/ OR DISTRIBUTION MARKETS | FORWARD OR BACKWARD INTEGRATION STRATEGIES | | | | |

FIGURE 3

objectives in mind. It follows that marketing will attempt to increase profits and cash flow from *existing* products and markets initially, because this is usually the easiest and least costly approach. Some examples however can illustrate the total pattern of strategy at work.

*Market penetration* – a Dutch ice-cream manufacturer successfully promoted the use of his product as a dessert and thereby increased the use of his product without changing either product or pack.

*Market development* – a British hotel chain has opened up a new market by offering 'leisure learning' weekends in its hotels.

*Product reformulation* – an Italian car manufacturer found that poor finish and subsequent rust were proving costly in terms of lost sales. A rust-proofing programme has not only won back dissatisfied customers but has attracted new customers who began to be critical of their current car and switched to the Italian manufacturer because of the promise of extra quality. By making the investment this manufacturer was able to reach new buyers and achieved a concurrent *market extension* strategy.

*Product-range extension* – a European breakfast cereal manufacturer found that his new variety pack became very popular amongst children who were no longer 'locked in' to one type until the pack was emptied.

*Market segmentation* – a German food manufacturer added a range of large-size packs to his range which was already selling well. This addition opened a new market segment with catering users.

*Product development* – a British electrical equipment manufacturer already selling industrial fittings very successfully in a competitive market introduced a range of fire security fittings which were an immediate success.

*Lateral diversification* – a successful French company in the materials handling market acquired a small warehouse design consultancy which then enabled the company to offer a complete package to its customers.

*Longitudinal diversification* – an Irish television rental company successfully launched an office equipment leasing company into an area hardly known before. Hitherto, office equipment was purchased. Leasing became an attractive and profitable alternative for both customers and the company.

*Forward integration* – a British wallpaper manufacturing company found that market share, profit and cash flow were all much improved by owning its own retail outlets.

*Backward integration* – a Dutch dairy producer found that moving back to own dairy herds smoothed out supply problems and improved service regularity.

*Further reading*

Levitt, T. M., *Marketing for Business Growth*, McGraw Hill, 1974

Luck, D. J., *Product Policy and Strategy*, Prentice Hall, 1972

**Self-audit questions**

8.1   *Can you define your business in terms of the benefits your products provide or the problems that they solve?*

8.2   *How could you measure the extent to which your current product range meets customers' benefit requirements?*

8.3   *What methods exist within your organization for reviewing the relative performance of each of your products?*

8.4   *Do you have a clearly defined product/market strategy?*

Question 9

# What products should we market?

*We have seen that the strategy a firm adopts towards its offering in the market place will determine its long-run viability as a successful entity. It needs to be recognized that for most organizations their product offering should be based upon a dynamic view of the market place. That is, over time the marketing environment will inevitably change and will thus necessitate a changed response from the firm. That response*

*takes the form of a programme of adjustment to their product/
market strategy.*

The majority of companies offer more than one product and
operate in more than one market. Decisions on product/market
strategy therefore must be made in the context of a product range
or *portfolio* and the defined segments in which this portfolio is
marketed.

Before examining the idea of the product portfolio in more
detail it is necessary to look at some of the factors influencing the
performance of individual products.

One of the most prevalent ideas to have emerged in the marketing literature over the last twenty years or so has been the concept of
the product life cycle. This seemingly simple notion suggests that
products move through identifiable stages over their life and typically exhibit the generalized pattern of sales, shown by FIGURE 4.

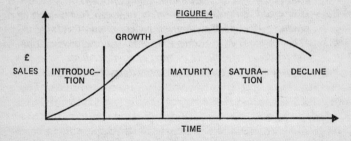

FIGURE 4

The product life-cycle model postulates that if the product is
successful in its initial introduction to the market (and many new
products fail at this stage) then as the product becomes established repeat purchase grows, word of mouth spreads, the more
cautious are persuaded to try the product and the rate of sales
growth increases. Often competitive organizations, seeing potential, will imitate the product and add their weight to the promotional expenditure and accelerate the increase in the total sales
of the product. But no market opportunity is infinite and ultimately the rate of sales slows as the product moves into its
maturity stage of life. Here there are few new sales to be obtained,
rather repeat purchases from loyal customers and some customers

won from competitors are the only way in which an increase in sales may be achieved.

As the product reaches market saturation there will normally be no further sales expansion unless the company modifies its marketing mix. Eventually the product moves through to the decline stage of its life cycle, where despite often desperate actions sales continue to decline.

This at least is the theory of the product life cycle. Indeed many products can be seen to have had sales histories that have conformed to such a pattern.

Nevertheless as a practical generalization the product life cycle may not be totally valid. It can be argued for example that the nature of a particular product life cycle is determined more by the activities of marketing management than it is by any underlying 'law'. For example, a German brand of cigarettes had exhibited a continued sales decline over a number of years and yet with the appointment of a new brand manager and a new advertising agency sales picked up and it is now the number-two brand in its product class! Had the management of that firm acceded to the literal view of the product life cycle then the brand would have been allowed to die.

It is also important to distinguish between the life cycle of a product *type* (e.g. cigarettes) as distinct from the product *form* (e.g. filter cigarettes) and the specific *brand* (e.g. Embassy No 6). Thus we may well be able to distinguish certain patterns of movement in sales of a brand but these have no relationship to basic trends in the overall market for the product form or the product type – and vice versa.

From a management point of view the product life-cycle concept is useful as it focuses our attention upon the likely shape of things to come if we take no corrective action. As we saw in Question 8 in the consideration of the product/market matrix there are several courses of action open to a company in its attempts to maintain sales of its products. FIGURE 5 illustrates how one British company in the automobile lubricants field was able to maintain market leadership through refusing to believe in the product life cycle as an inevitability. As growth in sales began to slow for the brand the company initiated a programme of product range extensions and market development which successfully took

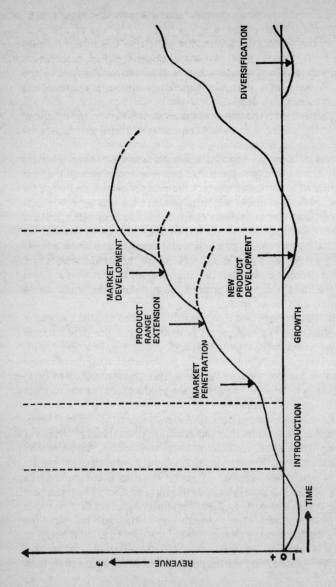

FIGURE 5

the brand into additional stages of growth. At the same time the company was aggressively seeking new products and even considering potential areas for diversification.

## The product portfolio

At any one moment in time the profitability of the firm will depend upon the individual profitability of each of the products in its portfolio.

We might imagine that a review of a company's product portfolio would typically reveal products in various stages of growth, maturity and decline. The precise balance of that portfolio would not only indicate today's profitability but would also be a fairly sound guide to tomorrow's profitability.

The idea of a product portfolio has many similarities with the investor's portfolio of stocks and shares. The investor, for example, may wish to achieve a balance between yield or income and capital growth; some shares might produce more of the latter and less of the former or vice versa. Again the investor might attempt to achieve a balance in terms of risk – some shares having a higher risk of capital loss attached against which must be balanced the prospect of higher returns.

The analogy fits the corporate product portfolio well. The company also will seek to assemble a portfolio that will meet its objectives – be they objectives of growth, cash flow, or risk. As individual products progress or decline and as markets grow or shrink then the overall nature of a company's product portfolio will change. It is imperative therefore that the whole portfolio is regularly reviewed and that an active policy towards new product development and divestment of aged products is pursued.

One approach towards product portfolio review that has gained considerable recognition in recent years is the so-called 'Boston matrix', named after its originators, the Boston Consulting Group.

The thinking behind the Boston matrix is simple yet it has profound implications for the firm.

Usually discussions of product life cycles are conducted in terms of the sales of the product or perhaps the profit accruals to it. However there is a further consideration which may be of even more importance in product portfolio decisions and that is cash flow. Profits are not always an appropriate indicator of portfolio performance as they will reflect changes in several assets of the company such as inventories, capital equipment, or receivables and thus do not indicate the scope for future development available to the firm.

Cash flow is a key determinant of the firm's ability to develop its product portfolio. To emphasize this the Boston Consulting Group developed a means of classifying products within the firm's portfolio according to their cash usage and their cash generation.

In their simple matrix, products are classified according to their positions on two dimensions: *relative market share*, and *market growth rate*. Market share is used because it indicates the extent to which the product should be capable of generating cash, market growth is used as an indicator of the product's cash requirements. The measure of market share used is the product's share relative to the largest competitor. This is important because it reflects the degree of dominance enjoyed by the product in the market.

The matrix shown in FIGURE 6 summarizes the categories.

FIGURE 6

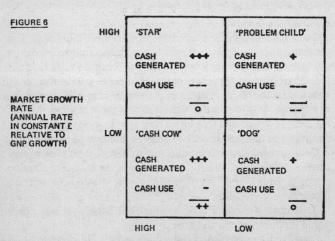

MARKET GROWTH
RATE
(ANNUAL RATE
IN CONSTANT £
RELATIVE TO
GNP GROWTH)

RELATIVE MARKET SHARE
(RATIO OF COMPANY SHARE TO SHARE OF
LARGEST COMPETITOR)

The somewhat graphic labels used to describe products in each of these quadrants, i.e. 'PROBLEM CHILD', 'STAR', 'CASH COW' and 'DOG', give some indications of the market position and prospects of a product in those categories. Thus the PROBLEM CHILD is a product which has not yet achieved a dominant market position and thus a high cash flow, or perhaps it once had such a position but has slipped back. It will be a high user of cash because it is in a growth market.

The STAR is probably a relatively new product that is still growing but has already achieved a high market share. On balance it probably is more or less 'self-financing' in cash terms. The CASH COWS are yesterday's stars which have retained their high market shares but are in markets where there is little additional growth.

As the name suggests, the DOGS are those products which have little future and may indeed be a cash drain on the company. They are probably candidates for divestment.

The art of product portfolio management is to develop a mix of products that in cash terms will be more or less self-funding in total. Thus over time in a well-managed business one might expect products to move through the matrix as in FIGURE 7 (a). The flow of funds within the firm might appear as in FIGURE 7 (b).

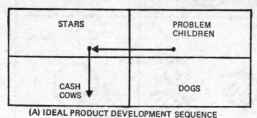

(A) IDEAL PRODUCT DEVELOPMENT SEQUENCE

FIGURE 7

(B) INTERNAL FLOW OF FUNDS

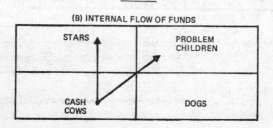

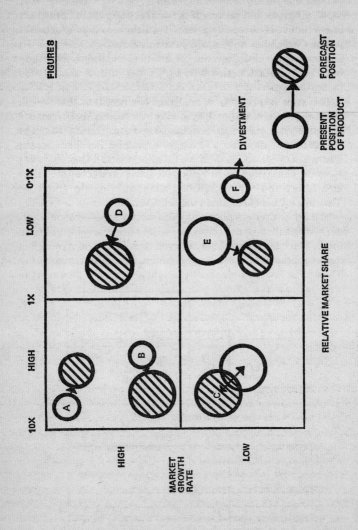

FIGURE 8

The Boston matrix may be used to develop a prognosis of how a company's portfolio might look in, say, five years' time. In the matrix shown in FIGURE 8 a manufacturer of office copiers and associated equipment has identified the current position of his product range and has also forecast the expected position in five years' time. The area of each circle is proportional to the product's contribution to total company sales volume.

The definition of high relative market share is conveniently taken to be a ratio of one and above. The cut-off point for high versus low market growth needs to be defined according to the specific circumstances prevailing in the markets in which this company operates but here the company have taken a figure of ten per cent.

This analysis enabled the company to formulate a policy towards new product development as well as to point towards the policies that needed to be pursued towards existing products in order that a balance could be maintained within their portfolio. This type of display is particularly useful to demonstrate to senior management the implications of different product/market strategies and can highlight potential weaknesses with current strategies.

*Further reading*

Abell, D. F., and Hammond, J. S., *Strategic Market Planning*, Prentice Hall, 1979

Luck, D. J., and Ferrell, D. C., *Marketing Strategy and Plans*, Prentice Hall, 1979

Dhalla, N. K., and Yuspeh, S., 'Forget the Product Life Cycle Concept!' *Harvard Business Review*, Jan/Feb 1976

**Self-audit questions**

9.1   *Can you identify life cycles for your company's products and for your company's markets?*

9.2   *Do you recognize the need to adjust your company's marketing mix strategies depending upon a product's position on its life cycle?*

9.3   *What are the objectives underlying your company's product portfolio strategy?*

9.4   *Can you identify 'problem children', 'stars', 'cash cows', and 'dogs' amongst your company's product range?*

9.5   *Will the portfolio be in 'balance' in five years' time?*

# Question 10

# How can we select and develop new products?

*A company's product development programme must be firmly based within the corporate plan. An audit of the overall state of affairs of the company should assess its current position and decide what its future direction should be. Such analysis permits the formulation of its objectives. By using an analysis of the gaps, the need for a range of strategic alternatives is noted and they can be developed. The gap analysis approach ensures that all product and market alternatives are thoroughly investigated for growth potential before perhaps more costly diversification alternatives are investigated. This is called 'macro' product/ market development. The 'micro' considerations define the range of factors that must be used when a product is assessed in terms of its fit within the product portfolio and for its contribution towards objectives. New Product ideas can arise from customers, scientists, competitors, salesmen and top management. When this is not enough, idea generation can be more structured and several approaches have been used with success. The ideas once generated must follow a rigorous evaluation and analysis procedure.*

In our reply to Question 8 we emphasized the need for explicit objectives with an agreed definition of the business, from which viable strategies could emerge. A matrix was developed which explored strategic alternatives that might be considered.

In arriving at both the objectives and the possible strategies it is usual to conduct a *position audit* of the company. A position audit involves a thorough evaluation of the company's internal and external operating environments. Internal factors are the company's basic *strengths* and *weaknesses*, external factors are the *opportunities* and *threats* facing the company over which it has no direct control.

For example, established customer loyalty can be seen as a strength. Products with high market shares ensuring good profits with strong cash flow positions are strengths. A large proportion of products in the decline stage of their product life cycles could be a distinct weakness. Clearly the identification of a weakness does provide an opportunity to rectify the situation, even to the extent of converting it into a strength.

The external factors may be viewed similarly. Opportunities and threats may be posed by political and regulatory events at home and overseas. The quadrupling of oil prices in recent years has had significant effects on almost all businesses. Long-term social changes should be examined and so too should technological developments.

The position audit helps the company ascertain where it currently is. Objectives help the company decide where it wants to be. Another technique, however, *gap analysis*, helps an organization analyse what is to be done. As FIGURE 9 shows, what an organization is trying to achieve and what it can expect from current operations often results in a gap between expectations and requirements. We can use the strategic alternatives discussed in answer to Question 8 to fill the gap.

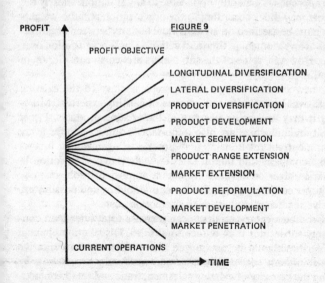

FIGURE 9

PROFIT

PROFIT OBJECTIVE

LONGITUDINAL DIVERSIFICATION

LATERAL DIVERSIFICATION

PRODUCT DIVERSIFICATION

PRODUCT DEVELOPMENT

MARKET SEGMENTATION

PRODUCT RANGE EXTENSION

MARKET EXTENSION

PRODUCT REFORMULATION

MARKET DEVELOPMENT

MARKET PENETRATION

CURRENT OPERATIONS

TIME

This macro approach sees that the company evaluates each possible alternative systematically. Clearly it is less expensive in terms of R and D activity, production and marketing to obtain growth from market penetration or market development strategies rather than from pursuit of diversification policies which may, in some events of necessity, require a major acquisition.

## New product micro strategy

Each organization requires a format or procedure in order that all possibilities which are conceived will be carefully considered. There are a number of approaches whereby weights are applied to each judgement factor depending upon its importance. A comparative matrix can be constructed to evaluate the relative importance of each factor. In this model each general area is given a relative weighting and this is sub-analysed for sub-factors. An illustration (opposite) clarifies the approach.

At the completion of such micro analysis the total can be compared against that set for all new products out of the total of 100. The approach is generally applicable to any situation. Clearly the factors may differ according to the organization and the weightings must be ascribed on an individual basis as between organizations at any moment in time and within a single organization over time. However, some of the sub-factors are worth considering in detail.

A new product idea, if it is complementary to the existing range, will be easier to sell because of existing expertise. Moreover it may well help sell more of the existing products. Price/quality relationships are also important. To move too far away from a current relationship may upset existing customer images of the company and inhibit sales. A wide range of variation in qualities, sizes or flavours presents a number of problems, e.g. customer confusion, excessive inventory holding and possibly excessive segmentation with high promotion costs.

If complementary products can increase total sales then conversely substitutes may reduce total sales. Distribution channel similarities should be maximized since this ensures an effective and minimum cost distribution and maximum penetration by using the capacity of existing salesmen, trade and retail contacts,

| MAIN FACTOR | SUB-FACTOR | WEIGHT (A) | COMPATIBILITY VALUES 0.1.2.3.4.5. 6.7.8.9.10 (B) | TOTAL (A × B) |
|---|---|---|---|---|
| **Marketing** (4.0) | Range complementarity | 0.15 | | |
| | Quality/price relationship | 0.20 | | |
| | Variants (sizes/flavours) | 0.10 | | |
| | Effects on current sales | 0.10 | | |
| | Channel synergy | 0.35 | | |
| | Physical distribution synergy | 0.20 | | |
| | Demand stability | 0.35 | | |
| | Market breadth | 0.20 | | |
| | Patent protection | 0.50 | | |
| | Investment protection | 0.25 | | |
| | Service features | 0.25 | | |
| | Competitive advantage | 0.60 | | |
| | Growth potential | 0.75 | | |
| | **Marketing total** | 4.00 | | Sub-total A × B |
| **Production** (2.0) | Plant usage | 0.25 | | |
| | Additional investment | 1.00 | | |
| | Personnel-technical | 0.50 | | |
| | Raw materials | 0.25 | | |
| | **Production total** | 2.00 | | Sub-total A × B |
| **Finance** (2.0) | Revenue-cashflow | 0.75 | | |
| | Profitability/objectives | 0.75 | | |
| | Risk | 0.25 | | |
| | Investment criteria | 0.25 | | |
| | **Finance total** | 2.00 | | Sub-total A × B |
| **Manpower** (1.0) | Management | 0.30 | | |
| | Supervisory | 0.30 | | |
| | Skilled | 0.20 | | |
| | Unskilled | 0.20 | | |
| | **Manpower total** | 1.00 | | Sub-total A × B |
| **Procurement** (1.0) | Domestic | 0.20 | | |
| | Known contacts | 0.10 | | |
| | Supplier concentration | 0.10 | | |
| | Lead times | 0.30 | | |
| | Price levels/time | 0.30 | | |
| | **Procurement total** | 1.00 | | Sub-total A × B |
| | | | | Grand total A × B |

and much the same can be said for all of physical distribution. This is a feature known as *synergy*, which could alternatively be described as the '2 + 2 = 5 effect'. It would normally prove far less profitable to introduce a product requiring exclusive distribution facilities, e.g. a dry goods grocery manufacturer introducing frozen foods, than to add another dry goods product.

An even level of demand throughout the year is preferable to seasonal fluctuations. Investment is recovered more quickly and there are no consequent problems of under-utilization of labour and facilities. Similarly a wide market can be preferable to one which is highly segmented.

A product which offers protection from competitive imitation either through patents or because of large capital requirements or long development times is preferable to one with little or no protection. Alternatively, the product itself may be an imitation, in which case the relative strengths and weaknesses of competitors should be assessed.

Since growth forms a basic objective for most companies, a new product should be one which demonstrates growth potential compatible with that required by company objectives. Service requirements must also be considered from at least two aspects. A technical product may well score highly because the design eliminates much of the maintenance required by its predecessors or competitors. It must also be considered from the point of view that the new product does have servicing needs and that the existing distribution channel may not have the ability to handle this work. This often proves a problem with diversification strategies.

For some products the *production considerations* may be just as important as the marketing factors and we may need to consider many more aspects, e.g. location and size considerations. Clearly the use that can be made of existing plant capacity is important. Equally the amount of additional investment is important. Technical personnel are highly trained and specialist and their transfer competence to a new field must be considered. A product requiring new raw materials may also require new handling and storage techniques which may prove expensive.

*Financial considerations* relate to the product's capability to perform within the product portfolio against the company's economic objectives. Thus cash generation and profitability are important. The risk of the investment measured against current products and their development costs and income streams over time, must be considered in view of company policy. Clearly the product must pass the investment vetting used by the company in terms of payback, average return, net present value or internal rate of return.

*Manpower requirements* will vary both with size and complexity of the product project. Whatever these may be the manpower considerations must be taken into consideration for planning purposes. The problems of industrial relations must never be overlooked particularly when new technologies are introduced.

The *procurement factors* are important. Domestic sourcing may be preferable because of quality and reliability considerations. Known vendor contacts are easier to deal with. Supplier concentration may suggest that price and suitability problems can be expected if there are few suppliers. Erratic lead times can cause havoc with production schedules if they are not previously known. At best they mean high buffer stocks to set as a safeguard against poor delivery. In a period of rapid inflation price trends over time must be watched for cyclic or other crucial traits.

## Product conception and gestation

There are a number of sources of new product ideas but the major ones are customers, scientists, competitors, company salesmen and management. Customers, at all levels of distribution, are never reticent in this area and a number of profitable ideas have been suggested. A Yorkshire supermarket group promoted the idea of mushy peas as a new frozen foodline to manufacturers.

Scientists often look for commercial applications for their work. A great deal of sponsored work in universities is to this end. Competitors often introduce new products that prove successful. A French earth-moving company successfully improved upon a unique sales feature of a competitor and moved ahead in market share.

Company salesmen by virtue of their proximity to the customer have firsthand experience of customers' unsatisfied needs – and of their complaints. This information can be obtained without too much difficulty by an appropriate reporting procedure. Top management knows the company's strengths and weaknesses and is in a good position to develop product policy. Based upon the company's strengths they are able to place such emphasis as seems necessary on the factors outlined above. Thus they may well direct the search along lines to seek products which are complementary, use existing distribution channels and physical facilities and so forth.

New product ideas are so vitally important for a growing company that a number of techniques have been developed and used quite successfully to ensure an adequate flow.

*Attribute listing* involves listing the attributes of an object and then modifying different attributes in a search for an improved specification for the object. For example one might list the attributes of a hand food mixer and consider modifications, e.g. nylon bearings, larger crank, or interchangeable beaters, to improve its performance.

*Forced relationships* is a technique in which product ideas are first listed then considered in relation to each other. An insurance company recently combined household effects insurance with personal effects insurance thus giving a lower per unit cost for each insurance policy issued but a higher value per policy sold.

*Brainstorming* is often described as a creative conference, the sole purpose of which is to produce a large number of ideas. A group of six to ten people is given a brief outline of a problem and such technical information as may be required to determine any constraints. The group meets one or two days later simply to generate ideas. No criticism or evaluation is permitted; the group generates ideas off the top of the head for *subsequent* evaluation. One major European oil company reported a successful brainstorming session to discover uses for a middle-distillate oil. In thirty minutes over one hundred ideas had been generated.

Operational creativity or *synectics* adapts brainstorming. Here the brief is defined so broadly that participants have no clue as to the precise nature of the problem. Proponents of this method suggest that brainstorming produces actual solutions too quickly, before a sufficient number of perspectives have a chance to develop. When the group appears to have exhausted the initial perspectives the coordinator can introduce facts which further refine the problem.

74

Arriving at any product idea is not easy; developing an idea to be ready for market is even more difficult. To minimize failure, and to ensure early rejection where appropriate, it is beneficial to follow a rigorous evaluation and analysis procedure. One such procedure which many companies have adopted as standard is:

| | |
|---|---|
| **Exploration** | the search for product ideas to meet company objectives |
| **Screening** | a quick analysis of the ideas to establish those which are relevant |
| **Business analysis** | the idea is examined in detail in terms of its commercial fit for the business – the micro strategy outlined above |
| **Development** | making the idea into hardware |
| **Testing** | market tests necessary to verify early business assessments |
| **Commercial-ization** | full-scale product launch, committing the company's reputation and resources |

The total time consumed in such a process varies substantially. A non-ethical drug, a cold cure, was developed in one year, but the zip fastener took as long as thirty years. Printed circuits took three years.

*Further reading*
Staudt, T. A., 'Higher Management Risks in Product Strategy', *Journal of Marketing*, 37, January 1973
Wills, G., *Technological Forecasting*, Penguin, 1971

**Self-audit questions**
10.1 *How do you currently select and develop new products in your organization?*
10.2 *Are you familiar with different procedures in other companies? If so, why do they differ?*
10.3 *What weightings are currently most appropriate for your company in assessing new product ideas?*

# Question 11
# Can we test new products before they reach the market?

*Whilst a steady flow of successful new products into the market place is a prerequisite for long-term corporate survival the introduction of such new products is not without its risks. To reduce the uncertainty surrounding the viability of proposed new products it is necessary to apply rigorous tests of market acceptability. Such tests must balance the cost of delay and the costs of information gathering against the benefits of reduced uncertainty.*

We have seen that new products are the life blood of a company in its attempt to survive in a dynamic and competitive marketing environment. The search for viable and profitable new products must be a continuing task of marketing management but it is a task that is fraught with risk. For the majority of companies the introduction of a new product into the market place involves a considerable investment, both in the development process and in the initial introductory stage when market acceptance has to be won if the product is to succeed. This investment can represent a considerable slice of a company's resources not only financial but physical and managerial, but there can be no cast iron guarantee that the investment will yield the sort of return that the company would consider acceptable. In some cases a single new product failure could spell disaster if the company had pinned all on success only to find that the outcome did not match expectations. Consider the case of Rolls-Royce and the RB211; here the company – prehaps wrongly with the aid of hindsight – had committed major resources to an engine which, whilst technically unimpeachable, did not match the wants of a large enough segment of the market to recoup the tremendous development costs and it led to the virtual collapse of the company.

This example can be matched by hundreds of others from consumer, industrial and service markets. Research has pointed to the fact that in some product areas up to eighty per cent of all new product launches fail in the sense that they do not meet marketing targets and are withdrawn soon after their introduction. Some product fields, such as grocery or cosmetics, are more prone to early deaths than others but whatever the context all the evidence seems to point to a high failure rate for new product introductions.

What then should be the role of marketing management in attempting to reduce the uncertainty that surrounds the new product launch?

There are no certain solutions that would produce crystal-ball revelations on the prospects for success or failure but there are means which can go some way towards a greater quantification of the risks implicit in a new product launch and it is the purpose of this question to explore some of these methods.

## When the testing has to stop

It is always an easy way out of decision making on crucial marketing issues to say: 'We need some more research.' The problem with continually putting off the moment of decision is that delay costs money. In the first case there is the actual cost of gathering further information which can be substantial; secondly, there is the 'opportunity cost' of forgoing profits which could be earned if the product was launched now and proved successful. However, to be balanced against these *costs of delay* are the *costs of proceeding too rapidly*. These latter costs relate directly to the risk of failure in the market place which decline, hopefully, with every additional stage in the research and testing programme. We can view the trade-off between these two costs schematically as in FIGURE 10.

Whilst our research technology is too primitive to allow us to determine where the optimum balance in this cost-benefit framework should be, the diagram serves to emphasize the nature of the new product testing decision, i.e. a process of balancing the uncertainty surrounding a new product launch against the costs of reducing that uncertainty still further.

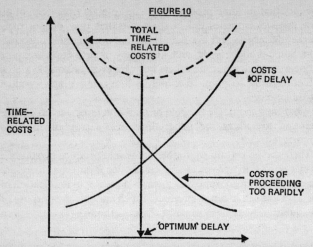

FIGURE 10

TIME FROM INITIATION OF NEW PRODUCT CONCEPT TO FINAL LAUNCH

## A sequence for new product testing

Let us consider the means available to a European manufacturer of sisal-based floor coverings who markets his products to the 'contract' market – a market where an intermediary, often an architect but also a purchasing agent, purchases the product for use in offices, hospitals, schools and so on. This is a fairly complex market with various alternative modes of floorcovering being available. It is a highly competitive market and frequently the floorcovering is specified on the basis of some total, overall scheme for interior decoration.

This company on the advice of marketing consultants was attempting to formalize its new product testing procedures. Previously they had endeavoured to ascertain trends in styles and colours on the basis of past sales and there had always been an attempt to perform a break-even analysis on the basis of projected costs and prices. Beyond this, new product testing was more a matter of technical assessment of product quality.

The process suggested by the consultants was essentially sequential with each stage in the analysis providing the opportunity to pause and make one of three decisions: launch the product now, collect further information, or abandon the product now. These decisions were given the short-hand of GO, ON and NO GO.

The testing sequence, illustrated in FIGURE 11, started with a test designed to give a broadbrush picture of how acceptable the product concept was to its potential market. The *concept test* was administered by means of a dozen interviews conducted by trained interviewers with architects and purchasing agents representative of the target market. The idea of the test was to expose them to details of the technical specification, possible colour ways and recommended uses. Sometimes artists' impressions of designs and colours were shown. The results of this stage of the test sequence were naturally entirely qualitative but they served to eliminate all those products which were complete non-starters. It was scarcely possible to make a GO decision at that stage.

The next stage was still qualitative, in fact it was termed the *qualitative screen*. As the name suggests it was a screening process which basically asked two questions: is the product concept compatible with company objectives and is it compatible with company resources? Considerations involved in the first question were such issues as: does the concept complement our existing market offering and is it compatible with the image that we seek and the segment of the market with which we identify? The second question raised issues such as: does the company have the capital to get this product to market and to develop an initial level of sales and does the company have the necessary knowhow and adequate physical facilities?

Assuming that the product concept survived this screening process the next stage in the testing sequence was the *economic analysis*. This analysis was designed to examine the economics of the project under differing assumptions of costs incurred and revenue achieved. It was conducted at a fairly simple level as the company at that time had only a limited knowledge of how the market would react to products priced outside the limited band that represented their experience. It was acknowledged that this stage of the testing sequence could be made considerably more sophisticated by applying the methods of investment appraisal that were in common use in other companies.

On occasion at this stage the company might feel sufficiently confident in the viability of the concept to move ahead to a full-scale market launch. Naturally such a decision would have to be based upon some highly positive results from these initial stages in the test sequence as the cost of setting up a production line, producing initial stock and developing and implementing a promotional programme is substantial. More often a decision would be taken to go on to the next, and more expensive, stage of the analysis: the *product test*. The product test was designed to gain impressions from a relatively large number of potential customers of how they would react to the physical product in comparison with competing products. Product testing involves the creation of the physical product in quantities at least sufficient to perform the test – hence the expense. The aim of the test is to identify a representative sample of the target market and to interpret the reactions of this sample to the product, especially their reactions relative to the competing products. This company recruited a panel of architects and purchasing agents and using trained interviewers they compared, according to a number of appropriate criteria, the proposed new products with selected competitive products. The analysis of these results enabled a picture to be built up of how the proposed new product compared with existing products on a number of key dimensions.

FIGURE 11

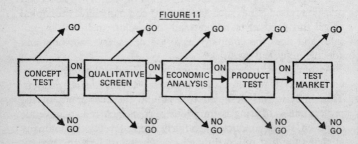

At this stage the company made the final decision: GO or NO GO. Clearly uncertainty about the new product's success would still remain but the sequential testing procedure had enabled this uncertainty to be reduced to acceptable levels. The company could have gone on, as many companies do, to conduct a *test market*. The test market, as the name implies, is an attempt to reproduce the conditions of a full-scale launch but on a much reduced basis. Often a town, or geographical area, chosen as representing the ultimate market, is selected and the product is launched in that town or area alone and its progress observed. As such a test is very much an 'experiment' it is necessary to ensure that conditions within the test market would be such that they could be fully reproduced on a national scale. For example no extra promotional effort should be expended other than an amount proportional to the total spend in the proposed full-scale launch.

Test markets can never be completely reliable indications of ultimate market performance because, quite apart from the problems of 'grossing up' small-scale test market results to provide a global picture, there is always a possibility of unusual competitive activities which may distort the results.

Whilst we have portrayed these steps as a sequence it should be clear that some of the stages could be conducted concurrently, e.g. the qualitative screen and the economic analysis. Whatever the sequence the purpose of new product testing remains the same: to reduce uncertainty surrounding the new product to a level acceptable to the company whilst still facilitating a launch to be made at the earliest possible time. The methods of product testing might vary from marketing situation to marketing situation but whether the product be a new airline service, heavy-duty transformers, or a vinyl wallpaper the principles are universal and the benefits considerable.

*Further reading*

Kraushar, P. M., *New Products and Diversification*, Business Books, 1969

Wills, G., Hayhurst, R. and Midgley, D., *Creating and Marketing New Products*, Staples Press, 1973

**Self-audit questions**

11.1   *How did you decide the timing of your most recent product launch? What were the costs of proceeding either more slowly or more rapidly?*

11.2 *Chart the sequences of a recent product launch. Which were the riskiest stages?*

11.3 *Can you suggest any improvements in the way your organization currently launches new products?*

# Question 12
# How can we estimate how much product we will sell?

*All estimates of future sales take place against a background of uncertainty. The environments in which the marketing activity is set require a constant monitoring. Because of this uncertainty sales estimation must be able to provide a flexible framework for marketing action and must recognize the probabilistic nature of sales levels.*

*It is suggested that the estimation of market potential and the share that our product might be expected to achieve is the central task of the sales forecast. This task will be influenced both by the forecasting horizon and the stability of the markets in which we operate.*

The problem of estimating the level of sales of any product, new or old, is ever present and may only be imperfectly solved. Knowing in advance what levels of sales could be achieved given a particular marketing mix and a particular marketing programme would reduce considerably the complexity of the marketing decision. Naturally the ability to make definitive statements about the future is only rarely encountered and the marketing decision maker has to fall back upon less precise devices.

Even some of the most carefully prepared forecasts of future sales have ways of being disproved by events. The wider environment in which the forecast is set changes in ways that are not always foreseen and thus not incorporated in the forecast. Energy crises, crop failures and drought, revolutions – these are just a few of the major impacts that can upset the forecast. It could indeed be suggested that if the world is so dynamic then what is the purpose of forecasting anyway? The answer is quite simply that any attempt to reduce the uncertainty that surrounds the future (and the future starts *now*) will, if used as a flexible input to a planning process, make us question the appropriateness of what we are currently doing. The key word in the previous sentence was flexible. The forecast should not be a straitjacket which directs our activities, as is so often the case when a sales forecast becomes a target with all the sanctity that numbers tend to be endowed with in management. Flexibility implies the use of forecasts in the planning process that cover a range of possibilities. Forecasts deal with contingencies not certainties. The head of planning in a large multinational chemical company says: 'We have to have alternative plans that can deal with either/or eventualities.' Establishing the nature of the 'either/or' is the task of the market forecaster. Parallel to this need for flexibility is the need to recognize that the output of the forecast should be expressed in terms of a *range* of possible outcomes. Because of the imprecision of most forecasting methods sales estimates so derived are clearly surrounded by a band of uncertainty anyway, but beyond this it must be recognized that the process whereby any sales level is achieved is essentially *probabilistic*. In other words chance has a central role in the outcome of any marketing process. Our forecasts can, and should, be made to incorporate the probabilities that are implicit in the marketing environment in which we operate.

How then do we start to grapple with the sales estimation problem?

## Understanding market potential

We have already raised the difference between actual and potential customers in a previous question and the same distinction is vital to sales estimation. The forecaster is concerned with what proportion of the total market potential his actual sales will account for. Market potential has been defined as the maximum possible sales opportunities for all sellers of a good or service. As such it refers to the potential sales that could be achieved at a given time, in a given environment by all the firms active in a specified product/market area or segment. Thus the concept of market potential extends our view of the 'market' for our product in that we see the product as competing against alternative means of satisfying the same need. Successful sales estimation will therefore depend upon the determination of the proportion of the market that can be achieved given a specific marketing mix and marketing programme. Graphically this situation could be shown as in FIGURE 12.

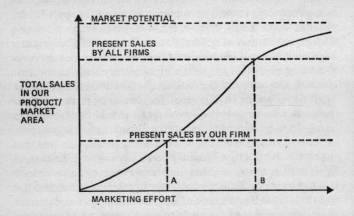

A= MARKETING EFFORT BY OUR FIRM

B= TOTAL MARKETING EFFORT BY ALL FIRMS IN OUR PRODUCT/MARKETING AREA

FIGURE 12

It will be realized that such a presentation is a static picture of actual and potential sales at a given time in a given environment and could be influenced both by environmental changes and by changes in marketing effort by any of the firms in that product/market area including ourselves.

Looking at the sales estimation problem in this light we see how it can be possible for such estimates to become 'self-fulfilling prophecies' in that the estimate and the marketing mix/programme are dependent upon each other. In a sense a given level of market achievement is predicated by what we believe to be potentially achievable.

## The forecasting horizon

Clearly the time period that we select for the forecasting exercise will influence our approach and our choice of estimation techniques. We are accustomed to thinking in terms of short-, medium- and long-term forecasting where the actual length of these periods is determined by our planning requirements. Thus for example a manufacturer of wine bottles in Spain considers his short-term forecasting requirements as being based upon his need to plan production schedules on a weekly basis. His medium-term requirements are determined by the industry demand over the period of time it takes to install and operationalize additional production capacity – in this case a year. And the longer term must take account of changing consumer requirements, e.g. easy-open bottles, and changing technology in the bottling and packaging fields.

The precise definition of what constitutes the short, medium and long term for any company will clearly vary but should ultimately depend upon the reaction time implicit in a company's activities and its organization. The reaction time for firms in ladies' fashion markets must necessarily be much shorter than for those companies engaged in the construction of hydroelectric power projects. Correspondingly their definition of the forecasting horizon will vary.

The firm's definition of that horizon will also be influenced by the variability of demand in their markets. For established products that variability may not be pronounced, particularly if seasonal variations are allowed for. Even though on a week-by-week basis sales may seem to fluctuate widely there will often be an underlying steady-state or a recognizable upward or downward direction in sales. The forecasting task for the manufacturers of beef stock cubes, a product in a steady state that has lasted for many years, is quite different from that facing the Swedish firm Uddeholm as they launch a new grade of stainless steel for use in the processing of fertilizers, a completely untried market.

## The techniques of estimation

Typically two broad approaches to market estimation have been employed by market forecasters in their attempts to estimate future sales levels. These may be termed macro or aggregate product/market estimates and micro or individual product estimates. These approaches are not alternatives but should complement each other in the information that they provide.

Let us first consider the macro approaches to estimation. Here the emphasis is upon observing the big picture and from that deducing the implications for the product/market in which we are interested. For this reason many business forecasters use leading indicators – that is indices of related or even non-related activities – that can be aids to estimate changes in market conditions at a macro level. For example in the United Kingdom the *Financial Times* Ordinary Share Index has tended in recent years to signal changes in general economic conditions about six months in advance. Similar UK leading indicators are: new housing starts (a lead of about 10 months), net acquisition of financial assets by companies (leading by about 12 months) and interest on 3-month bank bills (with a lead of approximately 18 months).

Such indicators however will only provide approximate pictures of general business conditions and cannot always be guaranteed to come right every time. On the other hand the forecaster may discern that there is a close fit between a seemingly unrelated activity and the sales performance of a particular product. One Danish manufacturer of garden furniture has established a satisfactory method predicting sales on the basis of an apparent correlation between the rise in real wages in Denmark and the sales of his product with a lag of eighteen months. This does not necessarily imply any causal relationship – simply a statistical association – but for the purpose of sales estimation in this case it seemed to provide a useful aid.

There has been a considerable growth in recent years in the use of *marketing models* to provide a macro-type basis for sales estimation. Generally these models will be based upon a number of statistically derived relationships drawn from empirical observations. Some of these can be relatively simple, embodying only a few relationships and requiring nothing more than a calculator to perform the manipulations. On the other hand one Europe-wide oil company has recently developed a sophisticated energy model to guide it in formulating its strategy on synthetic fuels. It covers all major energy forms, conversion technologies, transportation modes and demand. It also projects investment, financing, and resource depletion to the year 2025 and even attempts to predict prices on the basis of supply and demand. Not everybody shares this enthusiasm for large-scale models because of the problems of quantifying what are often qualitative and intangible relationships. Such relationships will often change considerably over time thus obsoleting the model.

These macro approaches, it was suggested earlier, are particularly suited to forecasting approaches which start at the top and work down. In themselves though they may not provide a complete answer to the company's sales estimation problem. The micro level approaches to estimation which tackle the problem from the other direction, i.e. the study of the sales prospects for an individual product, can often provide the missing pieces of the jigsaw.

Micro-type approaches are based upon building up, from an individual customer level, an estimate of what total sales of the product could be in a given period. Such methods will rely heavily on surveys of actual and/or potential customers of a sort we will be discussing in Questions 24 and 25. Essentially though, whilst they can be of a considerable sophistication, such studies rely upon indications from the respondents about their likely purchasing behaviour. For example, a German manufacturer of household electrical goods carries out a regular survey amongst a representative sample of actual and potential customers to ascertain the likelihood of their purchasing particular electrical appliances in the next twelve months. Using this device he can track the way in which first-time sales will move and also the way in which the replacement market is moving.

Many companies rely upon forecasts at the micro level which are based solely on an analysis of past sales. In other words past sales are charted with a view to identifying patterns and trends and thus enabling projections to be made. It will be recognized that projections are just that; they are extrapolations from past behaviour and are based upon an assumption that what has happened in the past will be a guide to what will happen in the future. This need not be so. One UK firm in the building products market expanded its production facilities on the basis of a sharp upturn in the early 1970s only to find that by late 1974 the market had collapsed. Perhaps the collapse was only temporary but it was long enough to seriously affect the firm's profitability and chances of long-run survival.

Successful marketing management must be based upon reliable estimates of market demand. It would probably be true to say that companies pay rather less attention to this crucial input to marketing decisions than they should. Success in the markets of the future will almost certainly require a reversal of this neglect.

*Further reading*

Hughes, G. D., *Demand Analysis for Marketing Decisions*, R. D. Irwin, 1973

Wood, D., and Fildes, R., *Forecasting for Business: Methods and Application*, Longman, 1976

**Self-audit questions**

12.1 *How do you distinguish currently between market potential, company potential and sales next year for your own market?*

12.2 *What forecasting techniques do you use?*

12.3 *How accurate are they, and what are the consequences of variances for finance, distribution and production managers?*

# Question 13
# How can we communicate with our customers?

*Organizations use both direct person-to-person methods of communications, such as when salesmen make visits to customers, and impersonal methods. The major impersonal method is*

*normally advertising although in industrial and service industries
this takes very different forms from that normally encountered
in consumer industries. In addition, any packaging an
organization uses communicates with customers as do the
organization's employees when the phone rings or a devliery is
made. Other forms of indirect communication are products
themselves and the prices which an organization asks for its
products or services and the multitude of word-of-mouth
comments that are made by customers and non-customers.*

Organizations communicate with their customers in a wide variety
of ways. A German manufacturer of recycling equipment for
plastic waste chose to meet his potential customers at a specially
convened technical briefing conference in Hamburg. He invited
his customers from throughout the EEC, whom he had defined
as public health and sanitation engineers together with the heads
of the various local government committees. The managing director of the company spent two days with the customers, firstly
indicating the general principles of the process; secondly, showing
all his guests an installation actually at work close by; and thirdly
by exploring the full extent of the commercial and social advantages which were accruing to the satisfied customer.

Then he turned over the leadership role of his technical briefing
conference to his economists and technical officers who spent
eight hours with the guests in small groups of six discussing the
particular nature of the problems each guest had back home in
his own local government activity. By the time they went home,
each guest had seen the process at work and had a grasp of the
sort of economic implications for his own activity. The mechanism chosen for communication had been to conduct person-to-
person exchanges and to explore in detail how the product could
meet the needs of each and every customer.

By contrast, when the British banking system launched its two
major credit cards – Barclaycard and Access – they went for a
mass advertising campaign. Few bank managers invited their
customers in for tea to discuss what were the merits and demerits
of a credit card from the clearing bank compared with American
Express. Instead, the national press was filled with display advertisements which were predominantly concerned with emphasiz-

ing that credit could 'take the waiting out of wanting'. Admittedly, with the strict control of credit limits operated they can only do it once or twice but stewardship of credit with relationship to an individual's total financial position was not emphasized. It would have been too expensive on the scale required to sign up enough cardholders. Instead, all holders of existing bank accounts which had been relatively trouble free were either encouraged to take a card, or sent one automatically. This was an impersonal approach to communicating with one's customers.

Both industries did, however, also employ what is called point-of-sale promotional literature. In the case of the German manufacturer of plastic recycling equipment technical documentation and costs and benefit data were provided to take away. In the case of the British banks the counters of their branches and the doormats of their customers were amply covered with explanatory leaflets.

It will be readily apparent that the above discussion only examines communication in a new launch situation. Such activities may create a high level of awareness of a product or service but they will often need supplementation in terms either of follow-up personal contact or reminder advertisements if enough potential customers are to acquire what is on offer. It can never be assumed that one communications impact on a customer is noted, let alone that it will form the basis without further support for a positive action like purchasing a product. Equally, we cannot assume that once a potential customer has made use of a product or service the task of communications is complete. Quite the contrary. The characteristics of the product or service in use, the nature of the contacts or service at the point of purchase, the after-sales service if needed; all these will communicate with the customer either to reinforce his judgement that he was correct in the way he chose or to deter him next time around. In either event, he is apt to talk, to convey impressions by word of mouth, about the organization to his colleagues and friends which will influence them. He communicates about the organization with potential customers and users.

## The communications mix

We have taken two examples in some detail to explore the communications activities of organizations with their customers and users. In general terms the recycling equipment was handled by person-to-person technical selling and the credit card service was mass promoted by advertising. There is, of course, a much bigger armoury of techniques of communication available to the marketer which he will seek to deploy both singly and in combination for the maximum effect within a given budget. The major media, as they are called, which are widely available in Europe are as follows:

*National and regional newspapers* appearing daily or weekly typically within just one country, but in recent years a number of links between the serious or quality dailies have appeared.

*Trade and professional magazines* covering everything from architects' materials, computers, caravans and model railways to the accountancy and professional marketing periodicals.

*National, regional and pan-European radio and television* which are self-explanatory.

*Exhibitions* held either on a national, European or international basis covering everything from dairy products to offset lithographic printing equipment and machine tools.

*Direct mail* employing circulars or leaflets conveyed through the post or delivered door-to-door. Such a medium is not only used for selling household items but widely used in industrial markets for introducing new products and services in the hope that subsequent follow-up sales calls can be more fruitfully made.

*Public relations* covering everything from the dissemination of information to the press and television for possible news coverage to the general development of an organization's image with the public which can often constitute a major asset in marketing terms.

*Back-up/point-of-sale literature* which covers the supporting literature organizations produce to supplement other communications. It includes catalogues, price lists and technical specifications as well as the use in consumer goods markets of special displays at the point-of-sale.

*Packaging* which must be viewed not only in terms of how it helps to persuade customers to purchase, typically an important influence in consumer markets, but also the extent to which it minimizes damaged goods that need to be returned or replaced thereby causing upset to customers and adverse communications impact.

*Personal selling* which we have left to last but which is by no means least important. Elsewhere a series of separate questions are devoted to it. Suffice it to observe here that it embraces the activities of individuals travelling on regular journeys to established customers to collect orders, the use of a telephone sales approach which is increasingly common in fast moving industrial markets, and the activities of the managing director in a capital goods industry, or a giant grocery concern selling to major supermarket chains that control ten to twenty per cent of his total business volume.

Marketing communicates with its customers by identifying how some or all of these possible media can be deployed. One on its own will seldom suffice. A Danish pharmaceutical manufacturer who sought to gain widespread sales for his ladies' hair colouring found that the chemist outlets into which he wished to sell his product to gain distribution were unwilling to respond to the blandishment of his sales ladies on a personal selling approach. They required reassurance that a major advertising campaign would be launched both on Danish television and in the fashionable ladies' magazines in order that the product would sell successfully from their counters.

In looking closely at this instance we can see the importance of the distinction we made earlier between customers and users or consumers. The hair colouring manufacturer had to communicate to two quite different groups – his customer and his customer's customers. If our customers, i.e. the chemists, were not confident that point-of-sale display and elegant packaging would be adequate as a total communications effort to pull the product through the channel of distribution to the ladies whose hair needed colouring, they would not stock it.

An alternative way of expending that organization's communications budget would be by direct personal selling on a home-by-home basis. The Avon organization has pioneered this system in Britain for a wide range of cosmetics. Their system is more typical of that used in industrial markets where sales or technical representatives combine their sales activities with advisory services on how best to tackle and solve problems.

The effective marketing organization is continually experimenting with the mix of communications media it employs to find out how to make a fixed expenditure more cost effective or alternatively to reduce its budget in achieving a similar level of effect.

## Indirect communications

Organizations also communicate with their customers in a series of less obvious ways, which we can term indirect. We have already referred to the image which an organization has in the mind of potential customers prior to receiving any new message about it. That image will, if one exists at all, have been built up from a range of past experience and hearsay. It will affect not only how customers perceive any particular communications message. It will also affect their behaviour or response as a result of receiving any communication. This indirect communication from the image is supplemented or reinforced by the way any inquiry or order is handled. In technical markets where products require installation, or service industries where a service relationship takes a while to settle down, the manner in which each customer contact is handled communicates with the customer.

So, of course, does the product or service itself. The type of arrangements KLM, British Airways or SAS make for their customers both on the ground and in-flight are vehicles for communication with the customer which will influence his attitude and perhaps his subsequent behaviour towards the particular carrier. The same can be said of the freight forwarder using the air cargo facilities of the same organizations. If delays, damages or misdirection occur these misfortunes communicate to him an impression of the airline which cannot fail to influence him later on. Pricing is also an extremely meaningful communications cue to customers. In unsophisticated markets where customers are unsure of the precise nature and criteria for judgement of a product or service – say wines, restaurants or hotel accommodation – price will frequently be used as an indication of quality. As the customer becomes more certain of himself he begins to rely more on his own judgement and does not fear to take a more discriminating view of price. Where the price is known to other colleagues or friends, however, the fact that it has been paid can also act as a communications message to such folk about the customer himself.

At this juncture we can perhaps return to reiterate the benefits of word-of-mouth communications. These are closely allied to the conspicuous visual display of products which have been purchased – be it the latest piece of electronic equipment in a factory or service industry, or new furnishing fabrics or garden furniture for the home. Other customers can both see and discuss the product in use. They can mull it over and receive advice from someone else who has already taken the risk and made a purchase. Such advice is seen as more objective than the salesman's word or the advertising. In user terms it usually is. If an organization can also get satisfied customers and users communicating for it in this way it is indeed blessed.

*Further reading*

Christopher, M. G., *Marketing-Below-the-Line*, Allen & Unwin, 1972

Crane, E., *Marketing Communications*, Wiley, 1972

**Self-audit questions**

13.1 *What communications mix was used in a recent new product/service launch by your organization?*

13.2 *What is the current communications mix of a major current product range item, and how and why has it changed in recent years?*

13.3 *How much does your organization depend on 'indirect communications' and are they consciously managed?*

13.4 *How does the use of personal selling relate to the use of impersonal advertising activities in your own organization?*

# Question 14

# How can we persuade our customers to buy our product?

*The process of persuasion can be analysed in many markets through a series of steps up which potential customers climb, covering initial awareness, interest, attitude formation, the emergence of intention and the decision to act. If our product or service has been matched with customer needs, the customer must normally be persuaded to want our particular organization's offering in preference to any other. Persuasion must also be sufficiently effective to divert attention from other alternative ways of spending money. This can often be accomplished by developing a psychologically unique appeal for our product or service, perhaps via branding, correctly judging the price and making the product available in a suitably convenient way.*

Successful persuasive appeals to customers to buy one's product depend fundamentally on acting from an understanding of how particular purchase decisions are reached. This requires both analysis of the decision-making process employed by the customer and the criteria used in arriving at a verdict. Nonetheless, the process of persuasion cannot begin unless awareness exists. Accordingly, it is useful to begin our answer to this question by emphasizing the need to create awareness of the existence of any product or service. This, as we have seen, can be accomplished in a variety of ways but without a favourable attitude and an intention to purchase, it will be of little benefit.

A large brewer in Britain distributed his draught beers in a limited number of public houses, predominantly those which were in the south, although some were located in other areas of the country. In order to promote his product, his advertising was placed on television throughout the whole country. An extremely high recall of the product and the message was achieved, but since the beer was only available in limited areas, much of the investment in awareness was wasted. Similar waste occurs in industrial markets when product advertising creates awareness but no further activity is undertaken to build upon it.

If awareness has been created in the mind of a potential customer, interest in learning more about the product or service will normally follow. Frequently the initial medium for arousing awareness may well include enough further information to facilitate this. Technical details or demonstration of potential benefits that can accrue can be an integral part of the initial communications message. In the context of these first two steps, attitudes may begin to form. They may reject the service offered, not believing that a draught beer brewed in London could possibly slake the thirst of an East Anglian farmer. Equally, the emergent attitude could be that an up-and-coming East Anglian farmer might well want to drink what the smart young men in London drink to wash down their ploughman's lunch in Fleet Street or on the King's Road.

The significance of *understanding* how the East Anglian farmer will react when he becomes aware of the draught beer will not have escaped notice. To persuade successfully requires the most careful attention to how attitudes towards particular products are formed. All the evidence available indicates that only a few generalizations can be made which cover more than a limited group of products or services. Nonetheless, we can confidently emphasize the necessity of maintaining consistency in our persuasive appeals, and that interest can be effectively stimulated to move towards the formulation of attitudes and beliefs by the presentation of appropriate material.

Information of itself never seems to *change* attitudes; if an attitude is well entrenched it will lead to a distorted perception of any information which is at variance with it, in order to make it fit. Hence, persuasive appeals must either create fresh attitudes or build upon those which are there already, and which are brought to bear to evaluate a product or service of which the potential customer has become aware, and in whom interest has been aroused.

Once the relevant attitudes have been located and understood, both sides of an argument are not normally necessary. Advocacy, effective advocacy, is what most of us wish to hear. It is the obverse process which we now encounter to the earlier rejection or distortion of information received. If the audience is well disposed, it will use the advocate's information to confirm and reinforce its own prior attitudes. It is reassuring to know that one is right, a point which must not be overlooked *after* the purchase incidentally.

We should perhaps pause here for a moment to reflect on the timeliness of these two stages, interest arousal and attitude development in the potential customer. Many purchasing officers in industrial companies, many housewives acting on behalf of the families they serve, many service organizations acting on behalf of clients, all may well be aware and interested but in no position to act. There may be no need for the product or service at the time when interest is at its height, and what seems inescapable from evidence culled in this field is that the investment made in taking customers up these early steps on the persuasion process can be all too easily dissipated. The favourable attitudes, the interest, even the awareness, can decay. A good filing system or a conscientious housewife might preserve the information for a while, but persuasion processes either move forward or back. Accordingly, it is crucial in directing one's marketing effort to persuade, to essay first to pinpoint those who are potentially in the market or can be brought to market by one's efforts. This point can be summed up in the expression *intention to buy*.

## The customer's decision to buy

ICI Paints Division sells non-drip emulsion paint. It is available both to tradesmen for use as professional decorators, and to the amateur do-it-yourself customer in homes across Europe. Television advertising creates an awareness of its brand and the content of the advertising arouses an interest. Both the tradesmen and the amateur decorators hold favourable images of ICI as a chemical company and have little doubt that the product will do the job adequately. ICI's dilemma is to ensure that at the decision-making stage its brand is preferred to others. Accordingly, it must identify what the decision criteria are as between one brand and the next, in order that on the key dimensions of that decision a relatively unique appeal can be created. After all, other companies such as Du Pont and the major French and

German companies are all active in the same markets, as well as firmly established British competitors in Crown Paints and Bergers. The decision transpired to be extremely complex. In almost all instances the decoration decision was a somewhat reluctant one for the end consumer of the paint, whether or not a professional tradesman was to be employed, or it was to be done on an amateur basis. The home would be disrupted and considerable expense would be involved. Paint was unlikely to be the only purchase considered in any event. Other items would be purchased also. Perhaps accessories would be required, and wallpaper may well be used in association with the paint. A simplified statement of the various elements leading up to the paint decision is given in FIGURE 13.

It will be apparent that the brand specification for paint is the last aspect of the total decision process. ICI's advertising could well trigger awareness, create interest, sway attitudes and crystallize intention, but it could then be unsuccessful if the correct colour did not appear on the colour card which blended with or matched the wallpaper. In any event, such a process inevitably makes ICI's position look weak in relation to other manufacturers whose range of products includes wallpapers.

In the British market, Crown form part of the Wallpaper Manufacturers' Group of companies. They were not slow to specify with their wallpapers which of their paint colours would go well. ICI entered the wallpaper market in the mid-sixties in a massive way.

Not only were ICI vulnerable in the decision-making process if an effective competitor were to exploit it, however. They were vulnerable also in distribution. Crown again owned a very considerable proportion of the specialist paint and wallpaper retailers, although they were not so strong in the merchants which supplied the trade decorators.

To persuade customers to buy ICI's paints, as opposed to any other brand with the appropriate colour, required the development of a brand loyalty or franchise – primarily with men since they generally specified the brand. Women were left with the colour choice by and large. Advertising activity could create the franchise provided a sufficiently wide range of retail outlets or merchants carried the product. One could hardly expect potential

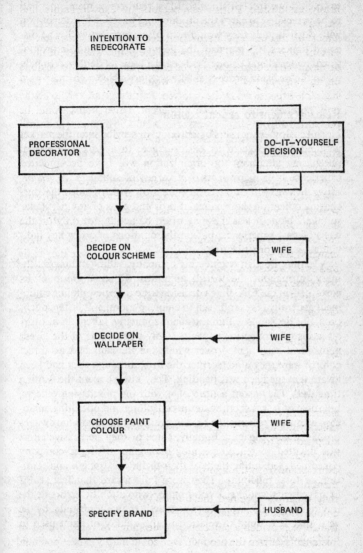

**FIGURE 13**

INTENTION TO REDECORATE

PROFESSIONAL DECORATOR

DO—IT—YOURSELF DECISION

DECIDE ON COLOUR SCHEME ← WIFE

DECIDE ON WALLPAPER ← WIFE

CHOOSE PAINT COLOUR ← WIFE

SPECIFY BRAND ← HUSBAND

customers to undertake a voyage of discovery around their town to track down the ICI stockist. Most retailers or merchants had to be persuaded to carry the product and to sell it in competition with other brands they would also often carry as well. The discount policies ICI pursued, the help with point-of-sale promotional material and colour shade cards, were all deployed to help make the decision process as likely as possible to go their way.

## Reinforcement to repeat custom

Not all customers or users of a product or service enter the market with no knowledge of its performance. In a typical industrial purchasing situation, the organization will have accumulated experience over many years of a variety of suppliers. A *vendor-rating scheme* will often be in operation which guides the purchasing officer on the balance of pros and cons of any particular supplier. Nonetheless, he may often be acting not only on the basis of past experience, but on the opinions of a few key individuals in the organization.

A leading Belgian engineering company, selling milling machinery throughout the world, identified within a group of its customers in the EEC that a decision to acquire new milling equipment generally takes fourteen to eighteen months. It is dependent on major decisions within the client company, taken about overall levels of production capacity. Only when some of the larger items have been agreed over which the Belgians had no direct control were they able to enter the lists, although they had been aware that the need was pending. They always spent the waiting time well. They spent a little of it with the purchasing officers, but most of it was spent with the consulting and operating engineers who were responsible for the design and operational switch-on of the new capacity. Equally, some of their persuasive effort was devoted to reaching senior management of the company concerned, reminding them of their technical strength and tradition of total reliability. They were fully aware that few senior managements would risk spoiling the whole job by errors at the milling machinery level. This was exactly the same attitude, by the way, that ICI found in relation to the quality of paint used in home decorating.

This Belgian company reinforced its image throughout the build-up to the final moment of decision. It knew that its activity of the fourteen- to eighteen-month period determined success at the decision time. It knew it must operate with different messages at different stages in the process at different levels within the client company. It is that type of understanding which companies need of how decisions are made if they wish to persuade their customers to buy their products. If that understanding can be matched with a product or service that matches the needs and wants of customers, then success is within an organization's reach.

*Further reading*
Crane, E., *Marketing Communications*, Wiley, 1972
Baker, M. J., *Marketing: An Introductory Text*, Macmillan, 2nd edition, 1975

**Self-audit questions**
14.1  *Describe the process by which a customer or consumer builds up to purchase your products/services for the first time.*
14.2  *How is repeat purchasing influenced?*
14.3  *Attempt to model the answer to 14.1 and 14.2 for a major competitor. Does he behave differently?*
14.4  *What could your oganization do better to ensure more new customers and more repeat sales?*

# Question 15
# How can we measure the effectiveness of our communications?

*The effectiveness of communications with customers in marketing can only be measured against clearly stated objectives. Furthermore, those objectives should broadly speaking be those*

*which can if necessary be achieved by communications activity
alone. Once clear objectives are identified, evaluative research
techniques are available to assess the extent to which they are
being achieved. Small experimental tests can be conducted before
any widespread deployment of communications, and then further
larger-scale analyses can assess the overall performance in the
market place. Communications objectives must always be clearly
distinguished from the marketing objectives of the organization.
Their successful accomplishment via an advertising or promotional
campaign, for example, cannot guarantee sales success unless all
other aspects of the marketing mix are effectively deployed as
well.*

Contrary to much folklore, communications effectiveness can be
measured with some degree of accuracy in marketing, provided
always that valid objectives have been set. It is important to emphasize at the outset the need for the objectives to be valid. We
have to know before we can make any communications decisions
precisely what role communications is expected to play in the
overall marketing effort. Is it expected to explain why the product
is more expensive than the customer might otherwise expect it to
be? Is it to communicate details about a completely new approach
to some task which will require rethinking of habitual practices
by an industrial purchasing officer? Is it intended to emphasize
that a service is widely and speedily available in event of a break-
down of machinery or plant, thereby reassuring a buying organization that he can expect few major problems if he buys from
that particular organization?

Each of these communications objectives can be effectively
achieved by a campaign of advertising or promotion, but the total
marketing operation could be a failure. The expensive product
may not be easily available, or fail to live up to performance expectations. The quality of service delivered may not be as effective as the buying organization had anticipated. In such instances,
which are not infrequent, there is little point in blaming the communications activity for raising customers' hopes which the rest
of the marketing activity dashes. The lesson is to see that the
communications objectives conform with the actuality of the
marketing effort overall, that they do not over-claim.

102

Communications can seldom make sales on their own; the only exceptional situations are direct response or point-of-sale advertising. Everywhere else they play their integral part in marketing success, or contribute to its failure. Accordingly, it is almost always appropriate to resist the temptation to relate communications expenditure to levels of sales achieved.

## Valid communications objectives

Recent studies at Cranfield with many of the leading British and European commercial organizations have shown that there are four major objectives which organizations traditionally set. They are as follows:

*Branding and image building* – whether the company is engaged in industrial products like the National Coal Board, British Petroleum and Dunlop, in consumer goods like CPC (Europe), Weetabix and Watney Mann, or services like the British Tourist Authority and the Midland Bank, they all seek to communicate an overall image of their organization and its work to their actual and potential customers. They see it as a communications' objective to ensure that the image is favourable in the belief that a favourably perceived brand name or image creates a constructive environment in which to market their outputs.

*Education and information* – organizations generally know far better within themselves than do their customers what they are trying to achieve in the way of product or service performance. In the well-organized marketing activity, that performance level will have been set on the basis of a very close analysis of customer and consumer needs and wants. The importance of ensuring that customers are aware of and comprehend the organization's offering and the benefits it can potentially bestow cannot be understated. It is all too easy to assume that customers are aware and understand. This objective is especially appropriate for market development strategies.

*Affecting attitudes* – a campaign of education and information is rarely a satisfactory goal except at early stages in the introduction of a new product or service to the market. Attitudes must be affected favourably also. We have already mentioned in answer to Question 13 the problems of seeking to change attitudes;

103

rather we must seek to build on or develop them. This was the communications goal set by Plessey when it launched its automatic ignition system for gas installations, especially domestic cookers. Cadbury's faced similar problems when they launched Marvel and Smash. In all three product instances, customers had historical attitudes to products of this type. In the first case, gas ignition systems had a long record of doubtful efficiency. Cadbury's were up against World War II stereotypes of dried milk and powdered potato, as well as being anxious not to damage their image as a manufacturer of chocolate which used *real* milk. In both cases, the image which the companies had nurtured enabled communications activities to develop attitudes towards the products on the basis that 'if a well established firm like that has produced the product it will be well worth trying, even though I would be extremely doubtful if an unknown firm had attempted it'.

*Loyalty reminding and reinforcement* – the fourth major objective has two dimensions. Companies wish to reinforce continually their customers' loyalties to their products or services. Customers need to be convinced that their pattern of habitual behaviour in always going to a particular supplier, or always shopping at a specific department store in Paris, London or Rome, is not shortsighted on their part. The communications objective will in such circumstances be to reinforce the feeling that the habit is correct and sensible and does not need breaking.

The corollary to loyalty reinforcement is, of course, reminder communications. One can so easily forget to keep adequate stock levels of products, or not avail oneself often enough of services. This is especially true in areas of discretionary purchasing or behaviour where failure to be reminded may well lead to another more recently communicated message having a greater influence on the customer. We can illustrate this point by referring to domestic or office decorations and furnishings. 'Old furniture must go' was a classic campaign by the furniture industry in the mid-sixties designed to encourage customers to enter a discretionary market. The same style of communications campaign is projected by brewers to remind us to use their pubs instead of watching televisions or following other social pursuits. Finally, the combination of loyalty and reminder communications will be intended to ensure that any custom generated does indeed come to the organization undertaking the campaign rather than to any conveniently available brand.

It will be apparent that one or other of these four major communications objectives will be more appropriate than the rest at any particular point in time. At the introductory stage of a product or service, the generation of awareness and the conveying of information are vitally important. Later in a product's life cycle branding, image, loyalty and reminding take on much greater significance. The effective marketing operation ensures that the appropriate communications goals are being set for each of its product ranges or groups of services offered, depending on the stage of market development.

## Pre-exposure testing of communications

No apology is required for devoting half the answer to this question to a discussion of communications objectives. As was observed at the outset, without them no real attempt can be made to measure effect. Once we have them, the creative generation of ideas for ways to communicate and to meet the objectives can be unleashed. This is a specialist task although most managers consider themselves gifted amateurs. Its outcome can be a sales presentation using a variety of media to communicate, some form of predominantly visual communication such as a brochure, direct mail circulars and press advertisements, an exhibition presentation with supporting materials and samples, or a television commercial.

Pretesting essentially involves presenting the communication to a sample of customers and measuring their reaction. It constitutes sensible insurance against errors in creative development and execution of ideas. It is a standard service available from most major marketing research organizations, with customers presented with the communication in as realistic a context as possible. They will have been questioned beforehand to establish a benchmark for their awareness, interest, attitudes, loyalty, and so forth. After exposure to the communication these characteristics will be measured again. In addition, the opportunity can be taken to get independent verbal customer reactions to the communications message. Negative aspects in the messages can be screened out. A frequent phenomenon that emerges is that the receiver of the communication is confused. It may try to say too much so that nothing registers with the customer. It may well be, as a leading Italian sports equipment manufacturer discovered when he used star personalities in promotional activities, that they had inappropriate associations in the mind of the customers.

Such procedures of pretesting can also be used to compare several alternative approaches or mixtures of communications activities to see which gives the better impact. Yardsticks for comparison with previous communications campaigns, booklets or sales presentations can emerge as data begins to build up. Comparisons can be made with the communications activities of competitors to see how well any particular campaign matches up. Furthermore, pre-exposure tests can be undertaken from the very earliest stages of development – using rough formats to test ideas and concepts.

## Post-exposure evaluation

The execution of the full communications campaign, once as many deficiencies as possible have been excluded by pretesting, is normally a considerably expensive affair. In consumer goods industries budgets for advertising run as high as thirty per cent of total sales income in, for example, cosmetics throughout Europe. For a major company this can mean several million pounds each year. The food industries of Europe have similarly massive advertising campaigns. In industrial markets the balance of communications expense tends to be more with personal contact of both a technical, advisory and after-sales service nature. Nonetheless, total expenditures on communications for industrial goods can reach very substantial levels.

Accordingly, it is normally only sensible to set aside some of the total communications budget to be in a position to measure how effective it was in practice. How much should be expended on evaluative research will depend on the benefits which will accrue from knowing how effective it has been. Certainly any organization going on in a subsequent year to spend further substantial sums is extremely unwise if it does not seek to learn most carefully from its expensively bought experience.

Once again, research methods involve survey work amongst customers both potential and actual. Whatever objectives were adopted for the communications campaign should be checked to see whether they have been communicated; and once again, it will be recalled that different levels of effect may be accomplished. Most customers may well have been aware of the campaign but failed to receive clearly the information it was intended to communicate, or they may have covered both of these stages and failed to develop or evolve their attitudes. Campaigns often have worthwhile effects, but effects that are somewhat at variance with what you hoped to achieve and what your pretests may well have led you to assume you could achieve.

The cause of slippage could be the media you employed in the major campaign. The pretesting methods cannot really simulate adequately a television commercial in mid-evening or a colour advertisement in the *Sunday Telegraph*, or a page in *Waterways World*. Such slippage as does occur, however, is vitally important evidence for the next campaign.

Measuring the effectiveness of any communications campaign is both possible and necessary. How much is spent on evaluating any particular campaign will, of necessity, be determined by what is at stake. What can be at stake is well demonstrated in the instance of a French consumer durable manufacturer based in the electronics industry. The size of the market was some Fr45–50 million per annum, and his was an old-established brand with some Fr one million spent annually on advertising in the media and a further Fr300,000 spent on point-of-sale activities. Private brands by retailers held some ten per cent of the market. He held a more considerable share. There were ten other branded competitors and the market was highly competitive between them all. The main communications objectives set were to convey the benefits to be derived from using the product, to develop and convey favourable attitudes towards the product and to maintain loyalty amongst current purchasers who repurchased relatively infrequently. For several years advertising for the product had tried to emphasize a key attribute of the product's performance but to no avail. However, some improvement occurred in some unintended directions which had the important effect of reducing the perceived relevance of that attribute for the current purchaser.

A switch in communications message built upon this accidental occurrence with great effect and further lessened the importance of the initial attribute.

*Further reading*

Corkindale, D., and Kennedy, S., *Managing Advertising Effectively*, MCB Books, 1975

Esomar Seminar Papers, *The Role of Market Research in the Creation of Advertising*, 1966

Henry, H., *How to Set Right Advertising Objectives*, Cranfield Broadsheet no 3, MCRC, 1979

**Self-audit questions**

15.1 *What are your organization's marketing communications objectives for its products? Examine one product/group in detail.*

15.2 *What procedures do you use to measure the expected effects of communications materials prior to the exposure? Could you sensibly do more?*

15.3 *How do you measure the impact of your communications after they have been exposed to customers and/or consumers?*

15.4 *How much do you think it is worth spending on evaluating communications effectiveness?*

# Question 16
# Do we need a sales force?

*Personal selling is a component element of the communication mix, the other most frequently encountered elements being advertising, sales promotion, and public relations. The role of personal selling in the communication mix can only be determined if a company has a thorough understanding of the relevant buying process, which consists of a number of phases, at each of which different people may well require different kinds of information. The efficiency of any element of communication is dependent on achieving a match between information required and information given.*

*Personal selling is a two-way form of communication that has a number of advantages, not the least of which is that the salesman can actually ask for an order. Other advantages include the flexibility that can be given to the sales message, the opportunity afforded to the prospective purchaser to ask questions, the opportunity the salesman has to overcome objections, and to relate his message to meet the express needs of the buyer.*

Sales force management has traditionally been a neglected area of marketing management, in spite of the fact that it has been around as an organized activity for considerably longer than marketing. Possible reasons for this are not too hard to find. Not all marketing and product managers have had experience in a personal selling or sales management role, consequently they tend not to consider it too carefully when making their marketing plans.

For their part, sales folk themselves sometimes encourage a distinction or division between sales and marketing by depicting themselves as 'the sharp end'. After all, isn't there something slightly daring about dealing with real live customers as opposed to sitting in an office planning, which is what marketing people are supposed to be doing?

That such reasoning is misleading will be obvious from what was said in our reply to Question 2 about the difference between selling and marketing. It will be recalled that unless a good deal of careful marketing planning has taken place prior to a salesman making his effort to persuade the customer to place an order, the probability of success is that much less.

It will also be clear by now that it is essential when planning for profitable sales to think not just about individual customers or individual products, but about *groups* of customers – or segments – and about how products relate to each other. It is also vital not

109

to concentrate solely on *today's* products, customers and problems but to think in terms of where *future* sales will be coming from.

Nevertheless, personal selling is still a crucial part of the total marketing process and needs to be as carefully considered and planned as any other element of the marketing mix. Indeed, it is an excellent idea for any manager responsible for marketing to go out on to a territory for a few days each year and have a go at trying to persuade customers to place orders. This is a good way of finding out what our customers really think about our marketing policies.

## The role of personal selling

Although its importance varies according to circumstances, in many businesses the sales force is the most expensive element in the marketing mix. Particularly in industrial goods companies, it is not unusual to find less than £10,000 being spent on other forms of communication and £150,000 or more being spent on the sales force in the form of salaries, cars and associated costs.

Yet in spite of its importance, it is not uncommon to discover that it is the most badly managed area of marketing, partly for the reasons referred to above. The authors of this book have investigated scores of European sales forces over the past decade and have found an alarming lack of planning and professionalism. Often salesmen have little idea of which products and which groups of customers to concentrate on, have too little knowledge about competitive activity, do not plan presentations well, rarely talk to customers in terms of *benefits*, make too little effort to close the sale, and make many calls without any clear objectives. Even worse, marketing management, because of their lack of knowledge and experience of personal selling, are rarely aware that this important and expensive element of the marketing mix is not being managed effectively.

A recent survey carried out on the effectiveness with which sales representatives made contact with those responsible for influencing purchasing decisions showed that on average only two contacts per visit were made in companies with over one thou-

110

sand employees in which there were about seven major influencers of the purchasing decision. A similar proportion of contacts was made on smaller companies. These results were not surprising when we pause to think how companies operate on a day-to-day basis and estimate the chances of any salesmen being able to see seven different executives in one visit.

Another survey showed that advertising in the trade and technical press was the major source of information for large companies, whilst personal visits from sales people was marginally the most important source of information for small companies. In both cases, exhibitions and direct mail were also important sources of information.

Such surveys, however, whilst they do illustrate that it is foolish to leave the communication task solely to the sales force, do not answer the question about the role of personal selling in the communication mix.

Whilst it is perfectly feasible to set specific quantifiable objectives in each marketing communication task, how much relative effort to devote to personal selling and other forms of communication can only be determined if a company has the clearest understanding of the *buying* process in its markets. In our response to Question 14 there was a simple model of the consumer purchase decision in relation to paints. During the past decade there has been a lot of research into the industrial buying process, for clearly this is equally as important as the consumer buying process, since few companies sell their goods direct to a consumer.

## Information required and given

The efficiency of any element of communication is dependent on achieving a match between information required and information given. To do this the marketer has to be aware of the different information requirements of different people at different stages in their buying process. Viewed in this way, the importance can be appreciated of directing the company's communication effort at *all* key points in the buying chain rather than assuming that the actual sale is the only event that takes place.

So, in order to determine the precise role of personal selling, a company needs to determine within channels who the major influencers are and what their information requirements are. It is now an accepted fact that most institutional buying decisions consist of about eight separate phases, starting with the recognition of a problem right through to performance evaluation and feedback of the product or service eventually purchased. Furthermore, the importance of each of these eight phases varies according to whether the buying situation is classified as a *new task*, a *modified rebuy* or a *straight rebuy*, for clearly the information needs will differ substantially accordingly.

It has been suggested that any market can be divided into three principal buying segments – pre-transactional, transactional, and post-transactional. It has been found that advertising and public relations are most frequently used to cultivate the market during the pre-transactional stage. Advertising is often used during the post-transactional stage to reinforce the purchaser's buying decision. Selling, however, is important in all three phases.

Personal selling has a number of obvious advantages over other elements of the communications mix. Personal selling is a two-way form of communication, thereby giving the prospective purchaser the opportunity to ask questions of the salesman about his product or service. The sales message itself is more flexible and can therefore be made more personal. The salesman can use in-depth product knowledge and relate his message to meet the perceived needs of the buyer and deal with his objections as they arise. Most importantly, the salesman can ask for the order.

Once an order has been obtained from a customer such that there is a high probability of a rebuy occurring, not only does the salesman's task change, but also the role of all communication changes more towards reinforcing the wisdom of the purchase decision.

In the grocery business, advertising and sales promotion are obviously extremely important elements in the communication process, whereas in the wholesale hardware business, frequent and regular face-to-face contact with retail outlets through a sales force is the key determinant of success. In industries where there are few customers, such as capital goods and specialized process materials, an in-depth understanding has to be built up of customer production processes, so again personal contact is of paramount importance. In contrast, many fast moving industrial goods are sold into fragmented markets for diverse uses, and here forms of communication other than personal selling take on added importance.

## Sales objectives

In our answer to Question 17, we shall be looking at the problem of how many salesmen we need and what we should ask them to do. For now, let us confine ourselves to establishing the relationship between corporate objectives and sales objectives.

All companies set themselves overall objectives which in turn imply the development of specific marketing objectives. In this question we have discussed the link between selling and the overall marketing activity. Thus, a hierarchy of objectives can be seen as *corporate objectives, marketing objectives, sales objectives*. The link is illustrated in FIGURE 14. The benefits to sales force management of following this approach are as follows:

1 Coordination between corporate and marketing objectives with actual sales effort
2 Establishment of a circular relationship between corporate objectives and customer wants
3 Understanding the corporate and marketing ramifications of sales decisions helps improve sales effectiveness.

The sales force of one company manufacturing stainless-steel containers was selling virtually any kind of container to virtually anybody who could buy, which caused severe production-planning and distribution problems that reverberated right back through the business chain, even to the purchase of raw materials. This seriously affected the company's profitability. Finally the sales force was instructed to concentrate on certain kinds of products and on certain kinds of user industries and this eventually led to economies of scale throughout the entire organization. The lesson which this company learned is that a sales force cannot be managed in isolation from other corporate and marketing objectives.

113

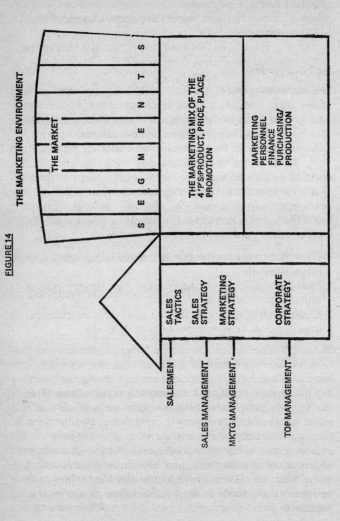

FIGURE 14

THE MARKETING ENVIRONMENT

THE MARKET

S  E  G  M  E  N  T  S

THE MARKETING MIX OF THE
4 'P'S:PRODUCT, PRICE, PLACE,
PROMOTION

MARKETING
PERSONNEL
FINANCE
PURCHASING/
PRODUCTION

SALES
TACTICS

SALES
STRATEGY

MARKETING
STRATEGY

CORPORATE
STRATEGY

SALESMEN

SALES MANAGEMENT

MKTG MANAGEMENT

TOP MANAGEMENT

*Further reading*

Frain, J., 'The Changing Role of the Salesman', *Selling Today*,
  March 1970

Wilson, L., 'How L'Oreal learned to Accept Change',
  *Marketing*, March 1979

Kotler, P., 'From Sales Obsession to Marketing Effectiveness',
  *Harvard Business Review*, Nov/Dec 1977

**Self-audit questions**

16.1   *Does your company need a sales force?*

16.2   *What is the role of personal selling in the marketing
       communications programme of your company?*

16.3   *What are the main information needs of the main
       influencers of what is bought?*

16.4   *What are the advantages of personal selling over other
       elements of your marketing communication mix?*

## Question 17
# How should our sales force be organized and managed?

*In determining how many salesmen you need, first establish
exactly what is happening now and the reasons why. Are there
any better ways of doing it? A salesman's workload consists of
making calls, travelling and administration work, all three of
which can be measured in order to determine the best territory
size to give a salesman the desired amount of work. Sales
objectives can be either quantitative or qualitative. Quantitative
objectives are concerned with what he sells, to whom he sells it,
and at what cost. Qualitative objectives should be related to the
salesman's performance on the job. Sales force motivation is a
function of money plus a sense of doing a worthwhile job and, in*

*order to improve performance, sales management should seek to increase incentives and decrease disincentives.*

Having established the strategic role of personal selling in the marketing mix, the following questions now need to be answered:
– how many salesmen do we need?
– what do we want them to do?
– how should they be managed?

## How many salesmen do we need?

In considering this question, a good starting point is to find out what is happening now. Start by listing all the things the current sales force actually does, which might include: opening new accounts; servicing existing accounts; demonstrating new products; taking repeat orders; merchandising; collecting debts. This should be followed by asking if there are any alternative ways of carrying out these responsibilities. For example, telephone selling has been shown to be a perfectly acceptable alternative to personal visits, particularly in respect of repeat business. This frees the sales force for missionary work, which is not so susceptible to the telephone approach. Can debts be collected by mail? Can products be demonstrated at exhibitions or showrooms? It is only by asking these kinds of questions that we can be certain that we have not fallen into the common trap of committing the company to a decision and then seeking data and reasons to justify the decision. A far better approach is to collect relevant, quantified data, then to use intuitive judgement and experience as necessary in coming to a decision.

Basically, all sales force activities can be categorized under three headings. A salesman:
– makes calls
– travels
– performs administrative functions.

These constitute what can be called his *workload*. If we first decide what constitutes a reasonable workload for a salesman, in hours per month, then we can begin to measure how long his current activities take, hence the exact extent of his current workload.

116

This measurement activity can be performed either by some independent third party, or preferably by the salesmen themselves. All they have to do is to record distance travelled, time in and out of calls, and the outlet type. This can then be easily analysed to indicate the average duration of a call by outlet type, the average distance travelled in a month, and the average speed according to the nature of the territory (i.e. city, suburbs, country). With the aid of a map, existing accounts, with their associated time values, can be allocated on a trial and error basis, together with the concomitant time values for clerical activities and travel. This way, equitable workloads can be calculated for the sales force, building in if necessary spare capacity for prospecting.

Sometimes, this kind of analysis produces surprising results in that the company's 'star' salesman is often found to have a smaller workload than the one with the worst results, who may be having to work much longer hours to achieve his sales because of the nature of his territory.

There are, of course, other ways of measuring workloads.

One major consumer goods company used its own work study department to measure sales force effectiveness. The results of this study are summarized in FIGURE 15, which is presented in bar chart form.

At least the company now knew how a salesman's time was spent and approximately how much was actually available for selling. One immediate action taken by the company was to initiate a training programme which enabled more time to be spent on selling as a result of better planning.

## What do we want our salesmen to do?

With so little time actually available for selling, it is vital that a company should know as precisely as possible what it wants its sales force to. do. Sales force objectives can be either *quantitative* or *qualitative*. Principal quantitative objectives are concerned with the following measures:
- how much to sell (the value or unit sales volume)
- what to sell (the mix of product lines to sell)
- where to sell (the markets and the individual customers that will take the company towards its marketing objectives)

## FIGURE 15

**SALESMAN'S TOTAL DAILY ACTIVITY**

| | | PER CENT OF DAY | MINUTES PER DAY | |
|---|---|---|---|---|
| OUTSIDE—CALL TIME | DRIVE TO AND FROM ROUTE | 15.9 | 81.28 | |
| | DRIVE ON ROUTE | 16.1 | 82.65 | |
| | WALK | 4.6 | 23.50 | |
| | REST AND BREAKS | 6.3 | 32.42 | |
| | PRE—CALL ADMIN | 1.4 | 7.26 | |
| | POST—CALL ADMIN | 5.3 | 27.11 | |
| | | 49.6 | 254.22 | =4 hr 14 mins |
| INSIDE—CALL TIME | BUSINESS TALKS | 11.5 | 59.6 | |
| | SELL | 5.9 | 30.20 | |
| | CHAT | 3.4 | 17.40 | |
| | RECEIPTS | 1.2 | 6.06 | |
| | MISC | 1.1 | 5.87 | |
| | DRINK | 1.7 | 8.41 | |
| | WAITING | 7.1 | 36.00 | |
| | | 31.9 | 163.44 | =2 hr 43 mins |
| EVENING WORK | DEPOT WORK | 9.8 | 50.0 | |
| | ENTERING PINKS | 3.9 | 20.0 | |
| | PRE—PLAN ROUTE | 4.8 | 25.0 | |
| | | 18.5 | 95.00 | = 1hr 35mins |
| | | | TOTAL | = 8 hr 32mins |

- the desired profit contribution (where relevant and where the company is set up to compute this)
- selling costs (in compensation, expenses, supervision, selling costs etc).

The first three types of objectives will be derived directly from the marketing objectives, which are discussed in detail in Question 27.

There are, of course, many other kinds of quantitative objectives which can be set for the sales force, including tasks to do with the point-of-sale advertising, reports, trade meetings, customer complaints and so on, but most of these will be subservient to the major objectives which are concerned with what is sold and to whom.

Qualitative objectives can be a potential source of problems if sales managers try to assess the performance of the sales force along dimensions which include abstract terms such as 'loyalty', 'enthusiasm', 'cooperation', since such terms are incapable of objective measurement. Instead, managers often resort to highly subjective interpretations, which cause resentment and frustration amongst those being assessed.

However, it is possible to set and measure qualitative objectives which actually relate to the performance of the sales force on the job. It is, for example, possible to assess the skill with which a person applies his product knowledge on the job, or the skill with which he plans his work, or the skill with which he overcomes objections during a sales interview. Whilst still qualitative in nature, they nevertheless relate to performance against standards understood by the sales force.

Given such standards, it is not too difficult for a competent field sales manager to determine deficiencies, get agreement on them, to coach in skills and techniques, to build attitudes of professionalism, to show how to self-train, to determine requirements that cannot be tackled in the field, and to evaluate improvements in performance and the effect of any past training.

One consumer goods company with thirty field sales managers discovered that most of them were spending much of the day in their offices engaged on administrative work, most of it self-made. So they took their offices away from them and insisted that they spend most of their time in the field, training their salesmen. To assist them in this task they trained them how to appraise sales-

119

men's performance in the field and how to improve salesmen's performance on the job. There was a dramatic increase in sales, and consequently in their own earnings, which incidentally rapidly overcame their resentment at losing their office!

## How should we manage our sales force?

Sales force motivation as a subject has received a great deal of attention in recent times, largely as a result of the work done by psychologists in other fields of management. Even though the word motivation is still bandied about by people with little understanding of its real meaning, there is now widespread appreciation of the fact that it is not sufficient merely to give someone a title and an office and expect to get good results. It is now widely acknowledged that effective leadership is as much follower-determined as it is determined by managerial leader.

Whilst for the purposes of this discussion it is not necessary to go into a detailed discussion of sales force motivation, it is worth mentioning briefly some important factors that contribute to effective sales force management.

If a sales manager's job is to improve the performance of his sales force, and if performance is a function of incentives minus disincentives, then the more we can increase incentives and reduce disincentives, the better will be performance. Of course incentives and disincentives are merely different sides of the same coin.

It has been shown through research that an important element of sales force motivation is a sense of doing a worthwhile job. In other words, desire for praise and recognition, the avoidance of boredom and monotony, the enhancement of self image, freedom from fear and worry, and the desire to belong to something believed to be worthwhile, all contribute to enhanced performance.

One well known piece of research carried out in the USA, on the reasons for the results of the twenty highest producing sales units in one company compared with the twenty lowest producing sales units, showed all the above factors to be major determinants of success. However, remuneration will always be a most important determinant of motivation. This does not necessarily mean paying the most money, although clearly unless there are significant nonfinancial motivations within a company, it is unlikely that people will stay.

In drawing up a compensation plan, which would normally include a basic salary plus some element for special effort, such as bonus or commission, the following objectives should be considered:

1 To attract and keep effective salesmen
2 To remain competitive
3 To reward salesmen in accordance with their individual performance
4 To provide a guaranteed income plus an orderly individual growth rate
5 To generate individual sales initiative
6 To encourage teamwork
7 To encourage the performance of essential non-selling tasks
8 To ensure that management can fairly administer and adjust compensation levels as a means of achieving sales objectives.

To summarize, the sales force is a vital but very expensive element of the marketing mix, and as much care should be devoted to its management as to any other area of marketing management. This will be most likely achieved if intuitive sense, which is obtained from experience, can be combined with logical frames of thinking according to the kind of ideas presented here.

*Further reading*

Downing, G. D., *Sales Management*, Wiley, 1969
Smallbone, D. W., *An Introduction to Sales Management*, Staples Press, 1968
Wilson, M. T., *Managing a Sales Force*, Gower Press, 1971

**Self-audit questions**

17.1 *What do you think is meant by the statement that the sales manager's effectiveness today depends more on his managerial abilities and behaviour than on technical or functional skills?*

17.2 *List the kinds of sales objectives that are set by your company. Do you think they are adequate?*

17.3 *What is the relationship in your company, if any, between sales objectives and corporate objectives?*

**17.4** *Why do you think psychological concepts should be considered in compensation strategy and tactics and how far does/could your company do so?*

# Question 18
# When should we use featured sales promotions?

*A wide range of tactical marketing support activities generally known as sales promotions are available to managers. They must, however, be used with precisely the same attention to objectives, testing and evaluation as is commended for advertising. The cost effectiveness of any sales promotions, including price reductions, needs establishing.*

*It is equally important to see sales promotional activity as integrated within the overall marketing plan for the organization. When carefully developed, industrial, trade and consumer markets are susceptible to tactical marketing support, and sales force bonuses and other incentives are equally included.*

*Sales promotions can be undertaken as a marketing tactic for any of the four 'P's.*

Our discussions in reply to earlier questions have indicated that all organizations have at their disposal a very considerable range of communications media including personal sales activity and the more impersonal advertising. At any moment an organization will have adopted a mix or balance of these means of communication and persuasion to purchase its products or services that interacts appropriately with the other three 'P's – price, product and place.

There is, however, one aspect which such a conceptual analysis sometimes overlooks – it is short-term or tactical marketing activity using some or all of the four 'P's. The tactical requirement may, for instance, be to secure additional product trial, or to increase distribution or display. It is such tactical marketing activity which we term *sales promotions*. The essence of sales promotions is that they feature an offer to defined customers or consumers within a specific time limit. To be termed a sales promotion an offer must be made over and above the normal terms of trade, the objectives being to enhance or promote sales to behave in a manner different from normal. The benefit offered must not be inherent in the product or service itself.

Seen this way it is apparent, as already indicated, that sales promotions are tactical marketing and can make use of the communications media, or of price, product or place – insofar as such fixed-period sales-enhancing tactics are an integral element of an organization's annual marketing plan. They constitute a subset of integrated marketing rather than element of the promotional 'P'. Accordingly, we devote a separate question here to sales promotions although discussion elsewhere of tactical aspects of each of the four 'P's covers similar ground.

## Tactical strategy

Because sales promotions are essentially used tactically, they often amount to little more than a series of spasmodic gimmicks lacking any coherence. Yet the very same managements that organize spasmodic sales promotions usually believe that pricing, distribution or advertising should conform to an overall marketing strategy, enshrined in an annual plan. Perhaps this is because marketing plans have always been based on a philosophy of building a long-term customer and consumer franchise in a consistent manner, whereas the basic rationale of sales promotions is to help the company gain and/or retain tactical marketing initiative.

Even so, there is no reason why there should not be a strategy for sales promotions, with each promotion increasing the effectiveness of the next. Then a bond between seller and buyer can be built up, thereby ensuring that tactical objectives are linked in with the overall plan, and there is generally a better application of resources.

That this is possible has been seen in recent years from sales promotional campaigns involving the Home Pride Flour Graders, who first appeared in the early sixties; from the twenty million enamel Golly brooches given out by Robertsons since the 1930s, from Mighty Ajax, Miss Pears, the Ovaltineys, and many other campaigns which have used schemes and devices which have been consistently incorporated into a product's total communications and marketing strategy.

More recent schemes, such as the Esso tiger, and the Smurfs, are proof that it is possible to establish a style of sales promotion which, if consistently applied, will help to establish the objectives of a product over a long period of time, which are flexible, and have staying power.

In Question 2 we asserted that industrial goods are always sold to other organizations and that this has the effect of changing the emphasis placed on certain elements of the marketing mix rather than having any fundamental effect on the relevance of the marketing concept.

It will not be surprising then to learn that the manner of consumer goods sales promotional techniques described above, and which are most familiar to us all, can be applied to industrial goods. Yet in spite of this, sales promotions are comparatively rare in industrial markets, perhaps partly from a belief born in the engineering discipline that if a firm has to promote its products that aggressively, there must be something wrong with them.

In recent years, however, industrial goods companies have begun to take note of the enormous success of campaigns such as Yorkshire Imperial Metal's 'golden spanner' and schemes in the Herbert Morris Group. They are becoming more aware of sales promotion as a flexible and competitive tactical tool in marketing. 3M recently offered a £50 coupon to prospective buyers of photocopiers via an advertisement in a Sunday newspaper. A major European industrial goods company with divisions spanning a range of products from fast-moving industrial to high-priced capital goods has developed a massive range of special promotion schemes. They are offering featured time period trade-in allowances; desk-top giveaways and custom-built guarantees – all made as featured offers outside and above the normal terms of trade.

# Making featured sales promotions effective

There is a widespread acknowledgement that sales promotions are often one of the most mismanaged facets of all marketing activities. This is mainly because of the confusion about what precisely a sales promotion is, which often results in expenditures not being properly recorded. Some companies include it with advertising, some as part of sales force expense, others as a general marketing expense, and yet others as a manufacturing expense as in the case of extra product, special labels, or packaging. The loss of unit sales revenue from special price reductions is often not recorded at all.

Few companies can afford not to set objectives for sales promotions or fail to evaluate results after the event. For example, a £1 case allowance on a product with a contribution rate of £3 per case has to increase sales by fifty per cent just to maintain the same level of contribution. Failure to attain this, or to meet alternative objectives set for the promotion, easily results in loss of control and a consequent reduction in profits.

In order to manage a company's sales promotions expense more effectively, there are two essential steps that must be taken. First, current spending must be analysed and categorized by type of activity, e.g. special packaging, special point-of-sale material or loss of revenue through price reductions. Next, within a total strategy for sales promotions, objectives for each promotion must be clearly stated, such as trial, repeat purchase, distribution, display, a shift in buying peaks or combating competition in a specified manner. Thereafter, the following process must always be applied:
- select the appropriate technique
- pretest the ideas
- mount the promotion
- evaluate its impact in depth.

A leading German company manufacturing self-assembly kitchens embarked on a heavy programme of sales promotion after a dramatic reduction in consumer demand. Whilst they managed to maintain turnover, they were worried that their sales promotional activities had been carried out in such a haphazard and piecemeal fashion that they were unable to evaluate the cost

FIGURE 16

| TYPE OF PROMOTION / TARGET MARKET | MONEY — DIRECT | MONEY — INDIRECT | GOODS — DIRECT | GOODS — INDIRECT | SERVICES — DIRECT | SERVICES — INDIRECT |
|---|---|---|---|---|---|---|
| **CONSUMER** | ● PRICE REDUCTION | ● COUPONS<br>● VOUCHERS<br>● MONEY EQUIVALENT<br>● COMPETITIONS | ● FREE GOODS<br>● PREMIUM OFFERS (e.g 13 for 12)<br>● FREE GIFTS<br>● TRADE-IN OFFERS | ● STAMPS<br>● COUPONS<br>● VOUCHERS<br>● MONEY EQUIVALENT<br>● COMPETITIONS | ● GUARANTEES<br>● GROUP PARTICIPATION<br>● SPECIAL EXHIBITIONS AND DISPLAYS | ● COOPERATIVE ADVERTISING<br>● STAMPS<br>● COUPONS<br>● VOUCHERS FOR SERVICES<br>● EVENTS<br>● ADMISSION<br>● COMPETITIONS |
| **TRADE** | ● DEALER LOADERS<br>● LOYALTY SCHEMES<br>● INCENTIVES<br>● FULL-RANGE BUYING SCHEMES | ● EXTENDED CREDIT<br>● DELAYED INVOICING<br>● SALE OR RETURN<br>● COUPONS<br>● VOUCHERS<br>● MONEY EQUIVALENTS | ● FREE GIFTS<br>● TRIAL OFFERS<br>● TRADE-IN OFFERS | ● COUPONS<br>● VOUCHERS<br>● MONEY EQUIVALENTS<br>● COMPETITIONS | ● GUARANTEES<br>● GROUP PARTICIPATION EVENTS<br>● FREE SERVICES<br>● RISK-REDUCTION SCHEMES<br>● TRAINING<br>● SPECIAL EXHIBITIONS AND DISPLAYS<br>● DEMONSTRATIONS<br>● RECIPROCAL TRADING SCHEMES | ● STAMPS<br>● COUPONS<br>● VOUCHERS FOR SERVICES<br>● COMPETITIONS |
| **SALES FORCE** | ● BONUS<br>● COMMISSION | ● COUPONS<br>● VOUCHERS<br>● POINTS SYSTEMS<br>● MONEY EQUIVALENTS<br>● COMPETITIONS | ● FREE GIFTS | ● COUPONS<br>● VOUCHERS<br>● POINTS SYSTEMS<br>● MONEY EQUIVALENTS | ● FREE SERVICES<br>● GROUP-PARTICIPATION EVENTS | ● COUPONS<br>● VOUCHERS<br>● POINT SYSTEMS FOR SERVICES<br>● EVENT<br>● ADMISSION<br>● COMPETITIONS |

effectiveness of what they had done. They were also very concerned about its effect on the company image and their long-term franchise with consumers. So they made a concentrated study of this area of expenditure which had come to represent over half their total communications budget. Next time round they had clear objectives, a clear promotional plan fully integrated into their marketing plans, and established means of assessment.

The company took their competitors by surprise and made substantial gains in market share. In one promotion alone they hired an entire hall at an international exhibition centre. They converted it into a giant showroom with forty kitchen displays and a 250-seat theatre. For an expenditure of £90,000 the company presented a new range to over 2,500 customers, obtained 900 display orders against a target of 750, and sold to their entire national distribution network in one operation. At the same time, they convinced the trade of their professional businesslike approach, and of their confidence in the future.

Some of the many and varied types of sales promotions that can be used are listed in FIGURE 16. Each of these different types is appropriate for different circumstances, and each has advantages and disadvantages. For example, case bonusing relates cost to volume, is fast and flexible, effective where the customer is profit conscious, can last as long as required, is simple to set up, administer and sell. On the other hand, it has no cumulative value to the customer, is unimaginative, and can often be seen as a prelude to a permanent price reduction.

Points schemes are flexible, have wide appeal, do not involve the company in holding stocks of gifts, customers cannot easily value gifts, and they are easy to administer. On the other hand, they offer no advantages in bulk buying, are difficult to budget, and they lack the immediacy of dealer loaders.

Great care is necessary, therefore, in selecting a scheme appropriate to the objective sought.

*Further reading*
Peterson C., 'The Strategic Role of Sales Promotion',
 *Marketing*, January 1977
Spillard P., 'How to Promote Industrial Products',
 *Marketing*, February 1977

Spillard P., 'Industrial Sales Promotion in Practice',
  *Marketing*, September 1977

**Self-audit questions**

18.1    *What is the difference between advertising and sales
        promotion?*
18.2    *How much money does your own company spend on each?*
18.3    *What strategy do you have for sales promotion?*
18.4    *How do you evaluate in depth your sales/promotional
        activities?*

# Question 19
# Where do our customers buy our products?

*Where our customers buy our products is logically determined by
the outlets at which those products are made available to them.
The planning of the firm's distributive activity should be based
upon a careful assessment of the market requirements and the
capability of the firm to meet those requirements. The
'marketing channel' through which our products move is a
network of institutions which themselves are linked by a series of
mutually beneficial relationships. The marketing channel is itself
dynamic, as are the markets that it serves. As such, decisions
regarding the choice of channel should be seen as an integral part
of the firm's marketing strategy subject to change and
adjustment in the light of circumstances.*

This problem might be restated as: 'what channels do our customers utilize in the acquisition of our products?' The answer is
vitally important because it stresses the importance in the company's marketing effort of the *marketing channel*. The 'right
product in the right place at the right time' is by now something
of a cliché but the message that it contains is central to our con-

cern with the channels of distribution that we use in marketing products and services in industrial and consumer markets.

We can view the marketing channel as the course taken in the transfer of title of a good or service from its original source of supply to its ultimate consumption. Such a consideration must take into account both the choice of the *route of exchange* and its administrative and financial control, and the *physical movement* of the product through that route. This latter point will be dealt with in detail in the response to Question 20 and it is the issues relating to marketing channel choice that are presently addressed.

Typically many companies will not give too much attention to the question of channel choice. It is not seen as being a variable in the marketing mix; frequently the marketing channel will have taken its current form as a result of unplanned and haphazard development. Such a disregard for this vital area of marketing discretion means that many opportunities for the profitable development of market potential are passed over. For example, one international chemical company selling into Europe via their own sales office direct to customers found that by using a chemical merchant or middleman they could reduce their own selling costs and take advantage of a ready-made sales organization.

Another company, a British shoe manufacturer producing good-quality shoes, found that they could open up a new and profitable market segment by including their products in the catalogue of a national mail-order firm. Thus they were able to sell the same shoes, at the same prices, to two, largely distinct, markets: the up-market speciality shoe shop as well as to the wider down-market audience reached via the mail-order catalogue.

Here then are two examples of the benefits of taking a fresh look at marketing channels. Both involved a reappraisal of the route by which the customer acquired the product and a comparison of the costs and benefits of using alternative routes.

Many companies use multiple channels of distribution to get their products to the market place. These companies may, for example, sell to different markets by means of different outlets, or the same market may be approached via a dual distribution channel with some products taking one route, and others taking a second. Alternatively a company may be considering the possibilities of using a different channel of distribution from its exist-

129

ing one. Whatever the situation, it is a necessary and a valuable exercise to look at the costs and benefits accruing through the use of a specific channel of distribution. The alternatives depicted in FIGURE 17 have quite distinctly different cost and revenue profiles.

FIGURE 17

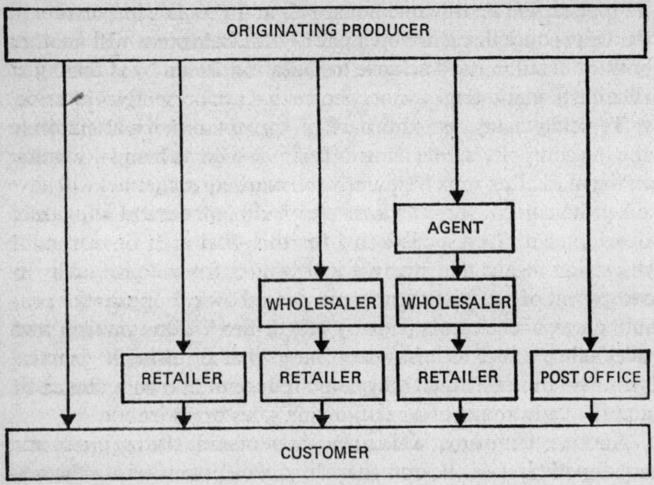

This cost/benefit appraisal needs to be undertaken in the widest context possible. It needs to consider questions of market strategy, the appropriateness of the channel to the product, customer requirements and so on as well as the question of the comparative costs of selling and distribution.

## Factors in the choice of channels

The ultimate purpose of the marketing channel is to reach the customer in a way appropriate to his requirements and to the firm's capabilities.

What are the requirements of the customer? Whilst these will clearly vary from market to market it is possible to generalize customer objectives relating to the decision on where to buy the product. These objectives could be summarized as optimizing

130

price/value considerations, maximizing convenience, and a surety of availability.

The *price/value* dimension is present to a greater or lesser extent in all markets and it implies that the consumer is seeking a certain level of value or utility from a good or service but that there is an implicit trade-off between that value and the price that is charged. In this way one housewife at an Asda supermarket in the UK is optimizing her own price/value balance whilst another housewife attempts to achieve a similar optimum by shopping at Harrods. In industrial and service markets the principles of price/value optimization on the part of the customer will similarly apply. Industrial purchasing officers do, for example, employ standard evaluative procedures such as *value analysis*.

The questions of *convenience* and *availability* are dealt with in some detail in the responses to Questions 20 and 21 but it should be emphasized at this juncture just what a key role they play in competitive markets. For example, the choice of supplier for providing the ancillary supplies to North Sea oil exploration and production companies has been largely determined in practice by the customers' need to have a convenient and sure source of supply – even to the extent of paying a higher price.

The selection of marketing channels must fit the requirements and capabilities of the company in addition to meeting the objectives of the customer. What sort of factors are involved here? Essentially we can look at two major facets of the firm's viewpoint on its channel decision. The first is the market, and the second is institutional considerations.

Let us consider how these factors might influence the firm. Sometimes the firm's market segmentation policy will require that particular channels of distribution be used. If we are marketing an insurance counselling service in Germany to individuals in the higher tax brackets then it would probably not be appropriate to set up a network of door-to-door salesmen. The company may well prefer to use an indirect channel of distribution which might rely upon intermediaries such as bank managers and accountants. Associated with the question of segmentation is that of *coverage* or penetration. In other words how far do we wish to gain distribution penetration in our target segments? To gain maximum coverage may well require the involvement of an intermediary.

One of the problems with indirect marketing channels, i.e. those that involve intermediaries, is that they almost always lead to a loss of close contact with the market place and to some loss of control over such key areas as customer-service policy. Also by implication there is the loss of margin to the firm in that intermediaries necessarily absorb some of the margin that would either have been available to the firm or to the customer. On the other hand they are often the only means of providing wider distribution without the very considerable costs of maintaining a direct marketing channel. The intermediary performs a very necessary function in many markets by consolidating what might be many small shipments from single producers to single customers into larger shipments comprising the products of multiple producers to multiple customers. This is best shown visually in the two diagrams in FIGURE 18 which compare the direct (a) and indirect (b) modes.

In some markets the intermediate function is performed by a wholesaler, in other cases a distribution service company, e.g. Pickfords, BRS, or SPD in Britain and Europe, will provide the

FIGURE 18

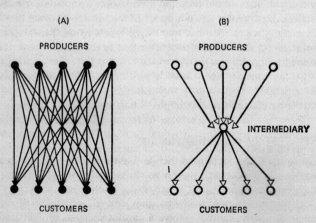

means of gaining the benefits of large-scale distribution at a fraction of the cost of going it alone.

It would be a mistake, however, to view relationships with channel intermediaries purely from an economic point of view. The marketing channel whereby the offering of the firm reaches the market place is a dynamic system, membership of which has considerable implications. In most channels one member will often emerge as the leader, determining the policy of other members of the channel – even extending its control over them. *Vertical integration* is a common phenomenon in marketing channels. Such integration could involve a company absorbing those firms who are its sources of supply, a backward integration, or a movement to control its markets – forward integration. Such a movement backwards or forwards need not always require ownership of the firms involved. Marks & Spencer, for example, is a retail operation in the UK which through its massive buying power exerts an almost total control over many of its suppliers. When you sell 100% of your output to one customer you are to all intents and purposes 'owned' by them. The motor car industry has a very similar relationship with its components suppliers too.

Even where integration through ownership or control does not exist, the institutional pressures within the channel can be considerable. Who should hold the inventory in the channel? How should the available margin be split? Can intermediaries lower down the channel be relied upon to follow through desired marketing strategy and promotional plans? The possibilities for conflict in the marketing channel are considerable. The likelihood of conflict is enhanced if each level of the channel attempts to maximize its own return. In situations such as this the return enjoyed overall in the channel may be reduced.

## Selecting the marketing channel

Given these considerations then and assuming that we are in a position to choose rather than be chosen, what are the circumstances that might prompt a reappraisal in our channel strategy?

The introduction of a new product, or even a merger with another company, should involve a careful analysis of the costs and benefits of utilizing present channels compared with possible alternatives. Likewise a change in our marketing strategy might involve a similar consideration. For example, an Italian manufacturer of specialist outdoor and climbing gear decided that the need for greater promotional and service support at the dealer level required a move from intensive to selective distribution. Or again the identification of new potential market segments might require a channel reappraisal. The market too can change, necessitating a reaction by the distributing firm. One firm that was adversely affected by too rigid a policy towards channels was an old established Belgian company in household products such as polishes and scourers. The company had traditionally sold its products through hardware wholesalers who distributed the products to hardware shops. When approached by a leading supermarket chain to produce 'own-label' brands for them the company refused on the grounds that such a move might not be well received by their existing outlets – the hardware shops. The problem was that hardware shops were a declining feature of the Belgian retailing scene and much of the business that had formerly gone to these stores had been captured by the supermarkets. Thus the company was locked in to a channel of distribution that was accounting for an ever-falling share of the market.

Situations like this can be avoided if our channels of distribution are viewed as a variable in the marketing mix, subjected to regular and searching review, and when necessary becoming the focus for vigorous and often necessarily courageous decision making.

*Further reading*

McVey, P., 'Are Channels of Distribution What the Textbooks Say?' *Journal of Marketing*, vol 24, January 1960

Lewis, E. H., *Marketing Channels: Structure and Strategy*, McGraw Hill, 1968

**Self-audit questions**

19.1    *Draw a diagram of your own organization's marketing channel or channels.*

19.2    *Do your competitors do things differently? Why?*

19.3    *What are the criteria you use to select new channel members?*

# Question 20
# How can we get our product to the customer?

*Getting the product to the customer cannot simply be viewed by marketing management as the concern of others. The distributive activity of the firm is as much a part of its marketing mix as are pricing, promotion and product decisions. Indeed in some markets the impact of the distribution effort upon sales can exceed that of the other mix elements. Seen in this light the means whereby the product reaches the customer assumes a vital importance in marketing strategy. The implications of this view of distribution's marketing role are considerable and involve a reappraisal of attitudes as well as of the means of distribution generally employed.*

*It is also suggested that the key to the successful development of the firm's distribution effort is the adoption of a total systems approach whereby an integrative view is taken of the various activities involved in that distribution effort.*

In an earlier discussion of the nature of the marketing mix, emphasis was placed upon the need to understand the impact of these mix elements upon our marketing effectiveness. In fact what is often the case in practice is that we concentrate on three elements – product, price and promotion – and leave the fourth element, *place*, to look after itself. In the quartet of the 'P's, place is the shorthand description for the means whereby the matching process between the needs of the market and the offering of the firm is actually achieved. It is clearly an activity of some importance in that it represents the addition of time and place utility to the product. Without this added value the product is worthless.

This distributive activity is referred to by a number of names: *physical distribution management (PDM), marketing logistics* and *materials management* are some of the descriptions that have been used in discussions of this neglected area of management.

Accompanying these different titles there has often been confusion surrounding the exact nature of the distributive task within the company.

This confusion may in part explain the neglect that has typically been demonstrated by marketing men. There has been a tendency in many companies to treat distribution as something of a necessary but mechanical activity that incurs costs and is something to do with transport. Too few companies have seen their distribution effort as potentially contributing in a vital and positive way to company profitability through its revenue-generating capability.

Let us see how one British company in the food business released the profit potential that was latent in its distributive system. With a sales turnover of nearly £100 million a year from four major lines the manufacturer was using a combination of fifteen public warehouses and company owned facilities for distributing 100,000 tons of goods each year. The company had separate sales and order processing organizations for each line with a total annual warehousing and transport bill of over £3 million. In recent years this figure had been growing alarmingly and yet turnover in real terms was static. A review by a team of consultants showed that there was little coordination between the distribution and marketing functions in the firm and that there was a considerable overlap in the selling and distributive activities. This overlap could be traced back to the somewhat complex organizational structure that had resulted when the present company was formed from a merger of three companies.

This audit of their activities resulted in a complete reappraisal of the way they sold and distributed their products. A single direct sales force was set up reducing the numbers of orders processed by almost 50% and by a consolidation of deliveries reduced transport costs by 20%. In addition the number of warehouses was cut to seven which reduced the total inventory holding in the system, as well as cutting storage and handling costs by 40%. The end result was a vast improvement in their delivery performance, and hence sales effectiveness, plus an overall reduction in total distribution costs of one-third.

Similar examples can be cited from markets as diverse as fuel pumps and baby foods. As more and more companies take a fresh look at the role of distribution in their marketing effort they are coming to similar conclusions. There is considerable scope for profit enhancement through distribution improvement. When it is considered that studies have estimated that the average European manufacturing company spends 21 % of its sales revenue on distribution-related activities it is not difficult to contemplate the benefits of such a reappraisal.

These benefits need not always come from cost savings in distribution. Frequently, profitability can be improved by spending more on some aspects of the total corporate distribution activity rather than less. International Computers, for example, have found that it pays to ship their computers from the UK by air freight to continental European customers rather than by surface transport. Although the costs of transport are clearly higher, savings are made on packaging and on port charges. Furthermore, faster deliveries mean lower inventory carrying costs for goods in transit and improved cash flow through a reduction in the time before customers can be invoiced.

If the marketing requirements of the company are to be consonant with its distribution capabilities then the meeting point between these two activities must be identified and subjected to scrutiny.

Such a scrutiny may well call for a realignment and a reappraisal of the conventional view of marketing and distribution in the company. If the marketing department is judged for performance in terms of sales and market shares, there will be a tendency to push the costs of distribution into someone else's cost centre. Indeed if distribution costs are not a consideration in the marketing budget this tendency is perfectly understandable. For example, one Dutch company in the machine-tool business experienced spiralling manufacturing costs because of the policy adopted by the marketing manager who insisted upon cutting delivery times by half. He had not thought through the implications of such a policy upon production scheduling and upon the requirements for stocks of sub-assemblies.

To overcome the problems caused by this compartmentalization of the company effort a new, integrative approach to marketing and distribution has appeared. This orientation is the *logistics concept*.

# Logistics is an integrative activity

The emphasis behind the logistics concept is on systems. It suggests that the *movement* activity in a company is so wide-reaching and pervasive in its impacts that it should be considered as a total system. Thus instead of marketing, production, distribution, purchasing etc. all working away oblivious of the others and attempting to optimize their own activity, the logistics concept suggests that it may be necessary for some, or all, of these areas to operate sub-optimally in order that the whole system may be more effective. So, for example, the marketing manager must be prepared if necessary to accept a lower level of service than he would like; or the production manager must be prepared to schedule shorter runs with more changes, if the overall effectiveness of the system is to be maximized.

To move this concept from the realms of theory to those of practice involves a consideration of the areas of concern to logistics management. There are five key decision areas that together constitute the *logistics mix*:

*Facility decisions* – these decisions are concerned with the problem of how many warehouses and plants should we have and where should they be located. Obviously for the majority of companies it is necessary to take the location of existing plants and warehouses as given in the short term but the question does arise in the longer term or indeed when new plants or warehouses are being considered.

*Inventory decisions* – a major element in many companies' total distribution costs is the cost of holding stock. Thus decisions about how much inventory to hold, where to hold it, in what quantities to order and so on are vital issues. Inventory levels, as we shall see in the response to Question 21, are also instrumental in determining the level of service that the company offers the customer.

*Communications decisions* – it must always be remembered that logistics is not only about the flows of materials through the distribution channel but also that a key determinant of efficient logistics systems is the flow of information. Here we are talking about the order-processing system, the invoicing system, the demand forecasting system and so on. Without effective communications support the logistics system will never be capable of providing satisfactory customer service at acceptable cost.

*Unitization decisions* – the way in which goods are packaged and then subsequently accumulated into larger unit sizes, e.g. a case load, can have a major bearing upon logistics economics. For example the ability to stack goods on a pallet which then becomes the unit load for movement and storage can lead to considerable cost savings in terms of handling and warehousing. Similarly the use of containers as the basic unit of movement has revolutionized international transport and, to a certain extent, domestic transport as well.

*Transport decisions* – last, but not necessarily least, are those decisions surrounding the transport function of the firm. The important aspects of the transport decision concern such issues as what mode of transport should we use, do we own our own vehicles or lease them, how do we schedule our deliveries, how often should we deliver and so on. Perhaps of these five decision areas it is transport that receives the greatest attention within the firm in that it is one of the more obvious facets of the distribution task.

Together these five areas constitute the total costs of distribution within a company. Further, however, it is frequently the case that a decision taken in one area will have an effect on the other four areas. Thus a decision to close a depot, a facility decision, will affect the transport costs, the inventory allocation and perhaps data processing costs – this is the idea of a *cost trade-off*. Managing the logistics function involves a continuous search for such trade-offs, the intention being to secure a reduction in total costs by changing the cost structure in one or more areas.

The important feature of this logistics mix concept is that transport is seen as being just one element amongst five. Conventionally in many companies transport *is* distribution; yet viewed in this total sense it may be that it accounts for only a small proportion of total logistics costs.

## Bringing sub-systems together

One of the major problems of conventional approaches to distribution is that responsibility for it is spread over many discrete functional areas. It has already been suggested that a too heavy emphasis on compartmentalization in the company leads to a sub-optimal situation overall. In one Swiss engineering company responsibility for stock levels throughout the system was in the hands of the production department; yet at the same time the purchasing manager was pursuing policies which conflicted with production policy, the distribution manager operated an inflexible delivery system and the marketing manager was driven to despair with the erratic service levels that resulted. All this resulted from a failure to take a systems approach to the logistics function within the company.

The acceptance of the integrative systems-based approach that characterizes the logistics concept implies a recognition that there is an interrelationship between the parts of the whole of such a nature that action affecting one part can well affect all others. Any action taken must therefore be considered in the light of its effect on all parts of the business and on the overriding objectives of the company. Thus the company can be viewed as a number of interlinked sub-systems which must somehow be united if overall effectiveness is to be maximized. The distribution planner under such an orientation must be concerned with the flow of

FIGURE 19

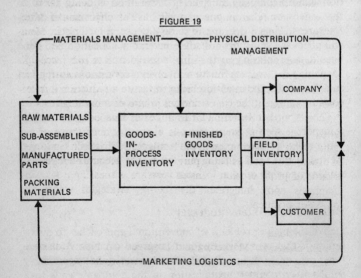

materials through the whole business process, from raw materials through to the finished goods arriving at the customer's premises.

FIGURE 19 brings together those aspects of the company's operations involving flows, either of materials or information, which are the core concern of an integrated approach to logistics management.

Thus, while physical distribution management is concerned only with those flows from the end of the production line to the consumer, the integrated approach of logistics encompasses the total flow of materials and related information into, through, and out of the corporate system.

## Distribution's role in tomorrow's markets

Recent years have seen a slow-down in the growth of many markets, unpredicted shortages of materials, shrinking margins and spiralling costs. In circumstances such as these an integrated distribution effort can make major impacts upon marketing performance and upon the total costs of corporate operations. There are signs that in some markets, distribution is being asked to provide the key to long-term survival. The chairman of Monsanto's European operations states for example: 'We in Monsanto increasingly regard distribution as having the same significance and making the same contribution to our success as skilful advertising, aggressive selling, efficient manufacturing and innovative research and development.' Such views are not necessarily confined to those businesses where distribution costs represent a high proportion of total costs; in consumer markets and in service industries there is a growing awareness of the crucial role of distribution in the firm's marketing mix. No longer is distribution seen as being purely a cost centre and an inevitable source of profit erosion – instead we are witnessing a growing emphasis upon integrated distribution strategies within the marketing context.

*Further reading*
Christopher, M., 'Marketing and Logistics – A New Area of Management Concern', *Industrial Marketing Management*, vol 2 no 2, 1973

Christopher, M., Walters, D. and Wills, G., *Effective Distribution Management*, MCB Publications, 1978
Van Buijtenen, P., *Business Logistics*, Martinus Nijhoff, 1976

**Self-audit questions**

20.1   *What do you understand by the 'logistics mix' as it applies to your organization?*

20.2   *What relationship does marketing planning have with logistics?*

20.3   *What are your total logistics costs and what major trade-offs have been taken advantage of in recent years?*

# Question 21
# What level of availability does our customer want?

*Logistics service is defined here as the provision of 'availability'. Availability is a major determinant of sales in all markets. Often it is the case that the company has no clearly defined policy towards customer service and will only rarely be able to quantify the costs of service or identify the direct customer benefits. The task implicit in the management of customer service is to achieve a balance between those costs and benefits at the margin. Methods of assessing appropriate levels of availability are proposed and the concept of a 'customer-service package' is discussed.*

Customer service is the output of a firm's logistics system. It may be defined in many ways. For the brewers of Oranjeboom Beer in Holland it is measured in terms of how frequently their sales outlets are out of stock. The National Westminster Bank in the UK consider their customer service offering in terms of the location of their banks, the availability of cash dispensers, the provision of budget accounts and so on. Monsanto Chemicals European Division, based in Brussels, define customer service in terms of the percentage of orders that they are able to fill within a specified period of time.

Another way to look at customer service is to see it simply as the provision of *availability*. If the company's product is not available at the time the customer needs it and in the location he specifies then the probability of making a sale is much reduced. In product/market areas where competing products are only weakly differentiated, as in the case of say sugar or butter, then availability will be the largest single determinant of sales. Research has shown that in many product fields availability considerations will overcome brand loyalty.

Thus customer service, however it is defined, is essentially the added value that availability contributes to the marketing effort behind our product offering.

It will be apparent that the provision of customer service in all its forms will involve the company in fairly large expenditures. In fact it can be demonstrated that once the level of service (defined here as the percentage of occasions the product is available to the customer, when and where he wants it) increases beyond the seventy-to-eighty per cent mark, the associated costs increase far more than proportionately. FIGURE 20 demonstrates the typical relationship between the level of availability and the cost of providing it.

The implications of this cost relationship are worth some attention. In the first place, many companies are simply unaware at what level of service they are operating. They do not have any laid down service policy. Even if the company does have a declared service policy it is often the case that service levels have been arbitrarily set. Offering a 97% level of service instead of a 95% level may have only a slight effect on customer demand, yet it will have a considerable effect on logistics costs – for 'normally' distributed demand this 2.1% increase in the level of service would lead to a 14% increase in safety stock requirement alone. This disturbing feature of logistics costs is at the hub of the question: What level of availability should we offer? The answer is simply put – at least in theory: management must be certain that the marketing advantage of an increase in service more than out-

FIGURE 20

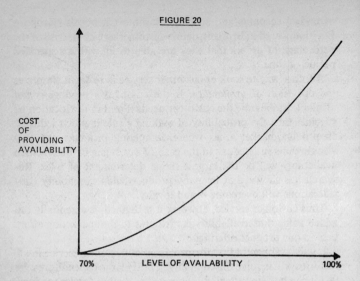

weighs the additional costs. However, what little empirical research there is has tended to suggest an S-shaped response curve to logistics service. At the very high levels of service the customer just cannot distinguish between small increments in the level of service. FIGURE 21 depicts this suggested relationship.

The requirement for marketing management is that it must recognize the cost implications of a service strategy. Indeed it is possible to go further and to suggest that by offering logistics service we are in fact absorbing a cost that would otherwise have been borne by the customer. For example if Nestlé delivers orders to Albert Hijn, the Dutch supermarket chain, twice a week instead of once a week, they are relieving them of a certain necessity for holding stock. Similarly if the manager of an Albert Hijn store knows that when he places an order with Nestlé they will rarely be out of stock on that item then again his stock holding can be lower. Because it costs money to hold stock – perhaps as much as twenty-five per cent of its value a year – Nestlé are absorbing some of this customer cost by their service offering.

Marketing and sales managers who insist on offering maximum

144

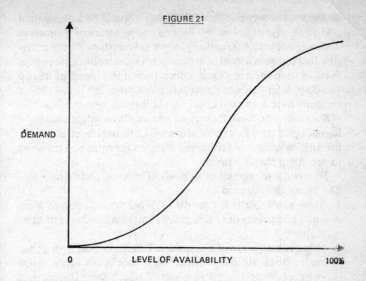

FIGURE 21

DEMAND

0                  LEVEL OF AVAILABILITY            100%

service to all customers, no matter the profitability and location of those customers, are, therefore, quite probably doing their company a disservice. By carefully reviewing customer service policy, perhaps even introducing differential service levels for different products or for different customers, marketing can enhance its contribution to corporate profitability.

## What is the right level of availability?

In most product/market situations logistics service will be a key element in a company's marketing mix – as important in its effects as say, promotion or price. Like any other marketing activity the provision of this service will cost money and therefore the company must become concerned to measure the costs and benefits of the various service alternatives available. Remembering that service offered implies customers' costs are absorbed, will the customer response be worthwhile?

Service too can provide new possibilities for market segmentation. A market can be segmented by the response of its members

145

to the level of service offered. Whether it would be a meaningful and viable segmentation will depend on the nature of the market and the product. Alternatively, upon examination it may transpire that too high a level of service is being offered in terms of the benefits which accrue. Thus a drop from a 99% level of service to a 95% level may not noticeably affect sales, but it will almost certainly have a marked effect on the logistics system costs.

Somewhere between these costs and benefits a balance has to be found. It will be at that point where the additional revenue returns for each increment of service are equal to the extra cost involved in providing that increment.

To attempt to ascertain this point of balance, certain information inputs are required.

1 How profitable is the product? What contribution to fixed costs and profits does this product make and what is its sales turnover?

2 What is the nature of the product? Is it a *critical item* as far as the customer is concerned where stock-outs at the point of supply would result in a loss of sales? Does the product have characteristics that result in high stockholding costs?

3 What is the nature of the market? Does the company operate in a sellers' or a buyers' market? How frequently is the product purchased? Are there ready substitutes? What are the stockholding practices of the purchasers? Which markets and customers are growing and which are declining?

4 What is the nature of the competition? How many companies are providing an alternative source of supply to our customers? What sort of service levels do they offer?

5 What is the nature of the channel of distribution through which the company sells? Does the company sell direct to the end customer, or through intermediaries? To what extent does the company control the channel and the activities of its members, such as stock levels and order policies?

This basic information is the raw material of the service level decision. To take an example, the level of service offered is less likely to have an effect on sales if in fact the company is the sole supplier of the product, and there are no substitutes. This situation is the case in some industrial markets and from a short-term point of view to offer a higher level of service, say 90% instead of

85% would probably have the effect of reducing the total profitability of the product.

## Developing a customer-service package

Experience in the market place suggests that customer service is a subjective, perceptual phenomenon that comprises a host of tangible and intangible features. It is a perception that arises from all the points of contact the customer has with the company in his search for solutions to his buying problems. It can in fact be seen as a 'package' in the sense that, whilst diverse, the contents of the package all have an effect on the customer's perception of logistics performance. Considering service offering as a package has a number of advantages, chief of which is that it forces us to take a global view of the customer's service requirements and thus encourages us to develop cohesive and integrated service policies. Inherent in this viewpoint is the idea that the service package can vary from customer to customer, from market to market or from area to area. Thus some of our customers may warrant special delivery service, or a greater technical back-up, or a more formalized channel of *reverse communications* or whatever – the service package can be designed with any of these requirements in mind and need not be the same for all customers or all segments of the market.

Assessing how the market will respond to a proposed customer service package is not easy. The concept of marketing experimentation is well established in other areas of the business. We are used to thinking of test markets for new product launches, advertising testing and so on. The development of similar experiments to search after cost-effective service policies is rather more novel. A number of companies have conducted experiments of this type and found the results to be extremely valuable. One company manufacturing a wide range of grocery products in the UK had developed good cost data which enabled it to estimate accurately what the cost implications of different levels of service would be. What they could not predict though was what the effect would be of those various service levels on sales revenue.

The way they tackled the problem was to identify two areas of the UK, each served from a different depot, and both as nearly identical to each other as possible in terms of sales, retail structure and demography. In one of these areas they deliberately reduced the level of service in terms of safety stock maintained at the depot; in the other area no change from the existing level was made.

The outcome of this experiment was that there was no significant difference in sales between the two areas. There was of course a major difference in the reduced stock investment required in the test region – thus suggesting that a lower level of service was indeed far more cost effective.

In this experiment only one variable in the customer-service package – stock levels – was subject to variation but similar tests could be envisaged which would enable the company to move closer to that balance between cost and benefits which is the ultimate aim of customer service management.

*Further reading*

Hutchinson, W. M., and Stolle, J. D., 'How to Manage Customer Service', *Harvard Business Review*, November/December 1968

Christopher, M., and Wills, G., 'Developing Customer Service Policies', *International Journal of Physical Distribution* (Monograph), vol 4, no 6, 1974

Christopher, M., Schary, P., and Skjott-Larsen, T., *Customer Service and Distribution Strategy*, Associated Business Press, 1979

**Self-audit questions**

21.1  *What levels of service do you currently give to customers? How consistent is it?*

21.2  *What level do you believe would be 'right'? Can you test out the validity of your belief?*

21.3  *What is your current customer-service package? How could you use it more aggressively as a marketing weapon?*

# Question 22
# What price should we charge our customer?

*Pricing decisions are of paramount importance in marketing strategy. Like the other elements in the firm's marketing mix the price of the product should be related to the achievement of marketing and corporate goals. Thus a clear view must be established as to the role of price in regard to such issues as the product life cycle, the requirements of the total product portfolio and sales and market share objectives. The procedures and methods adopted to meet these goals must be as dependent upon the market and competitive circumstances as they are upon costs. Indeed the market-oriented approach to pricing sees costs as a constraint which might determine a lower limit to the firm's pricing discretion rather than being themselves the basis upon which price is determined.*

In the economists' view of the world, price is regarded as the chief determinant of the level of sales of our product. Price is central to many of their models and the mechanism whereby prices are set has become a major field of study. At the governmental level too the price of goods and services is subjected to great scrutiny because of the implications for inflation and general social welfare.

In the light of this external interest in prices it is perhaps all the more surprising that many companies adopt relatively unsophisticated approaches to the determination of price. Surveys in several countries have shown that the price decision in the firm often tends to be automatic, to be based upon some rudimentary formula or rule of thumb. Only infrequently it would appear do pricing decisions form a part of some overall integrated marketing strategy where price is related in some specific way to the achievement of defined objectives.

Clearly the pricing decision is important. It is important for a number of reasons but primarily for its direct and indirect effect upon profits – price not only affects the margin through its revenue impact but affects the quantity sold through its influence on demand. The price of the product will also have an interactive effect with the other elements of the marketing mix and so, again, it is important that the price we set is appropriate to the marketing programme we have devised.

## Relating pricing objectives to marketing strategy

If an integrated marketing strategy is to be achieved then the pricing decision must be taken in the light of the objectives underlying that strategy. This implies first and foremost that the price of the product must fit the targeted *market position* planned for that product. By position here we mean the place that the product occupies, in comparison with its competitors, in the eyes of our customers or potential customers. Sometimes this position will be determined mainly by the perceived physical attributes of the product, e.g. a grade of industrial steel that occupies a particular market position in terms of its product characteristics. On other occasions the market position of a product may be affected considerably by perceptions of less tangible attributes, e.g. a toilet soap that has connotations of gracious living associated with it. Because price is one of the marketing mix elements that will contribute to a product's market position it is necessary that price should be consonant with that position – so a rock-bottom price on the toilet soap in the above example would scarcely be appropriate at all.

The price of the product must also relate to its life cycle and to our strategic views concerning that cycle. Let us take an example of a Norwegian manufacturer of a new type of Kraft paper. He is faced with a decision upon the launching of that product: which of two available price policies should he adopt? He could go for an initial high price or *skimming policy* or a lower price aimed at gaining maximum *market penetration*.

A skimming policy, as the name suggests, is based upon an entry to the market at a high price and then later, if necessary, lowering the price to gain acceptance in other price segments. It is an appropriate strategy in several circumstances, for example if the company feels that it has a sufficient lead over its competitors in the introduction of this product and can take advantage

150

of this lead to achieve an accelerated rate of recovery on its investment. It is important in such a situation for the innovating firm to be aware that a skimming policy can provide an umbrella which could encourage other manufacturers to enter the market. The key to success in these situations is to plan for a steady reduction in price once an initial market penetration has been established and once the cost recovery is underway. Such price reduction will normally be facilitated by the unit-cost reductions that should occur once cumulative output starts to grow – the so-called *experience effect*.

On the other hand our Norwegian paper manufacturer could take the opposite route by going for a penetration pricing policy. Here the price is deliberately set low with a number of objectives in mind. An initial low price makes it very difficult for would-be competitors to imitate innovations particularly in technological product areas. A penetration policy also ensures maximum adoption of the product in its early life thus leading to a more rapid experience effect. The problem associated with such a policy is chiefly the 'opportunity cost' of possible additional revenue foregone. The appropriateness of either of these policies will be determined to a large extent by the elasticity of demand in the market place. In other words, how responsive is demand to relative price levels? In some markets demand does not seem to be affected by price – up to a point. In such circumstances we say demand is inelastic as it is in the market for technical journals sold mainly to libraries. On the other hand some markets are more sensitive to price, for example urban bus services. Price elasticity by itself does not explain the response of markets to price levels but it should at least be included as a criterion in the choice of pricing strategy. In the case of our Norwegian paper manufacturer he would need to be sure that, in the markets at which his product was aimed, the choice of say a skimming strategy was compatible with the underlying price elasticity.

A further consideration facing the Norwegian paper manufacturer is the competitive situation. The Kraft paper market is an established one with a relatively large number of manufacturers supplying diverse markets around the globe. There are established *price brackets* for specific paper types and within these brackets there are a number of firms competing. Thus the question must be asked: are we a price 'maker' or a price 'taker'? In other words does our position in the market provide us with room to manoeuvre on price? In markets where the competitive product offerings are relatively undifferentiated this becomes a very real consideration.

Finally the company must recognize that pricing policies have a strategic importance in the context of sales and market share objectives and to the revenue requirements of the rest of the firm's product portfolio. If, for example, the chosen marketing strategy was to establish as quickly as possible a sizeable share of the market then sales maximization via a penetration pricing policy would seem to be indicated. In this case the company might even deem that the benefits of market share overrode the need for *initial* profitability, i.e. market share should be bought by a deliberate pricing policy. On the other hand in the case of an established product well into the maturity stage of its life cycle, the product might be viewed as a source of cash for financing the growth of other products in which circumstances the pressure would be to maintain price, even to increase it, at the expense of sales and market share.

In this latter context we are seeing price in its true strategic role. It is a variable that enables corporate marketing objectives across the complete product portfolio to be achieved. Thus the pricing decision on a specific product should be viewed in relation to the strategic requirements of the company's global market strategy as well as in terms of the product's own needs.


## Pricing procedures and methods

Given that pricing objectives have been established how might the decision on a specific price be taken? The conventional profit-maximizing model of the economist tells us that price should be set where marginal cost equals marginal revenue – in other words where the additional cost of producing and marketing an additional unit is equivalent to the additional revenue that its sale would generate. In its theoretical form the logic is indisputable; as a practical pricing tool however its use is somewhat limited. Why? It obviously requires a knowledge of the demand curve facing the product in the market place, it is based upon a notion of cost behaviour strictly limited to the short run, it does not take cognizance of any strategic objectives of the firm save profits, nor does it recognize that long-run goals can and frequently will be met by sacrificing short-run goals.

More often in practice we encounter pricing procedures which are based on simple, although often equally unsatisfactory, precepts. Many of these procedures are what might best be termed 'cost oriented'. A frequently encountered approach, based upon costs, is the *target return on costs* method. Using this approach the company would set itself a target level of profits to be achieved at a given level of sales such that an adequate return on costs would be achieved. A specialist book publisher in France uses this method, for example, whereby it makes a decision to produce 1,000 copies of a book at a total production and marketing budget of Fr30,000. It requires a twenty per cent return on this investment, i.e. Fr6,000, thus the required level of total revenue must be Fr36,000 – which on a sale of 1,000 implies a price of Fr36. This method is based in effect upon a break-even analysis of the form illustrated in FIGURE 22.

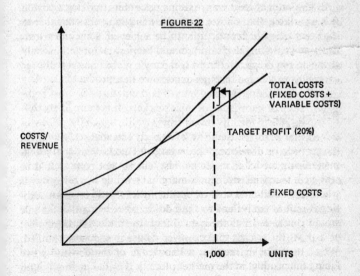

FIGURE 22

The problem with this approach is that it does not lead to a determinate solution to the pricing problem. This is because it assumes that if 1,000 copies of the book are produced they can be sold at the given price, whereas the price itself will likely have some effect on sales. Another problem occurs in some cases in the determination of total costs. This is particularly true in multi-product companies where many costs are common between products. There is also the danger that the method might lead us to seek a return on 'sunk' costs, i.e. those fixed costs which represent outlays made in the past and which should have no bearing on the price.

In contrast to such approaches to pricing based mainly upon costs is the *market-oriented approach* to pricing. Here costs are viewed solely as a constraint on the lower limit of pricing discretion. Instead the emphasis is placed upon such notions as: 'what the market will bear', competitive activity, price/quality perceptions, in addition to the overall strategic marketing goals of the sort outlined earlier.

The idea that a product should be priced according to market considerations rather than cost considerations is not new but it is surprising to find how many companies enter a pricing decision by first talking about costs. In a sense this is understandable as costs are tangible inputs, quantifiable even if sometimes misleadingly so, in any decision process. Market factors are usually harder to pin down. Getting a feel for what the market will bear can really only come through experience in a product field. Any talk of constructing demand curves is premature for most companies' state of knowledge of their markets. It is more likely that we will be able to identify broad bands within which the price will be acceptable to the majority of our chosen market. Some researchers have developed operational methods for determining what these price bands might be. They simply ask a representative sample of the target segment whether they would buy the product at a price P, and if the answer was 'no' they would be questioned to ascertain if the refusal was due to the price being too high, or too low in the sense that the quality of the product might be suspected. As these researchers say: 'The consumer intent on a purchase enters the market not with a set of demand schedules in mind, but simply with two price limits. He has a lower limit below which he would distrust the quality and an upper limit beyond which he would judge the article unduly expensive.'

This latter point introduces the concept of price having a qualitative dimension. In other words in many markets price is used by the customer as an indicator of quality. For example, Stella Artois is a Belgian beer marketed under licence in the UK. Their current promotional campaign is based amongst other things upon the premium price of the product. Their advertisements suggest that this is a high quality product and they deliberately major upon the fact that the price is in excess of competitive products. Other manufacturers have found that raising the price can have a beneficial effect on sales if the market cannot accept that a relatively low-priced product can in fact meet the claims that might be made about it. Thus the traditional view of price and demand being inversely related need not always hold in the relevant stretch of the market where a company is operating.

The market-oriented view of pricing attempts to relate the price of the product to the value that the customers believe they will derive from its purchase. In industrial markets the same principle holds. For example the Glacier Metal Company in Britain uses a method of pricing known as *product-analysis pricing* which is based upon the concept that the price the buyer pays for a product must be directly related to the various utilities that the user is seeking from the product and cost is seen solely as a lower limit beyond which the long-term price should not fall.

In almost all markets there is the added dimension to the price decision of the competitive structure of those markets. Often pricing discretion is limited by the fact that a going rate exists within a market and unless we occupy a dominant position in that market as a price leader this single fact will of necessity determine the price at which we must operate.

For the marketing manager these various aspects of the pricing decision can be seen as providing a framework which constrains his discretion for manoeuvre. For any one company this limiting framework can be viewed as in FIGURE 23.

As we have seen even this range of discretion might be circumscribed by competitive factors.

Overall, it will be apparent that the pricing decision is one which has so many ramifications both for profit and for strategy that it should be taken only in the light of a most careful analysis of the many factors outlined above.

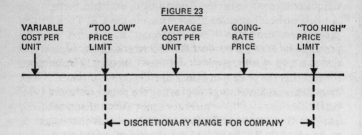

FIGURE 23

Further reading

Oxenfeldt, A. R., 'Multi-Stage Approach to Pricing', *Harvard Business Review*, July/August 1960

Wills, G., and Taylor, B., *Pricing Strategy*, Staples Press, 1969

Gabor, A., *Pricing: Principles and Practices*, Heinemann, 1977

**Self-audit questions**

22.1   *What are your company's pricing objectives and strategies?*

22.2   *How does your company currently determine prices at an operating level?*

22.3   *Have you any examples recently of a skim/penetrate strategy? Could the idea be applied more in your business?*

22.4   *What prices do your customers really want to pay?*

# Question 23

# What margins should we allow to our distributors?

*Conventional price theory does not help us greatly in the determination of policy towards distributor margins. The margins given to intermediaries should be viewed in terms of the 'value added' by them as product or service passes along the marketing channel. In return for the performance of various functions necessary to the efficient completion of the exchange process the firm will be willing to pass on some of the total channel margin available to it. The various types of margins that are commonly encountered are trade, quantity, promotional and cash discounts. It is suggested that the overall policy towards distributor margins should be considered in the wider context of the need of the firm to achieve its declared marketing goals. Likewise the question of margin levels must take into account the financial policy and capital structure of the firm.*

We have seen in response to earlier questions how crucial to the firm's marketing effort is the marketing channel that it employs. The intermediaries that constitute that channel perform a number of functions that enable the exchange transaction between producer and consumer to be fulfilled. In return for the functions that these institutions perform on the firm's behalf they naturally seek a reward. Put in its simplest terms this reward in total takes the form of the margin between the price of the goods at the factory gate and the price the consumer eventually pays. It is common to refer to this margin as the 'value added' by these intermediate functions. In perfectly competitive markets we might expect the nature of the reward for this value added to be determined solely in terms of economic criteria, that is an intermediary will earn at the margin an amount equivalent to the worth of the service he provides. If a higher reward was to be sought then other intermediaries would enter the market or the functions performed at that level would be performed elsewhere, thereby bringing the reward structure back into balance.

The actual case in most market environments is however somewhat different. In the place of perfectly competitive market structures one encounters *vertical marketing systems* where varying degrees of control and integration are administered by the more powerful members of the channel. This need not necessarily lead to dis-economies, indeed it may often lead to improvements in total channel efficiency. In the fragmented and unintegrated market structure implied by perfect competition the typically small size of intermediary unit will not be able to gain economies of scale in purchasing, handling and distribution. Similarly such a fragmented structure can lead to each individual unit in the channel attempting to maximize its own reward which could lead to a less than optimal situation in the channel overall.

The ideal reward structure in the marketing channel is based upon an acceptable rate of return on investment being earned at each level in the channel. This return would reflect the services and the functions that are performed at those levels – in other words a real reflection of value added. What occurs in practice is of course often less than this ideal. It has been suggested that the ultimate objective of marketing channel management should be to achieve a *non-zero sum game* situation. A zero sum game is one where 'I win, you lose'; on the other hand the non-zero sum game attempts to achieve a situation of 'I win, you win'. Our purpose now is thus to examine ways in which 'win/win' states might be achieved.

## Available discount options

Typically the firm will have available to it a number of devices for compensating the intermediaries in the channel. These will take the form of a number of discounts against some nominal price list. The most commonly encountered forms are:

(1) *Trade discount* – this is the discount against the list which the company will give to a channel intermediary in return for the service he makes available. Thus a wholesaler might purchase goods from the manufacturer at a twenty-per-cent discount in return for which he will provide such services as bulk breaking,

storage, and retail order filling. In turn the wholesaler will offer a trade discount to the retailer. In some cases the wholesaler will be bypassed and the discount normally passing to the wholesaler will either be retained by the manufacturer or passed on directly to the retailer. In some markets such as groceries the retailers have themselves taken on the functions of wholesalers and thus demand an increased discount to reflect this fact. The precise level of the trade discount is an issue to be explored later in this response.

(2) *Quantity discount* – a quantity discount is one which is offered in relation to the size of the order; the greater the order the greater the discount. A manufacturer offering this discount does so in order to encourage larger purchases than might otherwise be made. Such a discount can be to the benefit of both parties. Let us take the example of a Dutch manufacturer of household electrical appliances who offered a discount to wholesalers of 5% on orders for Fl 6,000 or more, a 7% discount on orders for Fl 10,000 and 12% discount for orders over Fl 15,000. These discounts were in addition to the normal 20% trade discount. Their rationale for such additional discounts on price was simple. In the first place the competitive environment demanded that discounts over and above the normal trade discount be given on larger orders. In addition the company believed there to be a number of economic advantages associated with such a quantity discount structure. The first of these was that they felt that the wholesaler would be encouraged to buy more and thus sell more. Secondly, by ordering in larger quantities, the wholesaler would carry a greater proportion of the total costs of holding inventory, costs that would otherwise have to be borne by the manufacturer. Thirdly it was felt that the encouragement to purchase in larger quantities could well lead to a decline in the number of orders placed by an individual wholesaler in a given period – with the effect of reducing the manufacturer's costs of meeting orders.

Naturally the wholesaler would want to be sure that the size of the discount more than compensated for his increased inventory carrying costs. A successful quantity discount scheme is a good example of a non-zero sum game.

(3) *Promotional discount* – in a number of markets, institutions in the channel in addition to the manufacturer are instrumental in

promoting the sale of that manufacturer's products. Such promotion might take the form of advertisements in various media informing the public that the manufacturer's products are available at particular outlets. Alternatively, and this is frequently encountered in fast moving consumer goods markets, the promotion may be in the form of in-store displays, or 'money-off' offers, or competitions and so on. This latter form of promotional activity has come to be known as *featured sales promotion* and in some markets is more heavily relied upon than the more traditional media promotion.

Whilst it might be argued that these various types of promotional activity are to the benefit of both the channel institution and the manufacturer there are a number of situations where the channel institution requires an additional discount in order to become involved in such activity. This is particularly true when a channel institution is the real power in a marketing channel. Thus in the UK a manufacturer of convenience food products has to offer an additional discount to the large supermarket chains in order that they will participate in a promotion that he is planning.

(4) *Cash discount* – in an attempt to encourage the prompt payment of accounts firms will often offer a cash discount to their customers. A typical example is a Belgian firm of office equipment manufacturers whose terms are thirty days credit but offer a discount of $2\frac{1}{2}\%$ for payment within ten days.

In times such as these when the management of cash flow becomes as important as making a profit it can be seen that the speedy payment of accounts by customers is vital. With a cost of capital of $20\%$ or more, this office equipment company, with Fr600 million annual sales, was facing an average account payment period of forty days – in other words some accounts were always overdue. Forty days represented approximately Fr96 million accounts outstanding at any one point in time (40/250 × 600) which represented an opportunity cost of Fr19.2 million a year (96 × $20\%$).

Clearly the $2\frac{1}{2}\%$ incentive to settle within ten days was having little effect. Their customers were in effect using their trade credit as a source of working capital and even at a discount of $2\frac{1}{2}\%$ forgone it was still cheap at the price. The problem of what level and what structure should be settled upon in determining cash discounts is difficult to solve. There is a limit to the extent to which the firm can eat further into its own margin to increase the discount for prompt payment. Likewise in competitive markets it is difficult to reduce the period of credit – or even to persuade the customer to respect the period of credit offered.

## Determining the policy towards margins

From the foregoing discussion it would seem that there are a number of problems surrounding the determination of margins to channel intermediaries. In a dynamic marketing channel there will be a constant pressure for the improvement of margins at all levels, the ultimate effect of which is often a shortening of the channel with the functions of some intermediaries being absorbed by others.

Because of these pressures the question of margins must be seen at a strategic as well as a tactical level. In those markets where there is a proliferation of products – say breakfast cereals in Europe – the problem of gaining distribution has to be solved by offering the largest part of the total margin available to the retailer. Such strategic implications as these will often determine our policy towards margins.

This whole area of *margin management*, as it is coming to be called, can be viewed as a series of trade-off-type decisions which determine how the total channel margin should be split. The concept of the total channel margin is simple. It is the difference between the level of price at which we wish to position our product in the ultimate market place and the cost of our product at the factory gate. Who takes what proportion of this difference is what margin management is about. The problem can be illustrated as in FIGURE 24.

It will be seen that the firm's channel requirements will only be achieved if it either carries them out itself or if it goes some way towards meeting the requirements of an intermediary who can perform those functions on his behalf. The objective of the firm in this respect could therefore be expressed in terms of a willingness to trade-off margin in order to achieve its marketing goals. Such a trade-off need not lead to a loss of *profitability*, indeed as

161

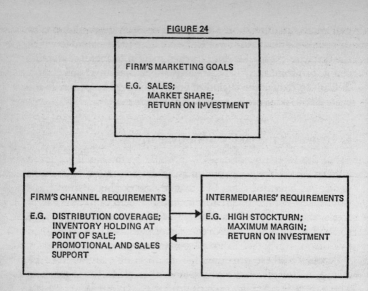

FIGURE 24

FIRM'S MARKETING GOALS

E.G. SALES;
     MARKET SHARE;
     RETURN ON INVESTMENT

FIRM'S CHANNEL REQUIREMENTS

E.G. DISTRIBUTION COVERAGE;
     INVENTORY HOLDING AT
     POINT OF SALE;
     PROMOTIONAL AND SALES
     SUPPORT

INTERMEDIARIES' REQUIREMENTS

E.G. HIGH STOCKTURN;
     MAXIMUM MARGIN;
     RETURN ON INVESTMENT

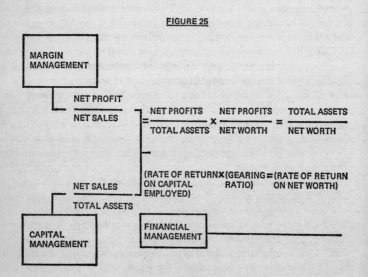

FIGURE 25

MARGIN MANAGEMENT

$$\frac{\text{NET PROFIT}}{\text{NET SALES}} = \frac{\text{NET PROFITS}}{\text{TOTAL ASSETS}} \times \frac{\text{NET PROFITS}}{\text{NET WORTH}} = \frac{\text{TOTAL ASSETS}}{\text{NET WORTH}}$$

(RATE OF RETURN ON CAPITAL EMPLOYED) X (GEARING RATIO) = (RATE OF RETURN ON NET WORTH)

$$\frac{\text{NET SALES}}{\text{TOTAL ASSETS}}$$

CAPITAL MANAGEMENT

FINANCIAL MANAGEMENT

FIGURE 25 suggests the margin is only one element in the determination of profitability.

Here profitability is more precisely defined as the rate of return on net worth, net worth being share capital and capital reserves plus retained profits.

It can be seen that by improving the utilization of capital assets (capital management) as well as by using a higher gearing it is possible to operate successfully on lower margins if this means that marketing goals can more effectively be achieved.

**FIGURE 26**

|  | COMPANY A<br>LOW MARGIN | COMPANY B<br>HIGHER MARGIN |
|---|---|---|
| NET PROFITS<br>———————<br>NET SALES | 2% | 4% |
| NET SALES<br>———————<br>TOTAL ASSETS | 7 | 5 |
| NET PROFITS<br>———————<br>TOTAL ASSETS | 14% | 20% |
| TOTAL ASSETS<br>———————<br>NET WORTH | 2 | 1 |
| NET PROFITS<br>———————<br>NET WORTH | 28% | 20% |

FIGURE 26 gives an example of two Spanish producers of welding rods. Company A operates on a low retained margin (2%), passing the rest of the margin on to other intermediaries in the channel. Company B operates on twice the margin (4%).

However because company A turns its capital over seven times a year compared with B with a capital turnover of only five and because company A makes use of debt funding whereas B does not, company A is able to produce a superior rate of return on net worth.

From the foregoing it will be apparent that the question of

rgins, both the margin retained by the firm and thus by implica-
n the margin allowed the distributor, cannot be examined without consideration of the wider implications of overall marketing
strategy and the financial policy and capital structure of the firm.

*Further reading*

Howard, K., and Christopher, M. G., 'Price and Discount
  Rationalization in a Multi-product Company', *Accounting
  and Business Research*, vol 3, no 11, summer 1973

McCammon, B. C., 'Perspectives for Distribution
  Programming', in Bucklin, L. P., (ed), *Vertical Marketing
  Systems*, Scott Foresman, 1970

**Self-audit questions**

23.1  *What management and marketing analysis underlies the
      margins you give to your distributors?*
23.2  *What is the current pattern of your margins to all
      customer segments?*
23.3  *What impact would higher or lower margins have in the
      short, medium and long term in your market?*


Question 24

# What is marketing research?

*Marketing research is an integral part of the marketing task.
It provides the manager with the means of identifying market
opportunities, it aids his understanding of marketing processes
and it can provide data for control of marketing programmes.
Recent years have seen the rapid growth in the use of marketing
research by companies in all sectors and also in the range of
technique available to the researcher. Whilst marketing research
must always be less than precise in that it deals with notoriously
unstable behavioural phenomena, it nevertheless provides an
invaluable means of contact with the market place.*

*This response examines the various approaches to the marketing research task that are commonly encountered today and considers their application to marketing problems. It is emphasized that much valuable marketing information can be gained from an examination of existing data which may be to hand within the company or from published sources.*

Many of the questions that we have addressed so far in this book have raised the need for gathering information from the market place. For example: 'Who are our customers?' 'Are all our customers the same?' 'How can we measure the effectiveness of our communications?' These and other queries can only be well answered in the light of knowledge about our customers, their behaviour, their beliefs and their reactions to our marketing effort.

As we have frequently noted the whole basis of the marketing concept is grounded in the notion that the profitable development of the firm can only be ensured through a constant attempt to match the capabilities of the firm to the needs of the customer. In order that these needs may be identified and the suitability of the firm's market offering assessed it is necessary that some type of information flow be instituted between the consumer and the firm. This is the role of marketing research.

A distinction is sometimes drawn between marketing research and market research. The former, it is suggested, is concerned with research into marketing processes whilst the latter is more specifically research about markets. However for the purposes of this response we shall use the term 'marketing research' to embrace both aspects.

The use of marketing research by European companies has grown considerably in the last ten years or so. Its use is not confined to manufacturers selling into consumer markets; some of the most interesting work to have been conducted in recent years has been on behalf of industrial marketing organizations, service companies such as banks, and social organizations such as voluntary and government agencies.

With this growth of marketing research has come an increasing sophistication in the use of the techniques available to the researcher, particularly through developments in the handling and analysis of *multivariate data*. The marketing researcher is now a professional whose advice is looked for more and more in marketing decision making. Likewise the growth of companies which provide specialist marketing research services has multiplied until it is now a major industry in its own right.

Thus the marketing manager has available to him the facility both to monitor the effectiveness of his marketing performance and also to gain a better feel for what opportunities exist in the market place. How this information can be integrated into the marketing planning and control task will be discussed in the response to Question 25. Our immediate concern is to consider what tools the marketing researcher has at his disposal and how and where these may be used.

## Forms of marketing research

Marketing research can be classified as being either *ad hoc* or *ongoing*. *Ad hoc* marketing research refers to situations where the identification of a research problem leads to a specific information requirement. So when a French manufacturer of proprietary pharmaceuticals found that sales of their long-established cough remedy were falling they decided to conduct a study of consumer attitudes and beliefs about cough remedies and used the information they gained to relaunch the brand. On the other hand, ongoing research, as the title implies, provides more of a monitoring function, providing a flow of information about the market place, our performance in it and so on. The Confederation of British Industry maintains a regular monitor, based upon surveys, of business confidence and investment intentions in the UK for example.

A further dichotomy may also be perceived between *external* marketing research and *internal* marketing research. The former research activity is conducted within the market and competitive environment in which the firm exists whereas internal research is based upon an analysis of performance gained from such information as sales trends, changes in the marketing mix such as price, advertising levels and so on. Much valuable intelligence can be gained from internal marketing analysis, and external information gathering should always be seen as a complement to such internal information.

**FIGURE 27**

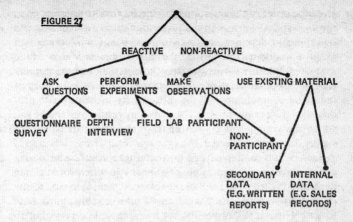

There are a number of headings under which the methods of marketing research might usefully be examined and FIGURE 27 provides a summary and useful framework for discussing the forms of marketing research activity that are commonly encountered today.

The basic split between reactive and non-reactive research is important. The reactive approach implies that information about the market place and the customers who inhabit it can be gained by 'poking a stick at it and seeing if and how it moves'. Non-reactive methods are based not upon reaction but upon interpretation of observed phenomena or extant data.

Reactive marketing research can involve us in either asking questions or in performing experiments, or both. Let us examine first the role of question asking in marketing research. This perhaps is what marketing research is about to many people, indeed the ubiquitous survey is a tried and trusted research device and the questionnaire the favoured means of data gathering.

The questionnaire is a flexible instrument. It can be administered by an interviewer or by the interviewee himself; it can take place on the respondent's doorstep, by telephone, or be sent by mail. There are, however, a number of pitfalls that can result from the use of a questionnaire without very careful pre-planning or checking. Everyone knows about the 'loaded' question or the dangers of ambiguity, yet they are not always so easily detectable.

Even the order of the questions can have a distorting effect upon the answers. The errors in the final population estimates from a questionnaire administered to a sample, arising from sources such as those mentioned, are termed the *bias* or *systematic error* of the estimates. In other words the true characteristics of the population, for example relative preferences between several types of industrial compressor, may be different from the estimate produced by the sample survey. This bias may result from the way in which the sample was chosen or from the means by which the survey data were collected.

Such pitfalls can be reduced by a careful approach to the design of the questionnaire and by *pilot testing* it – in other words giving it a trial run on a sub-group of the intended sample to isolate any problems that may arise. Sometimes it may be more appropriate to gather market information not by large-scale surveys but to attempt to draw insights for marketing action from smaller-scale, more detailed studies. Such studies are intended to provide qualitative cues rather than quantitative conclusions. For example the Meat and Livestock Commission asked us at Cranfield to conduct a series of *group discussions* amongst housewives to gain an understanding of their attitudes towards the purchase of frozen meat rather than fresh meat. A group discussion is a loosely structured interview where the leader – often a trained psychologist – attempts to draw from the group their feelings about the subject under discussion. The group is chosen to be representative of the population in which the researcher is interested although naturally any conclusions emerging from the discussions can only form the basis of qualitative generalizations about that population. Such interviews need not be conducted in groups but can be used to derive information from single individuals, this is called an extended or depth interview. Such a form of interview will often be utilized when information regarding specialized markets is required in industrial marketing research.

The other type of reactive marketing research is experimentation. In our earlier discussions of test marketing in the response to Question 11 we saw how one form of marketing experiment can provide a valuable source of information on market performance for new products. The marketing experiment can also help us gain a better understanding of how marketing processes work. For example a Swedish manufacturer of confectionery wanted to know if the effect on sales of a 'money-off' offer was greater than spending a similar sum on in-store merchandising improvements. The information he needed to answer this question could really only come from an experiment whereby a number of stores were selected in different areas of the country and used as the testing ground for these alternative promotional approaches. The stores chosen for the experiment were as near alike as possible in terms of turnover on the brand in question and served similar types of customers. One-third of the stores ran the 'money-off' promotion, one-third used the improved in-store merchandising, and the remaining third carried on selling the product without any changes. After a period of two months the manufacturer felt able to draw conclusions about the relative effectiveness of the two promotional methods by comparing store results with those stores where no changes were made.

Market experimentation need not necessarily involve the setting up of large-scale experimental designs such as the one just discussed. Sometimes laboratory-type situations can be used to test marketing stimuli. Often advertisements will be pre-tested in such laboratory conditions. Samples of the target audience for an advertisement will be exposed to the advertisement and their reactions obtained. In some cases more than the verbal reactions of the sample will be sought. Eye cameras, polygraphs and tachistoscopes are just some of the devices that have been used to record physical reactions to marketing stimuli.

Whilst the theory of market experimentation is sound enough, there are a number of drawbacks to its operation in practice. It is often difficult to set up experimental situations that are microcosms of the total market. There is always the problem of controlling all the variables in the experiment, for example actions of competitors, and of course the cost of setting up and maintaining market experiments can be prohibitive.

In contrast with such methods are those that are classified as *non-reactive* in that they do not rely upon data derived directly from respondents. *Observation* is such a technique and in appropriate situations can be very effective. How people behave in real world situations and how they react to stimuli can often best be discovered through watching and interpreting their reactions. Some observational methods such as a camera in a supermarket do not involve the direct participation of the researcher and this can be a limiting factor. Often the areas of activity in which we are particularly interested may only occur infrequently and the observation must be sustained over a period in order to capture a single activity. On the other hand *participant observation*, a phrase borrowed from anthropology, involves the observer in attempting to become a part of the activity that is under observation. This form of marketing research is very limited in its scope although one British research organization, Mass Observation, did some early pioneering work in this area in a number of studies, a famous example being a major study of consumer behaviour in public houses. One secondary source of observational data that is widely used is the *retail audit*. The retail audit has been developed and perfected as a technique over a period of time and, properly controlled, it can be a highly accurate source of marketing information on brand shares, market size, distribution coverage and sales trends. The audits conducted by A. C. Neilsen Ltd are perhaps the most widely known and work on a simple basis. Within a particular product field a representative sample of stockists is chosen and their cooperation obtained. At regular periods the investigator visits the stockists and notes two things: the current level of stocks of the product group being audited and the invoices or delivery notes for any goods in that group delivered since his last visit. With the information on stock levels obtained on his *last* visit it is a simple matter to determine sales of each item being audited during the period between visits, i.e. opening stock + deliveries between visits – closing stock = sales during period.

Another similar source of data is the *consumer panel*, which is a sample group of consumers in a particular product field who record their purchases and consumption over a period of time in a diary. This technique has been used in industrial as well as consumer markets and can provide continuous data on patterns of usage as well as other data such as media habits.

Last, but certainly not least in our scheme of marketing research methods, is the use of exising materials. The *desk research* study should in fact be the starting point of any marketing research programme. Desk research involves the use of existing information for determining the extent of prior knowledge about the subject under study. There is often a great wealth of material to be obtained from published and unpublished sources, which can reduce the need to 'rediscover the wheel'. Official statistics such as those published by governments, OECD, the EEC, the United Nations and so on can provide detailed data on markets and patterns within those markets. Other sources such as newspapers, technical journals, trade association publications and published market studies will provide a fill-in to any later field work that might be needed.

Similarly internal data derived from sales figures and salesmen's reports can also be a guide to the direction that later studies might need to take.

From this brief survey of research methods in marketing it can be seen that the scope of marketing research can be considerable. Yet at the same time it must be recognized that even the most carefully designed and conducted studies can at best only provide imperfect descriptions of market phenomena. Nevertheless marketing research remains the link between the identification of market opportunities and the successful exploitation of them by the firm.

*Further reading*

Elliott, K., and Christopher, M., *Research Methods in Marketing*, Holt, Rinehart & Winston, 1973

Seibert, J., and Wills, G., (eds), *Marketing Research*, Penguin 1970

Chisnall, P., *Marketing Research*, McGraw-Hill, 1973]

**Self-audit questions**

24.1　*What proportion of your marketing budget is spent on research to find out how effective it is?*

24.2　*How was that proportion determined? Do you feel that is the best way to do it?*

24.3　*What balance do you have between qualitative and quantitative studies? And between* ad hoc *and continuous? Why?*

## Question 25
# What role does marketing research play in effective marketing?

*Marketing research is the basic source of information on the markets we serve and the performance that we achieve within those markets. The successful marketing companies are those that have learnt how to convert marketing information into marketing action. One of the problems that faces many companies is that they have no shortage of marketing 'data', but marketing 'information' is in short supply. There is a crucial and vital difference between these two commodities.*

*One of the key questions posed must always be how can we place a value on marketing information? There is a real requirement for all information to be assessed in cost/benefit terms against previously defined needs that it is intended to meet. Providing such a definition of information needs is a necessary precursor of the effective integration of marketing research with marketing decision making.*

It is sometimes said that a prime management concern in marketing is 'the conversion of uncertainty into risk'. Uncertainty implies an inability to state the likelihood of any possible outcome occurring. By implication all outcomes must be treated as equally likely. Under uncertainty the manager must consider, say, the chance of failure in a new product launch to equal the chance of success. Risk, on the other hand, suggests that the likelihood of outcomes might be assessed more precisely. The marketing manager might feel that a particular new service launch has only a five per cent chance of failure. Our ability to make successful decisions is clearly enhanced if we are operating under conditions of known risk rather than uncertainty.

If this conversion of uncertainty into risk is the prime marketing management task, the second is surely the reduction or minimization of that risk.

To achieve either of these goals the manager requires information. Good information is a facilitator of successful marketing action and indeed, seen in this light marketing management becomes first and foremost an information processing activity. Marketing research is therefore concerned with much more than simply telling us something about the market place. Rather it is a *systematic and objective search for, and analysis of, information relevant to the identification and solution of any problem in the field of marketing.*

How should marketing managers approach the question of integrating marketing research with marketing action?

In the first place it is necessary to view marketing information as a resource. This means that we must be concerned with the problems of producing it, storing and distributing it. Marketing information also has a limited shelf life – it is perishable. Like other resources information has a value in use; the less the manager knows about a marketing problem and the greater the risk attached to a wrong decision, the more valuable the information becomes. This latter point is an important consideration in assessing marketing research budgets. It implies the need for a cost/benefit appraisal of all sources of marketing information. There is no point in investing more in such information than the return on it would justify. Naturally it is easier to determine the cost than the benefits. The managerial benefits of marketing research are difficult to pin down. They can be expressed in terms of the additional sales or profits that might be achieved through the spotlighting of marketing opportunities and also through the avoidance of marketing failures that could otherwise result without the use of information. One company involved in the development of an industrial application of heat exchangers in Germany believed that there was a twenty-per-cent chance that the product might not succeed, leaving them with a development and marketing bill of DMk2 millions. From this they inferred that the maximum *loss expectation* was DMk400,000 (i.e. DMk2,000,000 $\times$ 20%) and that it was worth paying up to this sum to acquire information that would help them avoid such a loss. Such a cost/benefit calculation implies that the information they could acquire would in itself be totally reliable. Because such perfect information can seldom, and here could not, be obtained they budgeted a smaller sum for marketing research which effectively discounted the likely inaccuracy of the information. Such an approach can be a valuable means of quantifying the value of marketing research in a managerial context.

## Data information and intelligence

Reference is frequently made to the information explosion, a phenomenon wherein the manager is confronted with a mass of data, often produced in an indigestible form with the aid of computer-based processing systems. More properly this should perhaps be referred to as the *data* explosion. Data are facts presented in some specific format; by themselves they do not represent *information*. Information on the other hand is data combined with direction, it is active whilst data are purely 'passive'. Without some purpose in mind, some marketing problem to identify or solve, data are of no value to the manager. The messages which the information contains and which are revealed by analysis should be the ultimate service sought from marketing research – a service that can be referred to as *intelligence*.

The differences between data, information and intelligence are more than semantic. They are crucial to a proper integration between research and marketing management. The problems of how data can be organized and analysed to provide information which will lead to marketing intelligence is an issue to which the marketer must continually address himself.

## Management decision and marketing research

Given that the appropriate analysis of marketing information can provide the basis of marketing action, what sort of decisions require what sort of information? This definition of management information needs is central to the successful construction of *marketing intelligence systems* (MIS) for the application of marketing information to marketing decisions. At its simplest we can identify three levels of marketing decisions where an input of information is essential. The first is marketing information for strategic, long-term decisions; the second is marketing information for tactical, short-term decisions and the third is marketing information for one-off marketing problems.

The first two situations require a continuous, on-going input of marketing information, whereas the last needs an *ad hoc* but speedy response from the marketing research function. Until the late 1960s marketing research was largely limited in application to this *ad hoc* and static analysis of marketing problems.

Although in the field of fast-moving consumer goods like pharmaceuticals such techniques as the retail sales audit and the consumer user diary panel frequently have more potential for dynamism, these activities were uncharacteristic of the great majority of organizations. Marketing research was not generally speaking employed to monitor the marketing environment on a continuous basis. However, a major shift in orientation by hitherto largely *ad hoc* users of marketing research, and the conversion of new organizations and service industries to the use of such techniques, has now led to substantial interest in the setting up and deployment of integrated marketing intelligence systems.

Today, international oil companies and airlines headquartered in Europe, for example, have marketing intelligence systems which enable their executives to know on a weekly basis what sales levels are for all products in all market areas, levels of inventory at all intermediate stations, their current production levels and capacity utilization. In addition their systems can provide trend data, market share estimates, cost information and data on the comparative profitability of all products or services on a market by market basis. All of this information existed previously within the organizations but before an MIS was introduced it was in a fragmented and uncoordinated form. By the adoption of a 'systems' approach to information requirements and by the use of existing computer facilities such companies are able to provide management with a *data bank* which is oriented to well defined information needs.

Such companies need not limit their MIS to the analysis of current and historical data. Information on consumer attitudes, advertising levels, changes in competitive marketing activity and similar information also now form an input to such systems in many areas of marketing endeavour.

FIGURE 28 describes the network of information and decision flows which were integrated through the establishment of an integrated MIS in a major European confectionery manufacturer

FIGURE 28

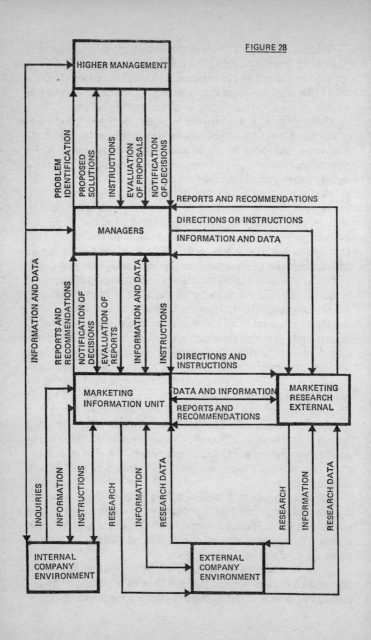

during the early 1970s. It also formed the starting point for analysis in the establishment of such an MIS by Cranfield faculty in a light engineering company based in the Midlands region of the UK.

The benefits of an integration of marketing information, from all sources internal to the company and external to it, lie chiefly in the 'direction' that is given to otherwise uncoordinated data. Such an integration does not necessarily imply the use of a computer although the power and flexibility of any MIS can be potentially increased greatly through such means. What is implied however is that management clearly defines its *information needs*. That is, they must examine the marketing decisions that they need to make and specify the information, both on-going and *ad hoc*, that they require in order to make those decisions effectively.

## Developing the marketing intelligence system

Any organization wishing to build an MIS faces a number of problems. How should we organize? How sophisticated should the system be? Do we build a total system or do we adopt a piecemeal approach? What should be the split between macro-level data and micro-level data? How much is it worth spending?

*Organization* – for most companies there will be the constraints of an existing organization structure which must be accommodated in the construction of the MIS. One team of experts in this field have suggested the appointment of a top-level 'information czar' or coordinator, who is capable of understanding both management information needs and systems problems. They suggest that this person should be the prime contractor who develops MIS plans and specifications, and coordinates and reviews the work of the various sub-contractors or suppliers contributing to the programme.

*Sophistication* – the question of sophistication of the system is crucial. Naive companies may attempt to introduce systems which do not reflect the level of sophistication actually required by managers in making decisions. Recent research in the marketing sphere has shown that many marketing managers, particularly those at the operating level, do not use explicit planning and control systems. The aim in building the MIS should be to strike

177

a balance between the sophistication of the system and that of its users.

*Total or piecemeal?* – it is always tempting when thinking in terms of systems to attempt to build a totally integrated MIS from first principles – a system that brings together financial, logistical and marketing information. Experience suggests that such attempts are rarely successful. As a general rule, it is better to think 'total' but to build 'piecemeal'. One company in the UK construction supply industry reports that it is adopting such an approach. It is building an MIS on the basis of putting together a number of building blocks each of which represents a sub-system for meeting a discrete information need. Together these building blocks will *eventually* form a total system. The process of development to the total system will be governed by experience and the growing sophistication of users.

*How much micro, how much macro?* – one of the most frequently encountered problems in marketing management is that data tends to be aggregated, that is to say the figures relate to total markets rather than segments, to countries rather than regions and so on. On the other hand, the manager can easily be overwhelmed if he is flooded with *dis*aggregated data. A key requirement of the MIS is therefore that whilst the system is based on a micro-data bank, the system should be capable of providing output at any requested level of aggregation.

*How much to spend?* – this problem has already been addressed earlier when the notion of information cost/benefit was raised. Building and developing the MIS is normally an expensive task. One major French company has so far spent well over Fr7 million developing an integrated, real-time system. Whilst this is an extreme example even the simplest MIS does not come cheaply. Management must specify the benefits that it expects to derive from the MIS and be prepared to put a value on them. In this way by concentrating on the *outputs* required from the MIS a surer basis for setting the information budget is provided. Such *output budgeting* approaches to information planning whilst fairly new to business have been applied in non-commercial fields for a decade or more.

The marketing manager occupies a vital position in any organization. He is a high-level information processor. He is positioned

178

between the multitude of data and feedback flows from the market place on the one hand, and internal information flows on corporate capabilities and performance on the other. Marketing research has thus a central role within the company of providing an organized means of maintaining and utilizing these disparate information flows and ensuring their effective conversion into marketing intelligence.

*Further reading*

Brien, R. H., and Stafford, J. E., 'Marketing Information Systems: A New Dimension for Marketing Research', *Journal of Marketing*, vol 32, no 3, July 1968

Schaffir, K. H., and Trentin, H. G., *Marketing Information Systems*, American Management Association, 1973

**Self-audit questions**

25.1  *Review a recent research study to see what benefits were achieved for the cost. What lessons does it afford?*

25.2  *How does your organization turn data into information and thence to intelligence?*

25.3  *Is there any scope for an MIS total analysis in your company? Why?*

## Question 26
# How can we organize a marketing department?

*The marketing department in any organization must act to achieve two goals. Firstly, it must develop a sufficient understanding of customers' needs and their future evolution in the market place to be able to contribute to the development of overall corporate objectives. Secondly, and equally important, it must act to develop and implement a regular process of active management of the product, price, promotion and place of sale for the organization. This involves the coordination, monitoring and control of all marketing activities of the organization, such as directing the sales force on a week-by-week schedule and deciding and checking on detailed promotional activities. Finally, the department must be certain that it is able to remain flexible in its deployment of resources within the marketing mix.*

At the outset of this series of questions, we identified marketing's role in any organization as needing to ensure that the four 'P's – product, price, promotion and place of sale – were successfully managed. Success means both that the customer is satisfied and that the organization's resources and capabilities are effectively deployed to that end. Typically, therefore, we can expect the marketing department to be organized in such a way that these goals are accomplished.

In practice it is easier said than done. A variety of different structures exist in companies because of the particular nature of the problems and tasks encountered. Nonetheless, the basic tasks will always remain and if they are neglected in times of short-term problems, the disadvantages will recur.

Marketing's job within the context of any particular time period is to generate the right mix of sales with customers at the right prices, in the right place with the right promotion. This means that the basic organization structure must include responsibilities for doing each of these things *and* for seeing that they are appropriately mixed together, that they are coordinated. In classical organization chart terms, this gives rise to a pattern of responsibilities as shown in FIGURE 29.

It will be seen that getting the product right involves the activity we have discussed in detail in answer to Questions 8, 9, 10 and 11. If a company has a great many products, it may well wish to group them; if it has a number of important brands, it will often ask a member of the marketing department to take particular care of them. Such a person is frequently known as the Brand Manager.

Getting the promotional activity right was discussed in answer to Questions 13, 14 and 15. We saw the need there to coordinate all the communications activities and then later in answer to

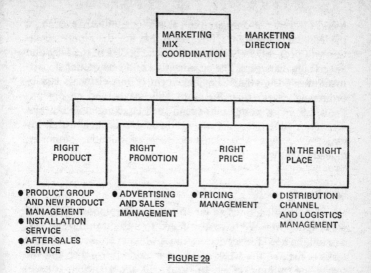

FIGURE 29

Questions 16 and 17 we examined in much greater detail how the sales activity, typically a very large element in marketing, can be successfully developed.

The marketing department must pull all these strands together as also it must in terms of pricing. And finally, as we saw in answer to Questions 19, 20 and 21, the product must be in the right place at the right time.

These are the specific operational responsibilities of the marketing department and the marketing director must act to manage them in such a way that the marketing objective of satisfying customer needs and wants is accomplished at the least cost, and the appropriate rate of profit or surplus. It is vitally important that he should be the focus of the coordination since he will often need to be tough in his attitudes and behaviour to particular elements in the marketing mix. He may well perceive that a massive increase in distribution service can more than offset the market advantage lost by a reduction in sales and advertising expenditure, thereby providing a better overall marketing outcome. If he is not in coordinative command of those three elements of the

181

mix, however, not only are the calculations unlikely ever to be made in the first instance, but even if they are, their implementation will probably only be over the dead bodies of the sales and advertising managers. The organization of the marketing department must ensure that all management of mix elements is subordinate to marketing direction. This may sound an obvious point, but many companies spend such large amounts on sales activity or advertising that they sometimes staff them with fairly senior executives who challenge such coordinative authority, indeed often usurp it.

## Marketing posts

We have been cautious so far to talk about responsibilities not particular posts. We have also failed to introduce into our discussion the need for services to those who undertake to fulfil the tasks – such as the work of the marketing researcher and the marketing training officer. In FIGURE 30, the particular roles in the marketing department of a Swiss textile fabric manufacturer are shown.

The roles allocated can be seen to be related to the specific nature of the organization. Its markets are with industrial purchasers and households. The Sales Manager has indeed three Controllers who report to him, two of them dividing household sales between them depending on whether the sales are sought direct from customers via direct mail response to advertising or occur through trade sales to wholesalers and retailers. This distinction is also present in the way the Design Manager, who has responsibility for the product, divides his activity, although the distinction noted earlier between direct and trade sales does not affect the design process. The Advertising Manager works through an agency which is accustomed to handling both industrial, trade and direct response advertising work. Similarly, the Pricing and Credit Control Manager handles all areas of activity.

The element missing in the coordination exercised by the Marketing Director is distribution, the role which determines which channels to use for reaching the end customer and in particular taking care to ensure that the correct level of logistical support is given. This was a serious bone of contention. Because

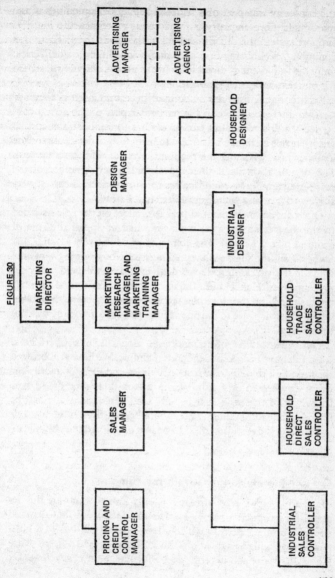

FIGURE 30

the company was part of a wider grouping of companies in the man-made fibre industry, it was required to use the logistics support system the other members of the group used. There was common warehousing and a common scheduling of deliveries. Only the fulfilment of direct response sales was uniquely designed for our textile fabric organization.

Such compromises are sometimes necessary even if they appear counterproductive to the particular part of the group concerned. In this case, after careful studies to establish the correct service levels a change was made to using sub-contractors for the logistics task who met the required levels at an economic cost. The organization itself then introduced a new member of the marketing team who exercised his role in precisely the same way as the Advertising Manager always had before.

Our final comment should perhaps reflect on the role ascribed to the marketing research manager which included the role of training officer as well. The company was relatively small – just SwFr 48 million sales each year. There were only some twenty-six staff in the marketing department including all field sales representatives. Hence, both the information gaining and presenting task and the training roles were not overwhelming. Nonetheless, this service role to the line executives in the company was not overlooked.

Our illustrations of a marketing department's operational structure have been kept deliberately simple. We have emphasized the need first to define the responsibilities and then to identify the posts we need to establish. We have seen that some of the performance of the tasks can be sub-contracted and some can be joined in one individual. What cannot be sacrificed is the marketing director's overriding need to be in a position to coordinate all the posts.

## Organizing marketing within the company

Marketing, as we have stressed, is only able to generate the demand for products or services. The satisfaction of that demand depends on the extent to which all the other functions of a business are working to agreed objectives. These agreed objectives are increasingly defined in terms of performance on *product/market missions*, and organizations will frequently coordinate their various lines of business in terms of a matrix structure. A matrix approach is employed at Cranfield for the conduct of its School of Management. Its vertical inputs to the organization are teaching inputs, and the horizontal outputs are improved managers. Education is, of course, an example of a non-profit service such as we discussed in answer to Question 4. Cranfield has three major teaching product/market missions, and each is coordinated by a director – for the MBA Programme, for Doctoral Studies and for Continuing Studies. Various professors head the subject groups which work together to make each mission a success. Success comes when all the groups work effectively together to achieve the output, which in Cranfield's case is a well educated or trained manager.

In FIGURE 31 this notion of the matrix is applied to a major Italian concern selling its products into catering establishments, grocery supermarkets and wholesalers.

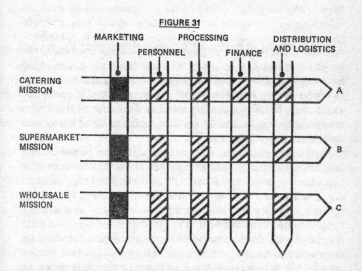

FIGURE 31

It will be seen that the marketing effort is just one part of the integrated activities of the company designed to take the right

185

processed food products to customers in catering establishments, to the Italian national supermarket chains and to wholesalers who supply the smaller retail grocery outlets. At each of the interstices in the matrix shown solidly, marketing will need to coordinate its activities in a different fashion in order to relate effectively with all other company activities and thereby induce the necessary customer satisfaction. The trade-offs we saw above which the Swiss textile company had to accept initially for its logistics activity are equally necessary on an internal company basis. The processing function may not be able within its existing plant to make the product mix which is ideally suited to the market. The development engineers may not be able to offer the requisite level of quality control. The finance function may not be able to raise or allocate the desired level of funds to support customer credit policies. Balancing out such competing claims within the total perspective of each product/market mission is, however, the ultimate necessity and it must be done on the basis of a customer orientation even if not entirely to the liking of marketing executives.

## The marketing department's role in developing the future

It can accordingly be seen now why marketing must plan ahead for more than the immediate period of operational activity. Its *viewpoint and its interpretation* of emergent customer needs and wants must be clearly countenanced at the tables of those who are taking the medium and long term decisions about any organization's future capabilities.

Marketing's colleagues in production, finance, personnel and distribution earnestly need and want to know what future viable paths the company can follow in its markets. Marketing must be continually exploring and displaying the alternatives. It can only do so by developing an adequate product policy and strategy based on understanding customers, what they will need and what they can be persuaded to want. Marketing must give its colleagues their bearings on the market place as they seek to invest in new manufacturing capacity to come on stream three years hence, or locate new facilities, or develop the skills of the workforce, or to analyse cash requirements to fund the business in the years ahead.

We can conclude by demonstrating this role in sharp yet realistic relief with the European airlines in 1975. They took delivery in 1975 of their TriStars, A300B European Airbuses or DC10 fleet in order to meet the levels of business activity forecast three years previously. Market demand was way down in 1975; twenty five per cent down in fact. The fleets were not needed but the product had arrived. It was relatively inflexible to the changed needs of the market situation. There was little flexibility for changed patterns of travel which the massive escalation in ticket expense had occasioned as between first class, tourist, part charter and charter flying. As we pointed out in answer to Question 12, forecasting is difficult so it must be flexible. European airlines were caught with a crisis as a result of a lack of flexibility in their forecasting and their planning, as well as from sheer bad luck. They are resolved to include a much deeper marketing involvement in future planning of organizational capability for the future. Every good marketing department should do the same.

*Further reading*

Hayhurst, R., and Wills, G., *Organizational Design for Marketing Futures*, Allen & Unwin, 1972

Corey, E. R., and Star, S. H., *Organizational Strategy: a Marketing Approach*, Harvard University Press, 1971

**Self-audit questions**

26.1  *Draw an organigram of how your organization integrates the management of the four 'P's.*

26.2  *Who is responsible for your organization's outputs as opposed to managing resource inputs?*

26.3  *What problems does/would a matrix structure pose for your organization? How would they be balanced by any advantage?*

26.4  *What role does your marketing department play in developing your company's future?*

# Question 27
# What is our marketing plan?

*Marketing planning is the planned application of marketing resources to achieve marketing objectives. It is the means by which a company seeks to monitor and control the hundreds of external and internal influences on its ability to achieve profitable sales, as well as providing an understanding throughout the organization of the particular competitive stance a company is planning to take to achieve its objectives. This helps managers of different functions to work together rather than pursuing their own functional objectives in isolation.*

*A marketing plan will contain a situation review, assumptions, overall objectives and strategies, and more detailed programmes containing responsibilities, timing and costs. The formality of the planning process will depend on the size and diversity of a company's operations, although the planning process itself is universally applicable.*

Any manager will readily agree that a sensible way to manage the sales and marketing function is to find a systematic way of identifying a range of options, to choose one or more of them, then to schedule and cost out what has to be done to achieve the objectives. This process can be defined as *marketing planning*, which is the planned application of marketing resources to achieve marketing objectives.

The problem is that, whilst as a process it is intellectually simple to understand, in practice it is the most difficult of all marketing tasks. The reason is that it involves bringing together into one coherent plan all the elements of marketing discussed in earlier questions in this book, and in order to do this at least some degree of institutionalized procedures are necessary, and it is this which seems to cause so much difficulty for companies. One reason for this difficulty is that there is not a lot of guidance available to management on how the process itself might be managed, proceeding as it does from reviews to objectives, strategies, programmes, budgets and back again, until some kind of acceptable compromise is reached between what is desirable and what is practicable, given all the constraints that any company has.

Another reason is that a planning system itself is little more than a structured approach to the process just described, but because of the varying size, complexity, character and diversity of commercial operations, there can be no such thing as an 'off the peg' system that can be implemented without some pretty fundamental amendments to suit the situation-specific requirement of each company.

Also, the degree to which any company can develop an integrated, coordinated and consistent plan depends on a deep understanding of the marketing planning process itself as a means of sharpening the focus of all levels of management within an organization.

## Why is marketing planning essential?

There can be little doubt that marketing planning is essential when we consider the increasingly hostile and complex environment in which companies operate. Hundreds of external and internal factors interact in a bafflingly complex way to affect our ability to achieve profitable sales. Also, let us consider for a moment the four typical objectives which companies set, of maximizing revenue, maximizing profits, maximizing return on investment, and minimizing costs. Each one of these has its own special appeal to different managers within the company, depending on the nature of their particular function. In reality, the best that can ever be achieved is a kind of optimal compromise', because each of these objectives is often basically in conflict with the others.

Managers of a company have to have some understanding or view about how all these variables interact and managers try to be rational about their business decisions, no matter how important intuition, feel and experience are as contributory factors in this process of rationality.

Most managers accept that some kind of formalized procedure for marketing planning helps sharpen this rationality so as to reduce the complexity of business operations and add a dimension of realism to the company's hopes for the future. Without some procedures for dealing with such issues, there is a danger that the company will exhaust much of its energies in internecine disputes, whilst its marketing may become little more than an uncoordinated mixture of interesting bits and pieces.

Ideally, what is required is some kind of institutionalized process designed to work out and write down in advance the particular competitive stance that the company plans to take. This should then be communicated throughout the company so that everyone is conscious of what has to be done to take the company towards its objectives. A useful way of achieving this synergy is through the marketing planning process.

## The marketing planning process

FIGURE 32 illustrates the several stages that have to be gone through in order to arrive at a marketing plan, which a recent study of leading French companies showed should contain:
– a summary of all the principal external factors which affected the company's marketing performance during the previous year, together with a statement of the company's strengths and weaknesses *vis-à-vis* the competition; this is often called a SWOT analysis (*strengths, weaknesses, opportunities, threats*).
– some assumptions about the key determinants of marketing success and failure
– overall marketing objectives and strategies
– programmes containing details of timing, responsibilities and costs.

Each of the stages illustrated in FIGURE 32 will be discussed in more detail in our answers to Questions 28, 29 and 30.

The dotted lines joining up steps 5, 6 and 7 are meant to indicate the reality of the planning process in that each of these steps is likely to have to be gone through more than once before final programmes can be written.

Although research has shown these marketing planning steps to be universally applicable, the degree to which each of the

**FIGURE 32**

**THE MARKETING PLANNING PROCESS**

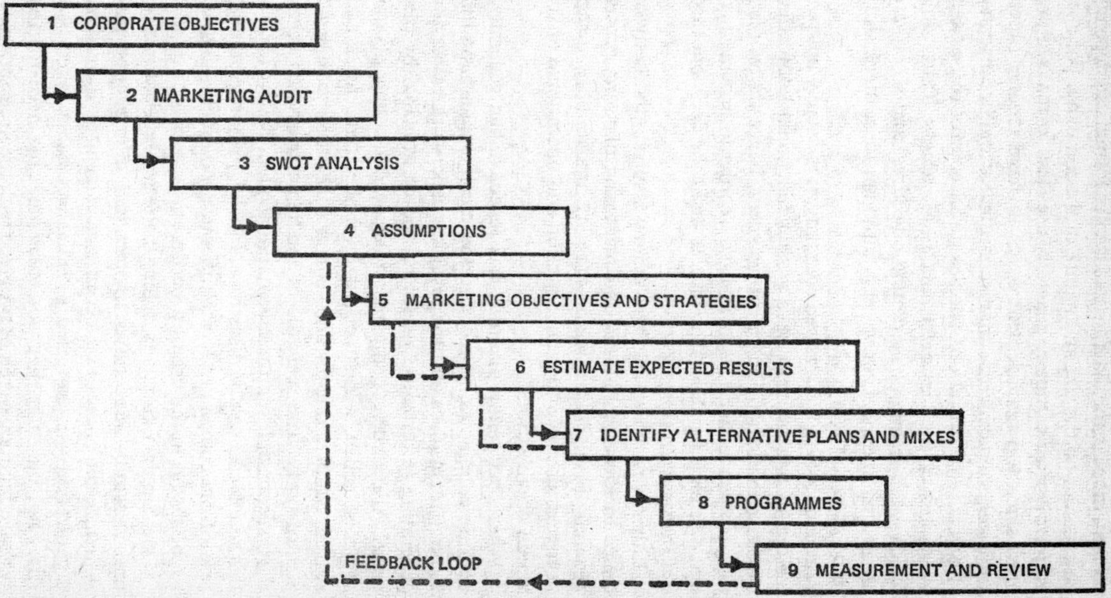

1 CORPORATE OBJECTIVES

2 MARKETING AUDIT

3 SWOT ANALYSIS

4 ASSUMPTIONS

5 MARKETING OBJECTIVES AND STRATEGIES

6 ESTIMATE EXPECTED RESULTS

7 IDENTIFY ALTERNATIVE PLANS AND MIXES

8 PROGRAMMES

9 MEASUREMENT AND REVIEW

FEEDBACK LOOP

separate steps in the diagram needs to be formalized depends to a large extent on the size and nature of the company. For example an *undiversified* company generally uses less formalized procedures, since top management tends to have greater functional knowledge and expertise than subordinates and because the lack of diversity of operations enables direct control to be exercised over most of the key determinants of success. Thus, situation reviews, the setting of marketing objectives, and so on, are not always made explicit in writing, although these steps still have to be gone through.

In contrast, in a *diversified* company, it is usually not possible for top management to have greater functional knowledge and expertise than subordinate management, hence the whole planning process tends to be formalized in order to provide a consistent discipline for those who have to make the decisions throughout the organization.

Either way, however, there is now a substantial body of evidence to show that formalized marketing planning procedures generally result in greater profitability and stability in the long term and also help to reduce friction and operational difficulties within organizations.

Where marketing planning has failed, it has generally been because companies have placed too much emphasis on the procedures themselves and the resulting paperwork rather than on generating information useful to and consumable by management. Also, where companies relegate marketing planning to someone called a 'planner', it invariably fails, for the simple reason that planning for line management cannot be delegated to a third party. The real role of the 'planner' should be to help those responsible for implementation to plan. Failure to recognize this simple fact can be disastrous. Finally, planning failures often result from companies trying too much too quickly and without training staff in the use of procedures.

One Swedish company selling batteries internationally tried unsuccessfully three times to introduce a marketing planning system, each one failing because management throughout the organization was confused by what was being asked of them. Also, not only did they not understand the need for the new systems, but they were not provided with the necessary resources to make the system work effectively. Training of managers and careful thought about resource requirements would have largely overcome this company's planning problems.

In contrast, a major multinational company, having suffered grave profitability and operational difficulties through not having an effective marketing planning system, introduced one over a three-year period that included a training programme in the use of the new procedures and the provision of adequate resources to make them work effectively. This company is now firmly in control of its diverse activities and has recovered its confidence and its profitability. In our replies to Question 28, 29 and 30 we deal with the marketing planning process in more detail, starting with a look at the *marketing audit*.

*Further reading*

Ames, B. C., 'Marketing Planning for Industrial Products', *Harvard Business Review*, vol 46, Sept/Oct 1968

Christopher, W. F., 'Marketing Planning that Gets Things Done', *Harvard Business Review*, Sept/Oct 1970

McDonald, M. H. B., 'Marketing Planning, Fact or Fiction', *Quarterly Review of Marketing*, summer 1979

**Self-audit questions**

27.1  *What problems are likely to arise in a company that does not produce a written marketing plan?*

27.2  *Describe the marketing planning procedures in your company.*

27.3  *How does corporate planning relate to marketing planning – and/or how should it – in your company?*

# Question 28
# How can we audit the effectiveness of our marketing plan?

*A marketing audit is a systematic critical review and appraisal of the environment and of the company's marketing operations. It is a powerful tool in ascertaining whether a company is in phase with its dynamic and rapidly changing marketing environment, in ensuring that advantage is taken of opportunities, that preparations are made for overcoming threats, that strengths are developed and that weaknesses are overcome. To be effective, four major points must be borne in mind: (1) audits should be carried out on a regular basis; (2) audit procedures should be institutionalized and defined in detail; (3) management should be trained to use these procedures effectively; and (4) to ensure that audits are action-oriented, the major impetus must come from top management.*

In our reply to Question 27 we looked at the need for marketing planning and outlined a series of steps that have to be gone through in order to arrive at a marketing plan. The purpose here is to go into more detail about one of the most important steps in the process – the *marketing audit*. Any plan will only be as good as the information on which it is based, and the marketing audit is the means by which information for planning is organized.

Auditing as a process is usually associated with the financial side of the business and is conducted according to a defined set of accounting standards, which are well documented, easily understood and which therefore lend themselves readily to the auditing process.

The total business process, although more complicated, innovative and relying more on judgement than on a set of rules, is still nevertheless capable of being audited. Basically, an audit is the means by which a company can understand how it relates to the environment in which it operates. It is the means by which a company can identify its own strengths and weaknesses as they relate to external opportunities and threats. It is thus a way of helping management to select a position in that environment based on known factors.

Expressed in its simplest form, if the purpose of a corporate plan is to answer three central questions:
– where is the company now?
– where does the company want to go?
– how should the company organize its resources to get there?
then the audit is the means by which the first of these questions is answered. An audit is a systematic, critical and unbiased review and appraisal of the environment and of the company's operations. A marketing audit is part of the larger *management audit* and is concerned with the marketing environment and marketing operations.

Often the need for an audit does not manifest itself until things start going wrong for a company, such as declining sales, falling margins, lost market share, under-utilized production capacity, and so on.

At times like these, management often attempts to treat the wrong symptoms. For example, introducing new products or dropping products, reorganizing the sales force, reducing prices, and cutting costs, are just some of the actions which could be taken. But such measures are unlikely to be effective if there are more fundamental problems which have not been identified. Of course, if the company could survive long enough, it might eventually solve its problems through a process of elimination! Essentially, the argument is that problems have to be properly defined, and the audit is a means of helping to define them. To summarize, the audit is a structured approach to the collection and analysis of data and information in the complex business environment as an essential prerequisite to problem solving.

## Audit format

Any company carrying out an audit will be faced with two kinds of variables. Firstly, there are variables over which the company has no direct control. These usually take the form of what can be described as *environmental* and *market* variables. Secondly, there are variables over which the company has complete control. These we can call *operational* variables.

195

## BUSINESS & ECONOMIC ENVIRONMENT

Economic
Political/fiscal
Social
Business
Legal
Technological
International
Intra-company

## THE MARKET, ENVIRONMENT

Total market
Segments
Channels
By products
By end use
By geography
By needs
By tastes
By attitudes
By habits
By purchasing ability
By stocks
By turnover
By profits
Out of stocks
Inventory
Customer classification
Customer buying power
Customer problems and
requirements
Customer methods of supplier
selection

## THE COMPETITIVE ENVIRONMENT

Products
Technology
Sales and market shares
Marketing skills
Marketing decision variables
Key success and failure factors

## OWN COMPANY

Sales (total, by geographical
location, by industrial type,
by customer, by product)
Market shares
Profit margins
Marketing procedures
Marketing organization
Sales/marketing control data
Marketing mix variables, as
follows:
– Market research
– Product development
– Product range
– Product quality
– Unit of sale
– Stock levels
– Distribution
– Dealer support
– Pricing, discounts, credit
– Packaging
– Samples
– Exhibitions
– Selling
– Sales aids
– Point of sale
– Advertising
– Sales promotion
– Public relations
– After-sales service
– Training

This gives us a clue as to how we can structure an audit. That is to say, in two parts:

– an *external audit*

– an *internal audit*.

The *external* audit is concerned with the *uncontrollable* variables, whilst the *internal* audit is concerned with the *controllable* variables. The *external* audit starts with an examination of information on the general economy and then moves on to the outlook for the health and growth of the markets served by the company.

The purpose of the *internal* audit is to assess the organization's resources as they relate to the environment and *vis-à-vis* the resources of competitors.

A checklist of areas which should be investigated as part of the marketing audit is given in the preceding tabulation.

Each one of these headings should be examined with a view to isolating those factors which are considered critical to the company's performance. Initially the auditor's task is to screen the enormous amount of data and information for validity and relevance. Some data and information will have to be reorganized into a more easily usable form, and judgement will have to be applied to decide what further data and information is necessary to a proper definition of the problem.

Thus, there are basically two phases which comprise the auditing process:

– the identification, measurement, collection and analysis of all the relevant *facts* and *opinions* which impinge on a company's problems

– the application of judgement to uncertain areas which are remaining following this analysis.

## When and how should the marketing audit be carried out?

A mistaken belief held by many people is that the marketing audit should be a last-ditch, 'end of the road' attempt to define a company's marketing problem, or at best something done by an independent body from time to time to ensure that a company is on the right lines.

However, since marketing is such a complex function, it seems illogical not to carry out a very thorough situation analysis at least once a year at the beginning of the planning cycle.

There is much evidence to show that many highly successful companies, as well as using normal information and control procedures and marketing research throughout the year, also start their planning cycle each year with a formal review through an audit-type process of everything which has had an important influence on marketing activities. Certainly in many leading consumer goods companies, the annual self audit approach is a well tried and tested self-discipline which is built into an integrated management process.

Occasionally it may be justified to hire outside consultants to carry out a marketing audit to check that a company is getting the most out of its resources. However, it seems an unnecessary expense to have this done every year. The answer, therefore, is to have an audit carried out annually by the company's own line managers on their own areas of responsibility.

Reluctance to do this usually centres around the problems of time and objectivity. In practice, these problems are usually overcome by institutionalizing procedures in as much detail as possible so that all managers have to conform to a disciplined approach, and secondly by thorough training in the use of the procedures themselves. However, even this will not result in the achievement of the purpose of an audit unless a rigorous discipline is applied from the highest levels down to the lowest levels of management involved in the audit. Such a discipline is usually successful in helping managers to avoid the sort of tunnel vision that often results from a lack of critical appraisal.

## What happens to the result of the audit?

The final all-important issue, of course, is what happens to the result of the audit. Some companies consume valuable resources carrying out audits that bring very little by way of actionable results. Indeed, there is always the danger that at the audit stage insufficient attention is paid to the need to concentrate on analysis that determines which trends and developments will actually affect the company. Whilst the checklist provided demonstrates the completeness of logic and analysis, the people carrying out the audit should discipline themselves to omit from their plans all information that is not central to the company's marketing problems. Thus, inclusion of research reports, or over-detailed sales performance histories by product which lead to no logical actions whatever, only serve to rob the audit of focus and reduce its relevance. Since the objective of the audit is to indicate what a company's marketing objectives and strategies should be, it follows that it would be helpful if some format could be found for organizing the major findings.

One useful way of doing this is in the form of a SWOT analysis, which was mentioned in response to Question 10. Let us just remind ourselves that this is a summary of the audit under the headings (internal) *strengths* and *weaknesses* as they relate to external *opportunities* and *threats*.

To summarize, carrying out a regular and thorough marketing audit in a structured way will go a long way towards giving a company a knowledge of the business, trends in the market, and where value is added by competitors, as the basis for setting realistic marketing objectives and strategies.

One company in the Spanish footwear business that was suffering a sudden decline in profitability had a marketing audit carried out which revealed fundamental weaknesses in almost every area of marketing, the most serious of which was that the company's sales were completely out of step with the trends in the market. Following the audit the company was quickly able to rectify many of the faults and this led to a gradual recovery of their market position and profitability. Since then the company has been sure to carry out itself a thorough marketing audit at the beginning of every planning cycle.

*Further reading*

Tirmann E. A., 'Should your Marketing be Audited?'
  *European Business*, autumn 1971

Kotler, P., 'The Marketing Audit comes of Age', *Sloan Management Review*, winter 1977

McDonald, M. H. B., *Handbook of Marketing Planning*, MCB Publications, 1980

**Self-audit questions**

28.1   *What is a marketing audit?*

28.2   *If you were to carry out a marketing audit in your own company, what are the major headings you would include for investigation?*

28.3   *Who would you ask to carry out a marketing audit in your own company?*

28.4   *Before setting marketing objectives in your company, what form of situation review takes place and at what levels?*

## Question 29
# How can we prepare our marketing plan?

*The marketing plan lies at the heart of a company's revenue-earning activities, since from it flow the timing of the cash flow, the size and character of the labour force, and so on. Thus it is not possible to plan a company's marketing activities in isolation from other business functions: consequently the marketing planning process should be firmly based in a total corporate planning system.*

*The key step in the marketing planning process is the setting of marketing objectives and strategies. Marketing objectives are about products and markets only and should not be confused with price, place and promotion, which are the strategies, or means, with which the objectives should be achieved. Objectives should be capable of measurement, otherwise they are not objectives.*

*The detailed programmes which follow the setting of marketing objectives and strategies may be organized according to functions, products, markets, geography or customers, depending on circumstances.*

*Marketing plans are an aid to effective management, not a substitute for it.*

In our replies to Questions 27 and 28 we discussed, respectively, the total marketing planning process, and one of the most important steps in the planning process – the marketing audit. Before finally turning our attention to the other important steps in the marketing planning process, it would be useful to discuss how marketing planning relates to the corporate planning process.

FIGURE 33 shows five steps in the corporate planning process. As can be seen, the starting point is usually a statement of corporate financial objectives for the long-range planning period of the company, which are often expressed in terms of turnover, profit before tax, and return on investment.

More often than not, this long-range planning horizon is five years, but the precise period should be determined by the nature of the markets in which the company operates. For example, five years would not be a long enough period for a glass manufacturer, since it takes that period of time to commission a new furnace, whereas in some fashion industries, five years would be too long a period. A useful guideline in determining the planning horizon is that there should be a market for the company products for long enough at least to amortize any capital investment associated with those products.

The next step is the management audit, of which we specifically discussed the marketing element in the last question but which can, of course, embrace all functions of a business. This is an obvious activity to follow on with, since a thorough situation review, particularly in the area of marketing, should enable the company to determine whether it will be able to meet the long-range financial targets with its current range of products in its current markets. Any projected gap can be filled by the various methods of product development or market extension which were discussed in response to Question 10.

Undoubtedly the most important and difficult of all stages in the corporate planning process is the third step, objective and strategy setting, since if this is not done properly everything that follows will be of little value.

Later in this section we will discuss marketing objectives and strategies in more detail. For now, the important point to make is that this is the time in the planning cycle when a compromise has to be reached between what is wanted by the several func-

## FIGURE 33

MARKETING PLANNING AND ITS PLACE IN THE CORPORATE PLANNING CYCLE

| STEP 1 | 2 MANAGEMENT AUDIT | 3 OBJECTIVE STRATEGY SETTING | 4 PLANS | 5 CORPORATE PLANS |
|---|---|---|---|---|
| CORPORATE FINANCIAL OBJECTIVES | MARKETING AUDIT<br>MARKETING | MARKETING OBJECTIVES, STRATEGIES | MARKETING PLAN | ISSUE OF CORPORATE PLAN, TO INCLUDE CORPORATE OBJECTIVES AND STRATEGIES, PRODUCTION OBJECTIVES AND STRATEGIES ETC.; LONG RANGE P & L ACCOUNTS AND BALANCE SHEETS |
| | DISTRIBUTION AUDIT<br>STOCKS AND CONTROL; TRANSPORTATION; WAREHOUSING | DISTRIBUTION OBJECTIVES, STRATEGIES | DISTRIBUTION PLAN | |
| | PRODUCTION AUDIT<br>VALUE ANALYSIS; ENGINEERING DEVELOPMENT; WORK STUDY; QUALITY CONTROL; LABOUR; MATERIALS, PLANT AND SPACE UTILISATION; PRODUCTION PLANNING; FACTORIES | PRODUCTION OBJECTIVES, STRATEGIES | PRODUCTION PLAN | |
| | FINANCIAL AUDIT<br>CREDIT, DEBT, CASH FLOW AND BUDGETARY CONTROL; RESOURCE ALLOCATION; CAPEX; LONG TERM FINANCE | FINANCIAL OBJECTIVES, STRATEGIES | FINANCIAL PLAN | |
| | PERSONNEL AUDIT<br>MANAGEMENT, TECHNICAL AND ADMINISTRATIVE ABILITY ETC. | PERSONNEL OBJECTIVES, STRATEGIES | | |

MEASUREMENT, REVIEW AND AMENDMENT (IF NECESSARY) OF OPERATING PLANS CONTINUOUS

tional departments and what is practicable, given all the constraints that any company has. For example, it is no good setting a marketing objective of penetrating a new market, if the company does not have the production capacity to cope with the new business, and if funds are not available for whatever investment and working capital is necessary.

At this stage, objectives and strategies will be set for five years, or for whatever the planning horizon is.

Step 4 involves producing detailed plans for one year, containing the responsibilities, timing and costs of carrying out the first year's objectives, and broad plans for the following years.

These plans can then be incorporated into the *corporate plan*, which will contain long-range corporate objectives, strategies, plans, profit and loss accounts and balance sheets.

At this point it is worth pointing out that one of the main purposes of a corporate plan is to provide a long-term vision of what the company is or is striving to become, taking account of shareholder expectations, environmental trends, resource market trends, consumption market trends, and the distinctive competence of the company as revealed by the management audit. What this means in practice is that the corporate plan will contain the following elements:

- desired level of profitability
- business boundaries
  - what kinds of products will be sold to what kinds of markets (*marketing*)
  - what kinds of facilities will be developed (*production and logistics*)
  - the size and character of the labour force (*personnel*)
  - funding (*finance*)
- other corporate objectives such as social responsibility, corporate image, stock market image, employee image.

Such a corporate plan, containing projected profit and loss accounts and balance sheets, being the result of the process described above, is more likely to provide long-term stability for a company than plans based on a more intuitive process and containing forecasts which tend to be little more than extrapolations of previous trends.

The headquarters of one major multinational company with a

sophisticated budgeting system used to receive 'plans' from all over the world and coordinate them in quantitative and cross functional terms, such as numbers of employees, units of sale, items of plant, square feet of production area, together with the associated financial implications. The trouble was that this whole complicated edifice was built on the initial sales forecasts, which were themselves little more than trend extrapolations, with the result that the whole corporate planning process developed into little more than a time-consuming numbers game. The really key strategic issues relating to products and markets were lost in all the financial activity, which eventually resulted in grave operational and profitability problems.

## Planning assumptions

Let us now return to the preparation of the marketing plan. Referring again to FIGURE 32, having completed our marketing audit and SWOT analysis, assumptions now have to be made and explicitly written down. There are certain key determinants of success in all companies about which assumptions have to be made before the planning process can proceed. It is really a question of standardizing the planning environment. For example, it would be no good receiving plans from two product managers, one of whom believed the economy was going to decline by 2 per cent, whilst the other believed the economy was going to grow by 10 per cent. Examples of assumptions might be:

'With respect to the company's industrial climate, it is assumed that:
1 Industrial overcapacity will increase from 105 per cent to 115 per cent as new industrial plants come into operation.
2 Price competition will force price levels down by 10 per cent across the board.
3 A new product will be introduced by our major competitor before the end of the second quarter.'

Assumptions should be few in number, and if a plan can be robust, i.e. is possible irrespective of any assumption made, then so much the better.

# Marketing objectives and strategies

The next step in marketing planning is the writing of marketing objectives and strategies, the key step in the whole process.

An *objective* is what you want to achieve. A *strategy* is how you plan to achieve your objectives. Thus, there can be objectives and strategies at all levels in marketing. For example, there can be advertising objectives and strategies, and pricing objectives and strategies.

However, the important point to remember about marketing objectives is that they are about *products* and *markets* only. Common sense will confirm that it is only by selling something to someone that the company's financial goals can be achieved, and that advertising, pricing, service levels and so on are the means (or strategies) by which we might succeed in doing this. Thus, pricing objectives, sales promotion objectives, advertising objectives and the like should not be confused with marketing objectives.

The simple matrix in response to Question 8 says all that needs to be said about marketing objectives, which are about one or more of the following:
- existing products in existing markets
- new products for existing markets
- existing products for new markets
- new products for new markets.

They should be capable of measurement, otherwise they are not objectives. Directional terms such as 'maximize', 'minimize', 'penetrate', 'increase' are only acceptable if quantitative measurement can be attached to them over the planning period.

Measurement should be in terms of sales volume, sterling, market share, percentage penetration of outlets, and so on.

Marketing strategies are the means by which marketing objectives will be achieved and generally are concerned with the four 'P's, as follows:

*Product* – the general policies for product deletions, modifications, addition, design, etc.

*Price* – the general pricing policies to be followed for product groups in market segments.

*Place* – the general policies for channels and customer service levels.

*Promotion* – the general policies of communicating with customers under the relevant headings, such as advertising, sales force, packaging, public relations, exhibitions, direct mail.

Having completed this major planning task, it is normal at this stage to employ judgement, analogous experience, field tests and so on, to test out the feasibility of the objectives and strategies in terms of market share, sales, costs, profits, and so on. It is also normally at this stage that alternative plans and mixes are delineated, if necessary, including featured sales promotions as discussed in Question 18.

## Programmes

The general marketing strategies are now developed into specific sub-objectives, each supported by more detailed strategy and action statements.

A company organized according to functions might have an advertising plan, a sales promotion plan, a pricing plan, and so on. A product-based company might have a product plan, with objectives, strategies and tactics for price, place and promotion as necessary. A market-based or geographically based company might have a market plan, with objectives, strategies and tactics for the four 'P's as necessary. Likewise a company with a few major customers might have a customer plan. Any combination of the above might be suitable, depending on circumstances.

## Use of marketing plans

A written marketing plan is the backcloth against which operational decisions are taken on an ongoing basis. Consequently too much detail should not be attempted. Its major function is to determine where the company is now, where it wants to go to, and how to get there. It lies at the heart of a company's revenue-generating activities and from it flow all other corporate activities, such as the timing of the cash flow, the size and character of the labour force.

The marketing plan should be distributed on a 'need to know' basis only. Finally, the marketing plan should be used as an aid to effective management. It cannot be a substitute for it.

*Further reading*

Ansoff, H. I., *Corporate Strategy*, Penguin Books, 1968

Stapleton, J., *How to Prepare a Marketing Plan*, Gower Press, 1971

Taylor, B., and Wills, G. S. C., *Long Range Planning for Marketing and Diversification*, Bradford University Press, Crosby Lockwood, 1971

**Self-audit questions**

29.1  *Describe the marketing planning process of your own company.*

29.2  *What weaknesses do you think there are in your current system?*

29.3  *Suggest some improvements that could be made to your current system.*

29.4  *What do you think would be the most suitable way to structure and develop your marketing plan?*

## Question 30
# How can we set the marketing budget?

*Marketing budgets can only be imaginatively created if an organization has a clear understanding of how sales and profitability respond to differing levels of marketing effort. Such understanding arises when sustained research and analysis of marketing activities are undertaken on a collaborative basis between financial and marketing managers. The identification of a realistic inventory of marketing expense and its appropriate allocation to tasks over time is the important starting point. Thereafter, determined management must seek to measure and isolate the time-related effects of such expenditures on demand. Whilst organizations are never able to understand the issue with total certainty, such analyses give rise to greatly reduced risks and a clearer appreciation of just how much marketing expense can be beneficially incurred. It also meets financial management's crucial need to assess the total cash and cash flow implications of marketing action.*

In the replies to Questions 27, 28 and 29 we have discussed in detail the prepartion of an organization's *marketing plan*. The completion of this process in terms of specific strategies and programmes will give rise to a clearer view of both revenue expectations and the estimated costs of implementation. These are the two key ingredients in the preparation of any marketing budget. Both can and will be monitored carefully as the year progresses and any necessary corrective actions taken to ensure a satisfactory outcome. In order to establish such managerial control, a clear understanding of the nature of the revenue flow and cost incidence is required. The most hazardous aspect usually is knowing the incremental revenue effects of any additional spending on the four 'P's.

Revenue forecasting poses a major problem since revenue is not directly under the control of the marketing manager. The best laid plans can be thrown off course by a competitive development that catches the imagination of customers in consumer markets. In industrial markets confidence in the economic future can have major effects on the sales of capital equipment as well as stock-holding policies. In a service industry such as tourism a movement in the exchange rate can cause switches in patronage from one country to another.

For reasons such as these, sales forecasting as described in the response to Question 12 must be most carefully conducted both for unit volumes as well as gross monetary values. At budget preparation time it is also foolhardy in most circumstances simply to take a single point forecast of sales. Anticipated sales outcomes must be imprecise because of factors that are external to the company. In addition, the company may sometimes experience problems in production or distribution that prevent fulfilment even if the sale has been made.

Such uncertainty frequently leads companies to adopt a safe approach to sales revenue forecasting, i.e. they only forecast what they are *very* confident they can achieve. This has the merit of limiting the scope for unpleasant surprises with concomitant hasty change of direction during the year but it can have disadvantages. In their zeal for reliable budgets such companies will often miss out on good opportunities within the market place, albeit with higher levels of risk.

Designing a system which takes a truly dynamic approach towards marketing budgets rather than a static annual view is a major challenge to the marketing and financial directors in all organizations. Whenever the response to a valid marketing opportunity is that 'the budget has been spent already this year', it is clear something is coming between the company and its effective prosperity. It is equally true that matters are none too satisfactory when uneconomic spending is continued in an organization simply 'in order to spend the budget'. This all too frequently occurs when organizations base subsequent years' budgets on previous levels.

The most satisfactory situation for a marketing director is typically that where he is required:

(1) to justify all his marketing expenditure each year from a zero base against the tasks he wishes to accomplish and for which he has clearly identified his gross revenue expectations;

(2) to review progress continually to ensure that no lapses in interdepartmental communications can hinder good marketing. This approach is the most logical result of tackling the problem of planning the company's marketing activities according to the process described in the replies to the three previous questions.

If those procedures are followed, a hierarchy of objectives is built up in such a way that every item of budgeted expenditure can be related directly back to the initial corporate financial objectives. Thus, having identified sales promotion as a major means of achieving an objective in a particular market, when sales promotional items appear in the programme, each one has a specific purpose which can be related back to a major objective. For example, the following entry appeared in a major British consumer goods company's plan for one of its sub-markets:

## Sales promotions – Product 1 (extract)

| Cost | Timing | Promotion | Anticipated results |
|---|---|---|---|
| £5,000 | Continuous with effect from period 1 | S.E. distribution and placement drive | To remedy major regional distribution weaknesses |
| £5,000 | periods 2 & 3 | National, all grocery trade sectors (case bonus 13 for 12) | To hold seasonal volume forecast and distribution during period of intensive competitive activity; also to extend distribution and placements wherever possible |
| £5,000 | periods 1–3 | Selected multiple tailor-made promotions | To develop fully the distribution and volume through the major multiple chains |
| £2,000 | Continuous with effect from period 1 | Sales manager's discretionary spend | For fast response to local and tactical promotions |
| £5,000 | Continuous from period 6 | Selected multiple tailor-made promotions | To develop fully the distribution and volume through the major multiple chains |
| £1,500 | period 6 | National grocery retail distribution and placement drive | To improve in-stock situation prior to Easter |

This extract was then built into the consolidated product promotional budget which appears opposite:

## Consolidated promotional budget – Product 1

| SPACE AND TIME | | £ | |
|---|---|---|---|
| | Consumer – press | 97,000 | |
| | tv | 177,200 | |
| | Trade | 48,700 | |
| | Miscellaneous | 1,000 | |
| | TOTAL SPACE | | 323,900 |
| PRODUCTION | Consumer – press | 24,000 | |
| | tv | 30,000 | |
| | Trade | 18,600 | |
| | Miscellaneous | 1,000 | |
| | TOTAL PRODUCTION | | 73,600 |
| | | | £397,500 |
| PROMOTIONS | Major national promotions | 26,750 | |
| | National and regional multiple tailor-made promotions | 44,000 | |
| | Scotland promotions | 12,300 | |
| | Group promotions | 5,300 | |
| | Discretionary spend: | | |
| | – Regional managers | 15,000 | |
| | – National a/cs manager | 2,750 | |
| | – Trade sales manager | 2,000 | |
| | – Grocery sales manager | 2,000 | |
| | TOTAL PROMOTIONS: | | £110,100 |
| DISPLAY | Posters | 50,902 | |
| | TOTAL DISPLAY | | £50,902 |
| PUBLIC RELATIONS | | | |
| | PR fees | 6,000 | |
| | PR activities | 17,050 | |
| | Factory visits | 1,000 | |
| | TOTAL PUBLIC RELATIONS | | £24,050 |
| EXHIBITIONS | | 2,250 | 2,250 |
| PACKAGING | | 5,000 | £5,000 |
| CONTINGENCY | | 21,460 | £21,460 |
| | | | £213,762 |
| | AGGREGATE TOTAL | = | £611,262 |

Doing it this way not only ensures that every item of expenditure is fully accounted for as part of a rational, objective and task approach, but also that when changes have to be made during the period to which the plan relates, such changes can be made in such a way that the least damage is caused to the company's long-term objectives.

## What is the marketing expense?

The incremental marketing expense is made up of all costs that are incurred after a product is made available in the factory or definite resource provision is made to offer a service, *other than* expenses involved in the physical movement of the product or service facility. This latter group of costs are typically called the distribution expense and whilst distribution may sensibly be regarded as an integral part of marketing, its costs represent a discrete sub-set.

It will always be a hazardous assignment to draw the line between marketing and distribution costs and sometimes there are problems between production and marketing. When, for instance, is packaging a marketing cost, when a distribution and when a production cost? Whilst there can be no universal answer, careful analysis tempered by the wisdom that continually seeks for simplicity in such circumstances, can normally yield an acceptable solution. Organizations that use all or some of their packaging simply to reduce damage normally call it a distribution cost, whereas those who use their packaging to sell – as in most consumer markets – typically regard much or all of it as a marketing cost.

The major areas of marketing cost any organization incurs arise from the four 'P's. It is useful to take each in turn to identify what should be considered.

*Product* – the most typical incremental marketing cost associated with product is its packaging with the caveats mentioned above. There will, however, also be a wastage or obsolescence expense on occasions as in the case of perishable products and services. British Rail recently reported that it has several million unsold seats on its trains each day that perish as a saleable service the moment the train leaves a station. Many factories also have

212

spare capacity available on a similar basis that could be producing product to sell. The extent, over a medium-term period, to which marketing fails to make use of such capacity is the cost of marketing failure. It constitutes lost opportunities. Few companies look at product or service costs this way, but when they begin to do so, marketing's attention can be constructively focused on the considerable challenges implicit in incremental contribution business or towards fresh strategies of segmentation.

One further area of product cost that is all too frequently overlooked arises from decisions taken by marketing on the different sizes or capability levels of a product to be offered. The implications in terms of inventory holding to afford stock cover are very real indeed but are seldom carefully analysed against the sought-for benefits of increased profitable customer offtake.

*Price* – there are three major elements of marketing cost under this heading which often escape careful attention. The first is any form of discounting that the organization may engage in that reduces its otherwise-to-be-expected gross income yield for each unit sold. These may take the form of quantity discounts, promotional discounts, loyalty rebates etc. The second element is customer credit given. Unpaid invoices cost money and customer credit is a standard device for gaining business. Its terms will often be varied with the net effect for a customer of transforming the total real price of the product or service. The third price related cost is commission typically paid to salesmen or agents and often on a scale that increases the more success they have in making sales. Such commissions whittle directly away from the gross revenue of the organization.

*Place* – these costs do (for these authors) encompass both the direct costs of marketing channel members to the company and the discrete physical movement or distribution costs that create availability. These marketing tasks have been discussed in detail in answer to Questions 18, 19 and 20. The channel member's cost is primarily termed the 'margin' or 'mark-up'. What level they should be set at was discussed in reply to Question 22. Suffice it to discern here that the margin or mark-up allowed to or taken by a channel member at one or more levels within a distribution system is a marketing cost. The recorded fact that many companies do not see fit to analyse such margins or mark-ups in the pattern of their overall marketing budget exercise is a mistake. Without such information a full view of the marketing activities for a company's products or services cannot be gained.

Distribution costs incurred in the physical movement of goods or making services available to customers are often a very extensive part of the total expenditure of many organizations and can therefore be a dominant element in marketing expense. The primary determinant of distribution cost is the level of availability that is deemed appropriate for the organization's success in the market place. High levels of customer service or availability will normally involve substantial investment in inventories and/or rapid transportation and delivery back-up. Distribution cost analysis is a major area of investigation in its own right; it is sufficient merely to observe here that its level is determined by a marketing judgement on the profitable responsiveness of sales to different levels of availability.

*Promotion* – there is perhaps nowhere better than in the area of promotion to demonstrate the divergence of expenditure as between industrial and consumer products. Industrial concerns incur few costs of advertising on television or in the national or international press whereas most consumer advertising appears there. Rather the industrial concern will incur costs on exhibitions, on sales and technical literature for the professional buyer or user of his product or services, on technical representatives making personal calls at clients and on advisory services on applications in diverse situations.

Organizations offering their products or services through distributors will also frequently be involved in back-up promotion support. The major supermarket retailers' weekly press advertising is frequently a shared cost with the manufacturers whose products are featured. In insurance and building society agencies, point-of-sale leaflets are made available on a continuous basis. The same is true for distributors of industrial items such as engineering equipment.

Sales force costs have already been mentioned. They are often a substantial expense and are on occasions treated separately. Whilst there can be no objection to a discrete sub-set of sales force costs being considered, it is absolutely indispensable that they, along with the earlier described distribution costs, are

214

## Two typical marketing budgets

| | A CONSUMER PRODUCT | % | AN INDUSTRIAL PRODUCT | % |
|---|---|---|---|---|
| GROSS SALES REVENUE FORECAST FOR YEAR | 3,000,000 | 100.00 | 2,000,000 | 100.00 |
| *Less* Cost of product ex factory | 1,000,000 | 33.30 | 1,000,000 | 50.00 |
| | 2,000,000 | 66.60 | 1,000,000 | 50.00 |
| *Less* Incremental marketing expenses as follows: | | | | |
| Packaging for display | 50,000 | 1.60 | 0 | 0.00 |
| Returns perished/damaged | 5,000 | 0.16 | 12,000 | 0.60 |
| Special discounts | 160,000 | 5.30 | 0 | 0.00 |
| Customer credit cost | 30,000 | 1.00 | 100,000 | 5.00 |
| Sales commissions | 0 | 0.00 | 20,000 | 1.00 |
| Distributors' margins | 500,000 | 16.60 | 0 | 0.00 |
| Distribution expense for customer service | 348,000 | 11.60 | 85,000 | 4.25 |
| Promotion – tv | 100,000 | 3.30 | 0 | 0.00 |
| press | 50,000 | 1.60 | 12,000 | 0.60 |
| technical | 0 | 0.00 | 12,000 | 0.60 |
| catalogues etc. | 1,000 | 0.03 | 8,000 | 0.40 |
| Sales force expense | 50,000 | 1.60 | 108,000 | 5.40 |
| Information costs | 45,000 | 1.50 | 30,000 | 1.50 |
| TOTAL INCREMENTAL MARKETING EXPENSE | 1,339,000 | 44.29 | 387,000 | 19.35 |
| NET CONTRIBUTION TO COMPANY GENERAL EXPENSE | £661,000 | 22.31 | £613,000 | 30.65 |

brought firmly into the total marketing budget of the organization. At the margin, sales force effort and customer service are marketing costs that can perhaps be better spent elsewhere on the marketing field of action.

## Information cost effects

We have already described in response to Question 24 how the collection of marketing information can enhance the effectiveness of marketing activity, i.e. a greater benefit is reaped than the cost of collecting the information. This gives rise to the obvious inclusion in any marketing budget of an information cost. It tends to occur as a fixed item each twelve months, with a long-term view about the level of appropriate expenditure required. Typically, this gives rise to mistaken levels of information usage. Whether information can sensibly be collected by any organization at any juncture must be dictated by the size of the perceived risk it wishes to take and by which it is confronted. New product or service launches, or moves into new international markets, are most likely to give rise to the need for heavy expenditure on information. Its benefit will, however, be spread over a much longer period than that in which the cost is incurred. Information is an investment in understanding a market situation which could hold true for one, two, five or even ten years. It is not necessarily a current expense like discounting or sales force commission, and it may well deserve a separate treatment in budgetary terms. Once again, the healthiest manner of treatment has been a zero-based dynamic budgeting approach.

*Further reading*

Sevin, C. H., *Marketing Productivity Analysis*, McGraw-Hill, 1965

Christopher, M., Walters, D. and Wills, G., 'Output Budgeting in Marketing', *Management Decision*, 9, 2, 1972

**Self-audit questions**

30.1   *What is your organization's total marketing expense? How does it compare with your competitors?*

30.2   *Have your expense ratios moved in recent years? Why?*

30.3   *How specific can you be in budget discussions of the likely impact of a reduction in funds available to the marketing director?*

30.4   *How much should your company spend on marketing?*

# Question 31
# Is international marketing different?

*International marketing is the performance of the marketing task across national boudaries. As such, the principles are the same. However, the environment in which international marketing takes place is different from the domestic environment; the control which it is possible to exercise over the four 'P's is different, and there is a different dimension of complexity to planning the marketing function internationally.*

*The most critical determinant of the way you market abroad is your method of entering a foreign market.*

*The key questions in international marketing are concerned with whether to market abroad, where to market abroad, what to market abroad, and finally how to market abroad.*

Perhaps the best way of beginning to answer this question is to remind ourselves that marketing is the way in which an organization matches its capabilities to the wants of its customers against the background of a dynamic environment. International marketing is simply that performance of the marketing task across national boundaries. Marketing research still has to be carried out, appropriate products developed, realistic pricing, packaging and branding policies adopted, sales forecasts made, effective communication with customers has to take place, and distribution policies still have to ensure that the product gets to the right place at the right time.

So, in principle, international marketing is no different from domestic marketing.

Yet, in reality, whenever a company begins to operate outside its domestic market, it is in the field of marketing that it most commonly stumbles. This has forced both academics and practitioners to pay increasing attention to the subject of international marketing, and they have begun to focus more and more on the *differences* rather than the *similarities* as a means of improving performance.

In a way, it is a bit like comparing a man and a woman. In principle, they are both the same. However, failure to take note of some important differences and to adapt your behaviour accordingly, could land you in all sorts of trouble!

International marketing has three unique elements:
– there are additional environmental variables.
– the control which it is possible to exercise over the four 'P's is different
– there is a different dimension of complexity to planning the marketing function internationally.

Let us look at each of these in some detail to see in what ways any differences there are have an impact on the marketing mix.

## The international environment

*Tariffs* – which are taxes on imports levied either *ad valorem* or on quantity in order to earn revenue and to protect home industries – affect the price of exported goods, making them less competitive than locally produced goods. Companies affected by tariffs often react by using marginal cost pricing policies, by modifying the product, by repositioning the product in a higher priced market segment, or by CKD shipping (completely knocked-down) for local assembly, thus attracting a lower rate of duty.

*Quotas* – which are direct barriers to imports – are much more serious because the firm has less flexibility in responding to them. Apart from attempting to get a fair share of quotas, virtually the only response is to set up local production if the market size warrants it.

*Exchange control* – this means that foreign exchange is in short supply and the government is rationing it rather than letting higher prices ration it. If a company is manufacturing in a country with exchange controls, it has to get on the government's favoured list to get exchange for imported supplies of raw materials or component parts, or develop local supplies irrespective of possible higher costs and indifferent quality. Also, such a country is unlikely to give high priority to profit remittance, whilst currency fluctuations can either wipe out a company's profit or create a windfall virtually overnight.

*Non-tariff barriers* – in the form of customs documentation, marks of origin, product formulation, packaging and labelling laws and so on – can similarly have a dramatic effect on a company's freedom over the management of the four 'P's.

*Political instability*, *boycotts*, *customs unions* – and other environmental factors – can also have a drastic effect on a company's marketing policy.

One German company selling perfume in Latin America lost most of its market share when the tariff was raised from twenty to fifty per cent. The options discussed by the local management at an emergency meeting were: to continue paying the high duty and change the product positioning to a high price segment; to import the primary ingredients and assemble locally; to ask for a lower price from the home factory; or to give up the market completely. Eventually the company realized that it had to take a longer-term view which took account of the potential in the *total* Latin American Free Trade Area, and that this should have been done at the market *entry* stage rather than after a heavy investment had been made in only one market. Eventually the company set up manufacturing facilities in one of the LAFTA countries and South America is now a profitable market for the company. But, above all, the company learned the hard way that it just did not enjoy the same degree of control over its marketing as in its home market.

## The cultural environment

If there are problems when marketing in different nation states over awareness and sensitivity to more readily discernible facets of trade and commerce, the problems are that much greater when it comes to differentiating between cultures. Intuitive skills can make a great contribution to successful marketing programmes in the home market, but behaviour according to the same cultural criteria in foreign markets can lead to the most elementary and expensive marketing mistakes.

Seven elements of culture which need careful attention can be readily identified:

*Material culture* – the extent to which culture is responsive to increased productivity and its consequent rewards as well as the current state of material wealth and its impact on purchasing inclinations and abilities.

*Language* – the most obvious perhaps, but an aspect of culture which requires the most careful attention in the choice, for example, of brand names and the communication of ideas.

*Aesthetics* – which again demands most careful understanding if promotional activities, packaging, product design, music as an integral part of life and colour with its host of special associations are not to be mishandled.

*Education* – which determines whether or not written communication is possible. High levels of illiteracy mean that instructions on packaging are pointless, and that training programmes for distributors and agents must take careful cognizance of the problems which result. The conduct of marketing research will also pose its own problems which can be severely restricting because such a high premium must of necessity be placed on objectively collated data in the face of an uncertain cultural situation.

*Religion* – like language, a readily identifiable aspect of cultural difference which we find both within and across national boundaries. Its taboos and predilections must be ascertained and their impact on economic behaviour studied with care.

*Attitudes and values* – most especially towards marketing and sales, will need to be ascertained and understood. Different cultures respond differently to the acquisition of conspicuous wealth, towards change in life styles and towards the taking of social risks.

*Social organization* – can most clearly be seen at work in the family or in the company's purchasing department. Certain cultures are respecters of age and status whilst others have developed a more meritocratic stance. Some have a greater respect for womenfolk than others. Some operate through a greatly extended concept of family, whereas in others the family has almost broken down as an effective social institution even for bringing up children.

Successful inter-cultural marketing activity is built upon an understanding of how local culture interacts with the four 'P's, which, incidentally, is precisely the same message as we conveyed in relation to different segments of any market we might wish to reach. The distinction here is that in an alien culture we need to proceed with great analysis and forethought; but then so do we in any segment with which we do not feel a close affinity.

## International control

Without doubt, the most critical determinant of the way you market abroad is your *method of entering* a foreign market, for this above all else decides the degrees of freedom you have over the management of the four 'P's.

Straightforward *exporting* can be either indirect or direct. Indirect exporting is when a third party arranges the documentation, shipping and selling of a company's goods abroad, and this usually represents the smallest level of commitment to international marketing. As foreign sales grow, however, the company begins to make a limited commitment, usually in the form of taking on the documentation task itself. It is often at this stage that overseas agents or distributors are appointed to carry out the selling task abroad, with the result that the company is now a direct exporter, although it is likely that the commitment is still limited to marginal production capacity with no additional fixed investment.

Recognition of the importance of overseas trading really happens when a limited fixed investment occurs, not just in the form of production capacity, but often also in the form of a marketing subsidiary abroad in recognition of the need for a more aggressive marketing approach.

*Foreign production* can take the form of licensing, contract manufacturing, local assembly or full manufacture either by joint ventures or wholly owned subsidiaries. With licensing, the company is hiring out its brand name, technical expertise, patent, trademark, or process rights. The licensee manufactures and markets abroad for the licensor. Whilst this avoids the need for a heavy investment, it can lead to an overdependence on the licensee, who quickly builds up both manufacturing and marketing expertise. Associated Engineering, the largest engine components manufacturer in the world, and Pilkington Glass are just two examples of successful licensing abroad.

Contract manufacturing is merely using someone else's production capacity and is usually only possible for technically simple products like food. It is a useful way of getting round tariff barriers as well as of gaining experience of a foreign market without the need for investment in capital and labour.

Similar advantages apply to local assembly, which is also a learning device, as well as enabling a company to avoid paying the higher tariffs on assembled goods, because bringing in unassembled goods helps local employment.

Sometimes, laws forbid one-hundred-per-cent foreign ownership of assets, especially in the less developed countries. So many companies set up joint ventures either with a foreign government or with local partners. It is certainly a way of sharing risk and of gaining experience using local expertise, but its major disadvantage lies in the loss of complete control, hence freedom of action, especially in the field of marketing.

One-hundred-per-cent ownership of foreign production plants represents a major commitment to international marketing and should only be done after much research. Most overseas manufacturing is related to where the markets are. ICI built a polyethylene plant in the south of France because this was the only way to get into the market. Likewise, GKN's big stake in the German components industry gave them a market share which could not be achieved by direct export from the UK.

From this discussion, it will be clear that there is a big difference between the marketing task of a company selling to a middleman as a final customer, with little concern about what happens to the product after the sale, and the task facing the company that assumes full responsibility for all stages of marketing right through to final user satisfaction. Regardless of the level of involvement in foreign marketing, companies are more and more finding it necessary to become marketing oriented in their international efforts.

The important point is that each of the options described above should not be considered as a series of steps to be followed *en route* to becoming a multinational company (in which all opportunities are assessed from the worldwide viewpoint, and in which the terms 'home' and 'foreign' are meaningless), but more as strategic alternatives. And since the method of market entry is the major determinant of the degree of control a company has over its marketing, each of the different options should be carefully considered before a decision is made.

A precision-components manufacturer appointed a distributor for Europe with a seven-year agreement. Whilst at first this provided some useful additional sales, when a downturn in the UK market took place, the company found itself at the mercy of an inefficient and unsympathetic distributor. Territorial expansion therefore ceased to be an option and the company had to initiate a very expensive diversification programme into new products.

## International coordination

The final difference between domestic and international marketing lies in the complexity of coordinating the international marketing effort, which will be discussed in answer to Question 32, where we shall look at some of the major problems of managing the four 'P's in international marketing.

To summarize, the key questions in international marketing concern the following issues:

– *whether* to sell abroad; geographical diversification may be more desirable than product diversification, depending of course on circumstances; however, the decision to sell abroad should not be taken lightly

– *where* to sell abroad is one of the major decisions for international marketing; choosing foreign markets on the basis of proximity and similarity is not necessarily the most potentially profitable option to go for

– *what* to sell abroad and the degree to which products should be altered to suit foreign needs is also one of the major problems of international marketing

– *how* to sell abroad is concerned not just with the issue of how to enter a foreign market, but also with the management of the four 'P's once a company arrives; finally, there is the difficult question of how to coordinate the marketing effort in many foreign countries.

*Further reading*

Terpstra, V., *International Marketing*, Dryden Press, 1978

Paulden, S., 'Marry in haste, repent at leisure', *Industrial Marketing Digest*, 3 (3), 1978

Walsh, L., 'How Compair went into West Germany', *Marketing*, February 1979

Yoshino, M. Y., *The Japanese Marketing System*, MIT Press, 1971 (for comparison with a very different system)

**Self-audit questions**

31.1 *What is the difference between domestic and international marketing?*

31.2 *What is the international marketing philosophy of your company?*

31.3 *Compare the marketing task of the exporter with that of the company with foreign plants.*

31.4 *Imagine that home market pressures have forced your company to consider looking abroad. What criteria would you use to decide the best way for your company to enter foreign markets and how would you choose where to go?*

## Question 32

# How can we be successful in international markets?

*International marketing intelligence is the systematic gathering, recording and analysis of data about problems relating to the marketing of goods and services internationally. It is concerned with where to go, how to enter, how to market (the four 'P's) and traditional marketing research questions within each market. The key questions in international product management are concerned with whether to adapt national products when selling them abroad and with what product line to sell in international markets. In pricing management, the identification of costs is often difficult, but apart from this there are numerous extraneous factors which complicate the pricing decision. These difficulties make it essential to have a pricing policy. One of the key issues in international marketing is the method of market entry, for this is what determines how we market our goods abroad. Also important, however, is channel strategy. Another key issue is international promotion. Finally, it is only by developing a standardized planning process that international companies will gain the real benefits of marketing internationally.*

In answer to Question 31 we concentrated on the *differences* between domestic and international marketing. These are largely the result of the effect of differences in the environment and the level of control which it is possible to exercise over the marketing mix rather than of any fundamental differences in the marketing concept. We now turn our attention to the question of international market intelligence, and the four 'P's, to see in what ways the application of the tools and techniques of marketing is affected by the international environment.

## International marketing intelligence (IMI)

IMI is simply the systematic gathering, recording and analysis of data about problems relating to the marketing of goods and services internationally. It is concerned with the following:
– where to go
– how to enter
– how to market (the four 'P's)
– traditional marketing research questions *within* each market.
IMI involves: marketing research studies as in the domestic market; the study of additional factors not usually present in domestic marketing; studies of *many* foreign markets individually
– multi-country studies.

This latter form of marketing research is often referred to as comparative analysis. It is a way of organizing information on international markets and involves comparing and grouping countries in ways useful to decision making, thus maximizing the use of a company's international experience. For example, grouping countries according to their geographic proximity, which some companies do for the purpose of marketing control, can be a mistake if they are not homogeneous in charactistics important to the company's marketing. Grouping countries according to, say, stage of economic development can be a useful way of filling data gaps, for the missing values can be assumed to be similar to those available in the same group. Also, the expense of researching in many small markets can often be avoided by carrying out research in a sample of countries and extrapolating the results to other countries in the same group.

A large electronics company carried out a comparative analysis of its markets worldwide by first identifying the characteristics that were important to its international marketing decisions, then grouped different countries according to their similarity on these dimensions. They found three distinct groupings and began to develop marketing strategies for these three groups rather than developing separate marketing strategies for each individual country as previously. This resulted in great savings for the company and also improved their control.

There are a great number of problems in IMI not normally present in domestic research. These centre around the cultural problems of language and social organization, technical problems, data problems and economic problems. In some parts of the world, only oral communication is possible, with several languages being spoken. But quite apart from such difficulties, it is often almost impossible to interview women, who in Moslem countries are not allowed to talk to men without their husbands being present. Mail and telephone surveys are impossible in some countries, which leaves virtually only personal interviews, often difficult because of geographic and cultural problems. Published data is less available and often unreliable, whilst different base years and different definitions are often used. Add to this the cost of researching foreign markets, and it will be seen at once that IMI is not just a simple extension of domestic techniques, although it must be said that as far as questionnaire design, sample sizes and so on are concerned, exactly the same rules apply.

# International product management

The key issues in international product management are concerned with the following questions:
- do we need to adapt our national products when we sell them abroad?
- what product line should we sell in world markets?

Economies of scale in production, R and D, marketing and other areas of business operations are the rewards for companies that can find ways of standardizing products. Militating against standardization are differing use conditions, legal and technical requirements, and other market factors. The story of the lack of success at first of Campbell's soups in Britain because of a failure to adapt to the different tastes of the British is well known.

However, the competitive advantages which can be gained by an international company from the economies of scale referred to above are great. Many successful companies reach a compromise between a totally unified product strategy and a totally fragmented strategy, but such a position has to be managed.

One accounting machine manufacturer successfully tackled the engineering problem of the different electrical supply conditions in different parts of the world and also managed to rationalize thirty different keyboards down to five.

Although it is generally easier for a large company with foreign production plants to adapt its products than an exporting company, the growing trend towards regionalism and internationalism is making it easier for all companies to tackle this difficult problem. The international product line is frequently smaller than a company's domestic range. Apart from financial constraints, companies often sell only their strongest products abroad, whilst competitive and the market situations also often act as constraints. For example, if a company is operating through an agent, or a licensee, it is often not possible to market the complete domestic range of products, whilst some products are just not in demand in certain countries. Also, with strong local competition in a major foreign market, the marketing costs of establishing a worthwhile market share might be prohibitive.

Notwithstanding these difficulties, however, operating internationally can have great benefits for a company in the management of its product line. For example, in more economically advanced countries, a product that may be in the saturation or even the decline stage, may only be in the early growth stage in other countries. Consequently, the opportunities for extending the product life cycle are that much greater.

## International pricing

Without doubt, one of the biggest problems in international marketing concerns pricing. Firstly, the identification of costs is often difficult, particularly in respect of special packaging, labelling, and other product adaptation costs. Added to this is the difficulty of export financing costs, especially as there is often such a long time lag between actually making the goods and actually getting paid for them.

Secondly, each market is potentially different. It is not just tariffs and exchange rates that differ, but the cost of living varies from country to country, as do competitive conditions and of course legislation. Many Third World countries have very stringent price controls, so it is often just not possible to impose a worldwide pricing policy. Then there are the difficulties of centrally controlled markets as opposed to 'demand' markets.

Other complicating features concern activities such as parallel imports and *entrepôt* trade, which is a mild form of smuggling that takes place especially where borders are highly permeable. Much trade is being done today by wholesalers buying goods in one country where the cost of living is low and shipping them to another where the goods are more expensive. The effect that such activities has on channel margins, hence on the reputation of manufacturers, is too obvious to mention.

It is for these and other reasons that international pricing is so difficult. It is wise not to play the game of marginal costing in order to gain a purely price advantage in foreign markets because there are so many variables outside a company's control. It does make sense, however, because of the growing internationalism of world markets, to try to have a pricing *policy*.

## International distribution management

We have already discussed in response to Question 31 the importance of the method of market entry. So often a company commits itself to a method of entry without considering the long-term implications of the decision and since this is the key determinant of international marketing success, great care should be exercised over the method of entry.

No less care should be devoted to the choice of channels within a foreign country. One camera company decided to sell to department stores in one country and the opticians, who were the major outlet for this kind of product, decided to cease trading with the company.

Channel *service* is also important. For example, how many calls by representatives are required, what training is required, what promotional support? Customer service levels must also be carefully determined as the output of logistics decisions on locally held inventory, etc.

The only certain way to ensure compatibility between the distribution choice and other elements of the marketing mix is by carefully researching the implications for the company of entering a foreign market.

## International promotion management

The same kinds of difficulties are encountered in the management of international promotion as in the management of other elements of the marketing mix. The two extremes are on the one hand total control from headquarters and on the other total autonomy at the local level. In practice, neither of these extremes really makes sense for the international company. For one thing, many of the differences already referred to in the discussion about IMI, product, price and place, militate against a completely standardized communications policy. Having said this, however, it would be very wasteful for any company not to pool its international experience.

One international confectionery company carried out expensive research in the UK on a new product concept, and then successfully developed the product in the British market. They were surprised to find that the product was quickly copied by its competitors and successfully introduced into European markets, thus proving that the UK research was equally valid in Europe. This shock caused the company to carry out an investigation into its worldwide activities. One of the major criticisms emerging from this investigation concerned advertising. Large amounts of money were being spent on different research and copy platforms throughout the world, much of it unnecessarily duplicated in markets which exhibited similar characteristics to others. The result was a concerted effort to pool its resources and derive the benefits of being an international company.

## International marketing planning

It will by now be obvious that the process described in answer to Questions 26, 27, 28 and 29 is even more vital for the international company if it is not to lose control and miss out on opportunities for economies of scale and the transfer of knowledge and ideas. It will also be clear that detailed marketing plans for foreign markets cannot be prepared by managers in London. What has to be controlled in international marketing are the *interactive* elements of the marketing mix, and these will be different for all companies. In other words, what can be controlled at local level without having an adverse effect on the total company operation should be left to local management. Thus it makes far more sense to be talking about a standardized *planning process* than standardized marketing programmes, for it is only by means of such a process that a sensible compromise will be reached between total local autonomy and control from headquarters. For international companies that can solve this problem, the rewards are great.

*Further reading*

McDonald, M. H. B., 'Marketing Unplanned', *Marketing*, April 1979

Terpstra, V., *International Marketing*, Dryden Press, 1978

Weichmann, U. E., 'Problems that Plague Multinational Marketers', *Harvard Business Review*, July/August 1979

**Self-audit questions**

32.1 *What are the problems which your company has in*

obtaining marketing information for foreign markets
which it does not experience in the home market?

32.2  What efforts have been made by your company to
standardize on product features in foreign markets?

32.3  What criteria does your company use for deciding how to
enter a foreign market?

32.4  Which elements of the marketing mix are controlled
locally and which centrally?


# Question 33
# How can consumerism affect marketing?

*Consumer complaints must by definition be a criticism of
marketing since they express dissatisfaction with how companies
match their capabilities with customer needs.*

*Accordingly, consumerism must act as a spur to redoubled
marketing effort, a fillip to devote even more care and attention
to understanding what consumers need. This means increased
attention to segmentation of markets and the development of more
suitable products or services for them.*

*Equally important, however, marketing must also take care to
present the true economic facts. More emphasis in
communications on what can reasonably be expected for a given
price level and the avoidance of over-claims must be important
steps in the right direction.*

In a perfectly market-based company, all the products or services
offered would meet the needs of its customers and consumers at
the requisite level of profits. If this is so, why do consumers
complain with an increasingly strident voice today about the way
businesses operate? Are the major companies not based soundly
on a marketing philosophy, or are the strident voices not representative of the wishes of the vast majority of customers?

Consumerism, the name given to a wide spread of activities in the past decade, focuses our attention on the problem. Is marketing failing to do its job well, or are a small collection of agitators making something of nothing? The truth in most cases is probably to be found in the 80:20 rule; eighty per cent of the problem is poor marketing, and twenty per cent is populist agitation *per se*.

Traditionally it has been argued that a bad product will only sell once. Its customers will reject it after unsatisfactory performance, and any organization which persists in offering such products or services cannot long survive. Consumerists increasingly argue that such a passive approach amounts to shutting the stable door after the horse has bolted. They usually want to see it made illegal for such products or services to be offered on the market in the first place. They have a worthy line of legislative enactments in most countries in their support. The doctrine of *caveat emptor* or 'customer beware' has been heavily eroded since the end of the nineteenth century, but there have been regulations of one form or another since time immemorial.

In most countries within the EEC today, customer groups have succeeded in obtaining massive legislative support. In Sweden it stretches perhaps furthest with its consumer ombudsman and 'market court'; but the UK has its own Director-General of Fair Trading and an impressive array of legislation. As an illustration we can perhaps take the concept of 'implied terms of sale'. In 1973 a statutory responsibility was laid upon a supplier of goods to ensure that any goods were indeed good for the purpose for which they were promoted and sold. This totally reversed the dictum *caveat emptor* to *caveat vendor*. And why not? Why all the resistance and complaints by businessmen? Surely no marketer would doubt that this is exactly what he wants to see happen in his relationship with his customers. That customer groups, or politicians with or without populist agitation, had to lobby and had to get laws passed to secure this sort of relationship with suppliers, is an indictment of marketing activities throughout Europe and beyond.

The problem can be well illustrated in relation to children's toys. The successful toy companies of today are those which advertise to the parents that their products are not potentially dangerous, not coated with lead paint, and not destroyed the hour after they are first pressed into active service. Fisher-Price is one of the most successful toy manufacturers. Since 1968, it has eschewed child manipulative promotion, carefully tested its products with children for durability, safety and purposeful play, and charged the prices necessary to make and market 'good' toys. Sales and profit margins are impressively good.

## Consumerism's way to better marketing

Consumerism is pro-marketing; it wants the marketing approach to business implemented sincerely not cynically. The cynical implementation, which consumerists claim has been all too widely practised, is no better than high pressure salesmanship or misleading puffery. The sincere implementation of the marketing approach entails respect for each individual customer you serve. Indeed, the consumerist argues eloquently that the sort of relationship found between a manufacturer and a customer in, say, a capital goods market should be created in consumer markets. And so far as that is both economically feasible *and* what the consumer really wants, marketers must surely want it also.

To move towards this more acceptable state of affairs in our society, consumerists broadly argue that they have:

*The right to be informed* of the true facts involved in any buyer/seller relationship. Some of the key aspects which have already been subject to legislation or regulation in Europe embrace the full cost of credit/loans taken up, often known as truth-in-lending; the true cost of an item under the slogan 'unit pricing'; the basic constituent elements of products, known as 'ingredient informative labelling', closely allied to nutritional labelling; the freshness of foods discussed generally as 'open-dating'; and 'truth-in-advertising'.

The case against producers is that they either mislead through puffery or fail to tell the whole truth on these issues. They believe the individual in society has the right to know these truths. Again, who can doubt that if that is what the customers want, then they should be told it? Who would be unwilling to tell an industrial purchaser the answer to these basic questions about any merchandise proffered for sale? What other information would our customers like? Can we not track it down *before* they clamour?

*The right to be protected* is also a major plank in the consumerist platform. All too often the consumer is placed in a position of great trust in the producer. This is most obviously true in relation to safety standards, medicines and the like. Here government agencies and statutory controls can ensure that minimum standards are required. Good marketing will go well beyond them, however, in most cases and not be slow to tell the customer that it does.

In areas where technical ignorance is not a problem, but the great power of a corporation can overcome the customer, as when unsatisfactory performance is not put right, legislation such as that covering implied terms of sale has adequately met the need; but once again, good marketing is well ahead of the law.

*The right to ensure quality of life* is the most challenging demand from consumerists that affects marketing activities. Nonetheless, if a meaningful segment of its market needs to perceive the products it purchases as furthering the quality of life, that is a need that should be respected. If packaging, for instance, offends through its non-biodegradability with a sufficiently large group of customers, and that group is prepared in the long run to meet the research and development costs and any ongoing costs of changing to an alternative which is more preferred, then good marketing will take an organization that way.

Let it be repeated loudly and clearly at this juncture; none of these rights are unfamiliar to the marketer of industrial or consumer products. He has been accustomed to taking them into account all along. What is different today is that the process of marketing is no longer done on the initiative of the marketer in a framework of *caveat emptor*. The framework is no longer paternalistic. Today, the customer works via representative institutions, even unions, and their cry is *caveat vendor*.

Consumerism will affect marketing by bringing into being a more informative approach to all forms of marketing communication. It must and will give rise to a greater integrity in the advertising and promotional puffery of our profession without one hopes making life too dull, too much like a company share

234

issue prospectus. It must give rise to a greater concern amongst all levels of business management with the longer-term social implications of the patterns of our materialistic society. What responsibility does the continual emphasis on next month's material expectations out of life have on delinquency amongst the under- and over-privileged in society? What are the implications for tomorrow of our present pattern of raw materials' usage or pollution of the environment? The outcry in France over the pollution of the sea shores by manufacturers was a recent instance of this; rapid action followed.

The consumerist argues we can certainly afford in most of Europe today to trade off some of today's advantages for the longer-term interests of society.

## Consumerism as an opportunity

The social emphasis of consumerism, particularly its demands for an enhanced quality of life, is no threat to profitable enterprise. Rather it is an indication of the direction in which the economic processes within our society are increasingly moving at present. The same movement precisely can incidentally be traced towards social factors at work, from the mid-nineteenth century to the present day. Unsafe machinery had to be fenced at greater cost to the manufacturer. Office furniture and equipment is better designed today for comfort at work, even though that better design often makes it more expensive at the outset. In the longer term, fewer accidents and a happier workforce can often make the overall profit outturn better. But even if they do not, society expects to pay the cost when it buys a product or service.

The progressive marketing-based company sees consumerism in the same light as it views safety at work. Consumerism as an articulate expression of customer needs demands a marketing response. It calls out for the reformulation and development of products and services to meet the requirements both of short-term satisfaction and longer-run benefits. This dichotomy is illustrated in FIGURE 34 which offers a basis for careful thinking.

Desirable and pleasing products are what marketing has tended to concentrate upon. It has often ignored the longer-term disadvantages in society. Consumerism has reminded us of them

FIGURE 34

|  |  | IMMEDIATE SATISFACTION | |
|---|---|---|---|
|  |  | LOW | HIGH |
| LONGER-RUN CONSUMER WELFARE | HIGH | SALUTARY PRODUCTS | DESIRABLE PRODUCTS |
|  | LOW | DEFICIENT PRODUCTS | PLEASING PRODUCTS |

vociferously and in a very real sense given us the opportunity to be better citizens. It is now, after all, really possible to design *and sell* a motor car that is considerably safer than its equivalent in 1960. Then, attempts to sell safety were conspicuously unsuccessful even though the car makers tried. It is possible to design and sell a more effective flameproof fabric for children's wear now than hitherto, because a much wider awareness of the need for it has been created. Consumerism, in other words, opens up market opportunities which the astute marketing-based organization will wish to meet – not cynically, but sincerely. Some examples can be cited such as phosphate-free detergents, reduced lead content petrol, degradable plastic containers for a host of products, synthetic tobaccos, new nutrient based breakfast cereals and low-pollution manufacturing systems.

In precisely the same way, retailing organizations have made great use of the popularization of 'unit pricing' to help them build their business. A major supermarket chain introduced unit pricing as a key service to its customers, inviting them to exercise their own judgements about relative prices compared with relative quality. New trade was developed and existing customers affirmed that they found the service of considerable value. It was, they reported, something they frequently tried to do themselves but found too difficult on the basis of a fresh exercise for each shopping trip.

The articulate customer movement known as consumerism is here to stay as a force acting upon companies in their market place. It can, respectfully used, be a significant further input of information in the process of matching the capabilities of the organization to the needs of its customers.

*Further reading*

Sapiro, A., and Lendrevie, J., 'On the Consumer Front in France, Japan, Sweden, UK and the USA', *European Business*, summer 1973

Meyer, M. S., 'Coping with Consumerism', *The Business Quarterly*, autumn 1972

Aaker, D. A., and Day, G. S., *Consumerism*, Free Press, 2nd edition, 1974

**Self-audit questions**

33.1    *What are the consumer pressures on your organization at present and what do you expect in the next five years?*

33.2    *How are you organized to respond to consumer pressures and turn them to your advantage in marketing terms?*

33.3    *What good, if any, would consumer directors do on the Board of your organization?*

# Question 34
# Is marketing unethical?

*Marketing has often been singled out for attack because of its allegedly unethical foundations. It has been accused of using dubious means to sell goods and services to people who have no basic need of them. Likewise marketing critics have argued that it contributes to materialism in society, that it elevates consumption to be an end in itself and that it leads to a wasteful misallocation of resources.*

*Many of these arguments are bound up in a questioning of the role of business activity generally in our late twentieth century society. It is argued in this question that the marketing systems we have are reflections of the requirements of society. As the socio-economic environments change so too must our approach to marketing.*

*Any discussion of ethics in marketing must inevitably involve value judgements. Indeed there would be little point in attempting a value-free debate on such a human activity as marketing. What is therefore contained in the response to this question is an exploration of what at the moment seem to be some of the major issues confronting marketing and what the arguments and counter-arguments are.*

Increasingly in recent years dissatisfaction has emerged amongst some sectors of our society with the structure of a system that seems to have consumption as both its means and its end. The unacceptable face of capitalism and the growth of an acquisitive and materialistic society are seen by some to be hand in glove. In the late sixties and early seventies there was a growing consciousness of the problems that the age of mass consumption had brought with it. A quite new awareness of alternatives that might be possible, indeed necessary, became apparent. This movement quickly found its chroniclers as books like Charles Reich's *The Greening of America*, Alvin Toffler's *Future Shock* and Theodore Roszak's *The Making of a Counter Culture* appeared on bookshelves around the world. The message articulated in these and other testaments of the movement was simple: people could no longer be thought of as 'consumers', as some aggregate variable in the grand design of marketing planning. They were individuals intent upon doing their own bidding.

It is not surprising in the light of such feelings as these that commercial activity of all sorts has been subjected to a more searching scrutiny than perhaps it has received for several centuries. As one of the more visible manifestations of such activity, marketing has been singled out for special attention.

Often marketing has been criticized because, according to its critics, it attempts by insidious means to convince the consumer that he or she must smoke this brand of cigarette or use this brand of deodorant, that without them their lives are somehow incomplete. This is the notion of the *defenceless consumer*, a person who is like clay in the hands of a wily marketer and thus in need of protection. Such a view of marketing tends to overstate the influence that the marketer can bring to bear in the market place. It imagines that the consumers' powers of perception are limited in the extreme and that their intelligence is minimal. It further implies that skilful marketing can *create needs*. This most certainly is not the case; marketing may well be able to persuade people that they *want* a product, but this is not the same. To this view the sceptic might answer for example: 'Nobody wanted television before it was invented, now it is a highly competitive market. That market must have been created.' This argument confuses needs and wants. Before the advent of television nobody wanted it but there has always been a need for in-home entertainment. Previously that need had been met by a piano, a book or parlour games or whatever. Now technology has made available a further means of satisfying that basic need for domestic entertainment – the television. The television has clearly provided a better way, for many consumers, of meeting that need than the piano. In a market such as this marketing's role has been concerned with identifying in as much detail as possible what the customer needs and then to persuade him or her that a specific product or brand will provide the most effective means of satisfying the expressed need.

Underlying this revised model of the consumer is the point of view that states that consumers have certain perceived buying problems. They have needs which can only be satisfied through the acquisition of specific goods and services and consumers seek satisfactory solutions to these problems first by acquiring information about available goods and services and their attributes and eventually by choosing that product which comes closest to solving the problem.

No. If marketing is to be criticized it must be on grounds other than these. The consumer is still sovereign as long as he is free to make choices – either choices between competing products, or the choice not to buy at all. Indeed it could be argued that by extending the choices that the consumer has available to him or her, marketing is enhancing consumer sovereignty rather than eroding it. Marketing is helping consumers in their need for self-actualization.

Nevertheless, as already observed, commercial activities of

all sorts including marketing are being reappraised in the light of society's current requirements and demands and it is only appropriate that we consider in this final question and answer what the implications of such reappraisal might be.

## Marketing and society

Any critical appraisal of marketing as an activity must take place within the context of the social and economic systems in which it is practised. A leading marketing scholar, the late Wroe Alderson, suggested the concept of *marketing ecology* as a viable means for interpreting marketing's wider role. By this he implied the study of the continual process of adaptation of marketing systems to their environments, the suggestion being that the marketing systems in existence at any point in time are simply reflections of the requirements of society. In systems terminology we are thus considering marketing as an 'organized' behavioural system which sustains itself by drawing upon the resources of the environment and which survives only by adapting to changes in that environment. These environments represent not only the immediate surroundings of our customers and our suppliers but also the wider phenomena which are embodied in technological, ideological, moral and social dimensions.

The pressures exerted by all these aspects upon a marketing system are very real and ever-present. Technology alone is stridently insistent for change in any marketing activity; shortening life cycles in all product fields bear witness to its clamorous effect. Many commentators have stressed the rate of technological change as one of the most forceful catalysts for marketing change. Even greater perhaps than this pressure, however, has been the impetus for change provided by a radically different moral and ideological climate in society at large. The basic purpose of business activities today has come to be questioned and not only by those committed to alternative systems of exchange.

An issue of *Time* magazine in 1975 had as its cover story a feature 'Can Capitalism Survive?' It pointed to the ever-growing problems of inflation combined with recession, the power of the giant corporations and unions, the widening gaps between rich and poor and the disenchantment of large sectors of society with the capitalist system. The article cited a declaration signed by seven Nobel prizewinners including economists Gunnar Myrdal and Kenneth Arrow, which condemned Western capitalism for bringing on a crisis by producing primarily for corporate profit. They called for an intensive search for alternatives to the prevailing Western economic systems.

Elsewhere similar doubts about capitalism's long-term future have been expressed. The Club of Rome's sponsored study *The Limits to Growth* and E. F. Schumacher's *Small is Beautiful* are just two testaments to present concerns about the directions in which our existing production and exchange systems are taking us.

David Bell, professor of sociology at Harvard, describes in his book *The Coming of Post-Industrial Society* a possible scenario for the near future as a society in which industrial production is no longer the dominant economic factor. Such a state has in fact already arrived in several Western economies including the USA. It is a society in which values, motivations, institutions and social structure are becoming very different from what we knew in the 1960s.

## Some current ethical concerns

It is perhaps no small wonder that, in a context such as this, the ethics of marketing have been called into question. In particular attention has been concentrated on a number of specific issues such as marketing's contribution to materialism; rising consumer expectations through marketing pressure; the elevation of the media to a position of unwarranted power; and the use of media to mislead and distort. Let us consider these in turn.

Marketing, it has been suggested, helps feed and in turn feeds upon the materialistic and acquisitive urges of society. Implicit in such a criticism is the value judgement that materialism and acquisitiveness are in themselves undersirable. Nevertheless, whether one holds with such a view or not there would seem to be a case to be answered. The prosecution in such a case would argue that marketing contributes to a general raising of the level of consumer expectations. These expectations are more than simple aspirations, they represent on the part of the consumer a desire to acquire a specific set of gratifications through the purchase of goods and services. The desire for these gratifications is fuelled by marketing's insistent messages. Further if the economic circumstances of the individual are not equal to the outlay involved to meet those expectations then this inevitably adds to a greater awareness of differences in society and to dissatisfaction and unrest amongst those so affected.

The counter-argument that must surely be used in defence is that materialism is no recent phenomenon correlated with the advent of mass marketing. Almost 2,000 years ago the Sermon on the Mount warned against the collection of treasures upon earth, *where moth and rust doth corrupt and where thieves break through and steal . . . Ye cannot serve God and mammon.* Similarly it can be argued that marketing itself does not contribute to rising expectations and thus to differences in society; it merely makes people *aware* and better informed of the differences that might exist. Indeed the advocates of the cause of marketing could well claim that in this respect its effects are beneficial since it supports, even hastens, pressures for redistribution.

Much of the criticism levelled at marketing is in fact directed at one aspect of it, advertising. Advertising men themselves are fully conscious of these criticisms. One booklet published by the world's largest advertising agency, J. Walter Thompson, was entitled: *Advertising – Is this the sort of work that an honest man can take pride in?* Within that publication were summarized six of the major arguments used by the critics of advertising:

That advertising makes *misleading claims* about the product or service advertised.

That by implication or association it offers *misleading promises of other benefits* which purchase and use of the product will bring.

That it uses hidden, *dangerously powerful techniques* of persuasion.

That by *encouraging undesirable attitudes* it has adverse social effects.

That it works by the *exploitation of human inadequacy.*

That it *wastes skills and talents* which could be better employed in other jobs.

Others have commented upon the increasingly pervasive influence of the media upon our lives. Marshall McLuhan, an early commentator on the effects of media, suggested that tv particularly has 'changed our sense-lives and our mental processes. It has created a taste for all experience in depth . . .' Some would see the effects of media upon our lives as far more sinister than this. Sociologists would point to the fact that media in general, but tv in particular, have become the major source of what they call 'socialization' for many children. In other words the values and morals that traditionally have been inculcated in children by their parents are now acquired through tv viewing.

On the other hand the supporters of advertising would point to the fact that advertising in all its forms is heavily controlled in most Western societies, either by self-imposed codes such as the British Code of Advertising Practice or by legislation such as the Trade Descriptions Acts. Besides which, it is claimed, you might be able to persuade people to buy something once through offering all manner of subtle inducements in the way of advertising claims but there is no way that sustained patterns of repeat purchase can be built up if the product itself is not perceived by the consumer to provide the gratifications he or she seeks. For example we might be persuaded that Martini is indeed 'the right one' as its promoters claim and to give it a trial but if it fails to do the things we want it to do – to meet the needs we wish to satisfy – we will quickly drink something else or seek to gratify our needs another way.

## Marketing reflects our socio-economic systems

Economic historians can trace the development of the exchange process over time and can illustrate how a society moved from a pre-industrial state through industrialization to the emerging post-industrial state. So too have our marketing systems adjusted to meet the changed requirements of society. In pre-industrial times marketing was about trading, about exchanging goods for money or bartering for other goods. The medieval market is a manifestation of the marketing response to the requirements of the time with its very strong discipline of weights and measures. With the advent of industrialization and the growth of mass markets, the task of marketing was radically altered. Now the need was to find the means of gearing the massive capacity that existed to produce goods and services for the needs of the market place and, further, in the highly competitive environment that generally prevailed, to inform the market place of what was available. Control and discipline in weights and measures was naturally and of necessity supplemented by control and discipline of the process of informing customers.

With the coming of the post-industrial society the task of marketing will change once again. There is already a noticeable movement by many of the larger companies to recognize a 'fourth estate' in addition to the three traditional areas of business responsibility, i.e. a responsibility to the customer, the shareholder and the employee. That fourth estate is *society*.

This more positive acknowledgement of the social dimension of corporate activity could well see the deliberate use of marketing and marketing technology as an agent of *social* change. Already we have seen the adoption of a marketing approach by government agencies in, for example, attempts to change behaviour in regard to drinking and driving, the wearing of safety belts in cars, the acceptance of nuclear power stations near our homes, the smoking of cigarettes. Such a development will give rise to a need once again for a thoughtfully agreed pattern of control and discipline as we proceed.

Thus when we talk about marketing we are referring to more than just a set of techniques and procedures. We are alluding to an organized behaviour system which is constantly changing as it adapts to the evolving requirements of society. Society really can and does get the sort of marketing systems that it needs.

*Further reading*

Fisk, G., 'Criteria for a Theory of Responsible Consumption', *Journal of Marketing*, vol 37, no 2, 1973

Wills, G. S. C., 'The European Customer in a Technological Society', *Inaugural Lecture at Cranfield*, 1973

Moyer, R., *Macro Marketing: A Social Perspective*, Wiley, 1972

**Self-audit questions**

34.1   *Do you think marketing is unethical?*

34.2   *What would be your main headings for a code of ethics in marketing?*

34.3   *What would you believe should be society's sanctions against companies or individual managers therein who broke any code of ethics?*

# Index

249

Peter F. Drucker
# Management £2.95

Peter Drucker's aim in this major book is 'to prepare today's and tomorrow's managers for performance'. He presents his philosophy of management, refined as a craft with specific skills: decision making, communication, control and measurement, analysis – skills essential for effective and responsible management in the late twentieth century.

'Crisp, often arresting ... A host of stories and case histories from Sears Roebuck, Marks and Spencer, IBM, Siemens, Mitsubishi and other modern giants lend colour and credibility to the points he makes' ECONOMIST

## The Effective Executive £1.75

'A specific and practical book about how to be an executive who *contributes* ... The purpose of this book is to induce the executive to concentrate on his own contribution and performance, with his attention directed to improving the organization by serving outsiders better. I believe Mr Drucker achieves this purpose simply and brilliantly – and in the course of doing so offers many insights into executive work and suggestions for improving executive performance. I can conscientiously recommend that this book be given the very highest priority for executive reading and even rereading' DIRECTOR

## Managing for Results £2.50

'A guide to do-it-yourself management ... contains first-class suggestions that have the great virtue that they are likely to be widely and easily applicable to almost every business' TIMES REVIEW OF INDUSTRY

'Excellent ... well-supported examples of what has happened in practice to companies that have thought in this analytical way' FINANCIAL TIMES

Peter F. Drucker
**The Practice of Management** £2.95

'Peter Drucker has three outstanding gifts as a writer on business –
acute perception, brilliant skill as a reporter and unlimited self-
confidence ... his penetrating accounts of the Ford Company ...
Sears Roebuck ... IBM ... are worth a library of formal business
histories' NEW STATESMAN

'Those who now manage ought to read it: those who try to teach
management ought to buy it'
TIMES EDUCATIONAL SUPPLEMENT

Rosemary Stewart
**The Reality of Organizations** £1.75

'Addressed to managers whether in industry, commerce, hospitals,
public administration or elsewhere and includes examples from these
latter fields ... its style is excellent, concise and free of jargon'
PUBLIC ADMINISTRATION

**The Reality of Management** £1.75

'Not just another manual for executives, it is rather more like a set of
compass bearings to help the manager plot his course in his career
and his social life' NEW SOCIETY

Martin Christopher et al
## Effective Distribution Management £1.95

Reliable and efficient distribution is crucial to business success – products must reach their markets on time and in good condition. Efficient distribution brings the opportunity of increased sales and lower costs. *Effective Distribution Management* pinpoints difficulties and provides solutions in this key area of business planning. A thoroughly practical guide, it is geared to the needs both of managers and of students on management courses. A concise question-and-answer format is adopted in the text, backed up by case studies which illustrate common distribution problems.

John Fenton
## The A–Z of Sales Management £2.25

A book for the sales manager determined to succeed. This humorous yet highly practical book covers the ins and outs of managing a sales force from Advertising to Zest, taking in all the vital aspects: credit control, meetings and conferences, decision-making, sales forecasting, remuneration schemes, job specifications, motivation, planning and control, leadership, expense accounts and – last but not least – how to achieve consistently good sales results.

John Fenton
## How to Double Your Profits Within the Year £2.25

A programme of improvements, applicable to all types of business, to help you at least double your profits within twelve months. Fictional but highly practical, the book is an extended memorandum, an action plan, written by the MD of an imaginary company to his top managers. It shows, for example, how you can choose which customers contribute most to your profitability; recruit the right people; improve production efficiency; price for maximum profit; control your sales force. In the few hours it takes to read the book, you will be convinced that the title's claim is a modest understatement.

## Desmond Goch
## Finance and Accounts for Managers £1.95

The art of accountancy is now the most important instrument of control in the management armoury. This comprehensive guide will enable managers – even those without formal training in business finance – to formulate trading policies, forecast future trends and effectively administer their departments.

## Graham Mott
## Investment Appraisal for Managers £1.95

a guide to profit planning for all managers

Every responsible manager wants a say in how his company uses its resources. This text provides non-accountants with sufficient financial knowledge to evaluate profit opportunities and contribute effectively when investment decisions are made. The clear and uncomplicated treatment is also geared to the requirements of students on the relevant professional courses. The author identifies the main assessment techniques, and looks in detail at yearly cash flows, taxation and effects of inflation, with examples and case studies.

## Terry Rowan
## Managing with Computers £2.95

A book to dispel the myth that computers are special and that they deserve special treatment. *Managing with Computers* helps managers recognize the powerful capabilities of computers and how they can be usefully exploited; what systems are available and the tasks they can perform; how managers can select the source of computing power most suitable for their needs; the essential steps in implementing and developing a computer system; and how a business may need to adapt itself to the presence of a computer. An invaluable guide to an indispensable management skill.

## Management

| | | |
|---|---|---|
| ☐ **Introducing Management** | Christopher, McDonald and Wills | £1.95p |
| ☐ **The Effective Executive** | } Peter Drucker | £1.75p |
| ☐ **Management** | | £2.95p |
| ☐ **Under New Management** | Tony Eccles | £2.95p |
| ☐ **How to Double Your Profits** | John Fenton | £2.25p |
| ☐ **Inside Business Law** | } David Field | £2.95p |
| ☐ **Inside Employment Law** | | £2.50p |
| ☐ **How to Win Customers** | Heinz Goldmann | £2.95p |
| ☐ **Gods of Management** | Charles Handy | £1.25p |
| ☐ **The Black Economy** | Arnold Heertje *et al.* | £1.95p |
| ☐ **Managing People at Work** | John Hunt | £2.50p |
| ☐ **Investment Appraisal for Managers** | Graham Mott | £1.95p |
| ☐ **Managing With Computers** | Terry Rowan | £2.95p |
| ☐ **Guide to Saving and Investment** | James Rowlatt | £2.50p |
| ☐ **Reality of Management** | } Rosemary Stewart | £1.75p |
| ☐ **Reality of Organisations** | | £1.75p |
| ☐ **The Fifth Estate: Britain's Unions in the Modern World** | Robert Taylor | £1.95p |
| ☐ **Bargaining for Results** | John Winkler | £1.95p |
| ☐ **Dictionary of Economics and Commerce** | | £1.50p |
| ☐ **Multilingual Commercial Dictionary** | | £3.95p |

All these books are available at your local bookshop or newsagent, or can be ordered direct from the publisher. Indicate the number of copies required and fill in the form below

9

..............................................................................................................................

Name_____
(Block letters please)

Address_____

_____

Send to Pan Books (CS Department), Cavaye Place, London SW10 9PG
Please enclose remittance to the value of the cover price plus:
35p for the first book plus 15p per copy for each additional book ordered
to a maximum charge of £1.25 to cover postage and packing
Applicable only in the UK

While every effort is made to keep prices low, it is sometimes necessary to increase prices at short notice. Pan Books reserve the right to show on covers and charge new retail prices which may differ from those advertised in the text or elsewhere